M & E
ANNOTATED STUDENT TEXTS

M & E ANNOTATED STUDENT TEXTS

TENNYSON: POEMS OF 1842: ed. Christopher Ricks
WORDSWORTH AND COLERIDGE: LYRICAL BALLADS: ed. D. S. Roper
BROWNING: DRAMATIS PERSONAE: ed. F. B. Pinion
HAZLITT: THE SPIRIT OF THE AGE: ed. E. D. Mackerness
KEATS: POEMS OF 1820: ed. D. G. Gillham
BYRON: DON JUAN (1819): ed. Brian Lee
RUSKIN: 'UNTO THIS LAST': ed. P. M. Yarker
BLAKE: SONGS OF INNOCENCE AND OF EXPERIENCE AND OTHER
WORKS: ed. R. B. Kennedy
SHELLEY: ALASTOR AND OTHER POEMS; PROMETHEUS UNBOUND
WITH OTHER POEMS; ADONAIS: ed. P. H. Butter

M & E ANNOTATED STUDENT TEXTS

PERCY BYSSHE SHELLEY

Alastor
and Other Poems

Prometheus Unbound
with Other Poems

Adonais

Edited by

P. H. BUTTER, M.A.
Regius Professor of English Language and Literature
University of Glasgow

MACDONALD AND EVANS

Macdonald & Evans Ltd
Estover, Plymouth PL6 7PZ

First published 1970
Reprinted 1981

ISBN: 0 7121 0145 4

Printed and bound in Great Britain by
Butler & Tanner Ltd
Frome and London

General Preface

The principal aim of this series is to encourage the reader above all to *read the text* of the author he is studying. The annotation, accordingly, is designed as a tool with which to read the text. The conventional introduction has been eliminated and is replaced by a brief preface indicating the principal topics that scholars and critics discuss in connection with an author's work.

Authors are not represented in this series by volumes of selections of the kind that is now so familiar. In a volume of selections the pieces selected and the context they create for other pieces exercise a great influence upon the reader's impression of the author. When the present series was planned, it was felt that it would be much better to choose from an author's work, not individual pieces, but so far as possible what are by common consent *key volumes*, so that each piece might appear in its original context. In this way, the overall impression of each volume is put firmly back in the hands of its author.

Editors have been asked to produce 'standard' texts on conventional lines, and the text of a poem in one of these volumes, therefore, will normally be that which the reader is most likely to meet in other contexts. Each editor, however, has been given a wide measure of freedom to make what seems to him the most sensible decision in the case of his own particular text, and the textual status of each volume is fully described in the Note on the Text with which it begins. In addition, important variants are recorded in the editorial commentary.

MARK ROBERTS

Contents

Note on the Text of this Edition	9
Prefatory Note	11
Principal Dates in Shelley's Life	13
Alastor and Other Poems	15
Prometheus Unbound, with Other Poems	61
Adonais	211
Notes	235
Critical Extracts	352
Bibliography	361
Index of Titles	367
Index of First Lines	368

Acknowledgments

The Editors and Publishers desire to make grateful acknowledgment to the following for permission to include copyright material as stated:

Owen Barfield, Esq., Trustee of the Estate of the late C. S. Lewis, and Oxford University Press, for the extract from 'Shelley, Dryden and Mr. Eliot' from *Rehabilitations and Other Essays*, by C. S. Lewis;

The Clarendon Press, Oxford, for the extract from the introduction by G. M. Matthews to *Shelley: Selected Poems and Prose*;

Heinemann Educational Books Ltd. for the extract from the introduction by John Holloway to *Selected Poems of Percy Bysshe Shelley*;

Oxford University Press for the extract from *Defending Ancient Springs*, by Kathleen Raine.

The Editor wishes to acknowledge his indebtedness to the General Editors, especially to Mr. Derek Roper, and to Mr. W. T. McLeod of Collins for many valuable suggestions.

Note on the Text
of this Edition

THE TWO VOLUMES originally published under Shelley's own supervision have been reproduced as closely as possible consistent with the policy of modernizing spelling and punctuation laid down for the series. *Prometheus Unbound: with Other Poems* presents special problems.

The first edition of *Alastor and Other Poems*, published in 1816 when Shelley was still in England, has been reproduced except for the correction of obvious errors and some modernization of spelling and punctuation.

Prometheus Unbound: with Other Poems was published in 1820 under the supervision of Thomas Love Peacock after Shelley had gone to Italy. When Shelley received it, he was dismayed by the number of errors in it. The other chief authorities are Mrs Shelley's editions (1839), for which she used a list of errata compiled by Shelley, but into which she introduced some new errors; a MS of *Prometheus Unbound* in Shelley's hand in the Bodleian (of great value, but not the final draft prepared for the printer); MSS of some of the minor poems in the Bodleian; and a MS notebook in Harvard University library, which contains some of the minor poems, some in Mrs Shelley's hand, some in Shelley's own. Since neither the first edition nor the MS of *Prometheus Unbound* is satisfactory, a modern edition had to be used as the base text. C. D. Locock's text in his edition of Shelley's *Poems* (1911) was chosen, but this has been extensively revised to conform to the policy of the series and to take account of recent research. Professor L. J. Zillman's variorum edition of *Prometheus Unbound* (1959) has been an invaluable guide, and his modernized edition of that poem (1968) has been referred to during revision. Because of the deficiencies of the first edition the modernization has been carried out more extensively than in the other volumes.

After his unhappy experience with *Prometheus Unbound* Shelley had *Adonais* (1821) printed at Pisa, where he was living, so that he could ensure that it was done correctly. The Pisa edition, therefore, has been reproduced with very few changes. Punctuation has been changed where the original might confuse a modern reader, but this has been done more sparingly than in the other volumes. Some amendments introduced by Mrs Shelley in 1839, clearly with Shelley's authority, have been incorporated.

With regard to capitals—much more freely used then than now—the editor has tried to combine modernization with respect for the author's intentions. This is not quite so small nor easy a matter as it may seem. It is easy to say that modern practice demands that capitals should be removed from such words as Earth, Ocean, Sun, and Moon except when a personification is intended. But in Shelley there is no absolute distinction between Earth the goddess and the earth; for from the E(e ?)arth's heart quickening life bursts in spring, and she is left a corpse by the departure of the golden D(d ?)ay. For such a poet personification is not just a literary device, but a means of expressing a sense of nature as alive, and it is not possible to draw a clear line between what is and what is not personification. In *Adonais*, over which Shelley took trouble, the capitals have been left; but from *Prometheus Unbound*, where there is no satisfactory authority to follow, many capitals have been removed, and a few have been added. In the end each reader must decide for himself from the context when and to what extent a personification is intended.

Prefatory Note

THIS VOLUME contains most of Shelley's greatest poetry, and it brings together a sufficiently wide range of his poems to show his development and his mastery of a variety of different kinds of poetry and of metrical forms. By comparing the earliest-written poems in *Alastor and Other Poems* with *Alastor* itself we see him coming to maturity. *Prometheus Unbound* is his greatest completed work. Some of the poems published with it are among his best lyrics; others would not be likely to be chosen for an ordinary selection, but are of value for showing his versatility. *Adonais* he considered the least imperfect of his compositions; and it embodies, more fully than any other of his poems of moderate length, his mature vision of life.

An annotator is necessarily concerned with explaining allusions, pointing to sources, referring to the ideas behind his author's poems. What he provides will be helpful rather than harmful only if the reader uses it tactfully, and is not encouraged to read the poems as versified speculation. Shelley was very intelligent, well read in several languages, passionately interested in ideas, deeply concerned about morals and politics; he had a stronger grasp on the actual than is often allowed him. But he would not be of interest to us now if he had not been primarily a poet, with at his best an unusual power to speak to the imagination through rhythm and symbolic image. One should start with the poems, submit oneself to the enchantment of the rhythms and images. Later one will find oneself asking questions, and may turn to the critics and commentators to see if they provide any helpful answers.

The elderly Wordsworth is reported to have said: 'Shelley is one of the best artists of us all: I mean in workmanship of style.' A just and critical appreciation of him as an artist has been hindered by dislike or misunderstanding of, and indeed by enthusiasm for, his opinions. Nowadays it is not his radicalism nor his scepticism that are likely to be felt as barriers so much as his visionary idealism, his Utopianism. We should not be put off by misunderstanding. He had a clear, perhaps an exaggerated, sense of present evil; and did not think that a perfect society would be easily or soon achieved, if at all. If he had also a sense of what man potentially is, of what human society might be, of the joy that is possible even in the midst of pain, these feelings also are a part, a valuable part, of our experience. A sceptical visionary, one who drew on the wisdom of the past while whole-heartedly accepting change, he should find a sympathetic hearing in our time. His best poetry asks us, enables us, to see rather than to assent to any doctrine. The sense of joy, as well as of sorrow and aspiration, that it conveys cannot be refuted. Poetry, he says, 'may be defined as the expression of the imagination.' It 'awakens and enlarges the mind itself by rendering it the receptacle of a thousand unapprehended combinations of thought. Poetry lifts the veil from the hidden beauty of the world, and makes familiar objects be as if they were not familiar.'

Principal Dates in Shelley's Life

1792   Born, August 4th, at Field Place, Horsham, Sussex; son of Timothy Shelley, landowner and Whig M.P., later a Baronet.

1802–4   At Syon House Academy, Brentford.

1804–10   At Eton. Interested in science as well as in literature. Wrote novels in the fashionable 'Gothic' manner, *Zastrozzi* (published 1810) and *St. Irvyne* (1811), and much verse, *Original Poetry by Victor and Cazire* (in collaboration with his sister; published 1810) and *The Wandering Jew* (not published until 1831).

1810–11   At University College, Oxford. Friendship with T. J. Hogg. Wrote *Posthumous Fragments of Margaret Nicholson* (1810). Read Godwin's *Political Justice*. Expelled after writing a pamphlet, *The Necessity of Atheism*.

1811   Eloped to Edinburgh with Harriet Westbrook, and married her.

1812   In Ireland (Feb.-April), speaking and writing in favour of Irish unity and emancipation. Correspondence and meeting with Godwin. Meeting with T. L. Peacock. In Wales (winter), helping with plan for model village and dam. Writing *Queen Mab* (finished and privately printed 1813; pirated edition published 1821).

1813   In London (spring). Daughter Ianthe born (June). In Bracknell and Windsor in Berkshire (July-spring 1814). Becoming estranged from Harriet. Wrote *Refutation of Deism* (published 1814).

1814   Elopement to Continent with Mary Godwin (July-Sep.). Returned to London. Financial straits. Son Charles born to Harriet (Nov.).

1815   Income increased after death of grandfather, Sir Bysshe Shelley. Large gifts to Godwin. At Bishopsgate near Windsor (summer). Wrote *Alastor* (published 1816), having done little writing since *Queen Mab*.

1816   Son William born (Jan.). Continental tour (summer); with Byron on Lake of Geneva. Mary began *Frankenstein* (published 1818). Suicide of Harriet (Nov.). Marriage to Mary (Dec.).

1817   At Marlowe on the Thames (spring). Help to poor. Friendship with Peacock. Wrote *The Revolt of Islam* (published 1818) and *A Proposal for Putting Reform to the Vote* (1817). Daughter Clara born (Sep.).

1818   *Rosalind and Helen* begun (completed in Italy; published 1819). Departure for Italy (Mar.). At Leghorn (May), Bagni di Lucca (summer), Venice and Este (autumn), Naples (winter). Translated Plato's *Symposium*, began *Julian and Maddalo* and *Prometheus Unbound* (both completed 1819). Clara died (Sep.).

1819   At Rome (spring), Leghorn (summer), Florence (winter). William died (June); Percy Florence born (Nov.). Wrote *The Cenci* (published 1819). Stirred by news of the 'massacre' of Peterloo, wrote *The Mask of Anarchy* (published 1832) and other poems. Began *A Philosophical View of Reform* (finished 1820; not published until 1920).

1820   At Pisa and nearby Bagni di San Giuliano except for summer visit to Leghorn. Wrote *The Sensitive Plant, Ode to Liberty, The Witch of Atlas, Swellfoot the Tyrant* (published 1820), etc. *Prometheus Unbound* published. Met Emilia Viviani (Dec.).

1821   At Pisa. Edward and Jane Williams arrived (Jan.). Wrote *Epipsychidion* (Feb.; published 1821), *A Defence of Poetry* (Feb.-Mar.; not published until 1840), *Hellas* (Oct.-Nov.; published 1822). Byron arrived (Nov.).

1822   Moved in spring to Casa Magni, near Lerici, in the Gulf of Spezia. Wrote *The Triumph of Life* (unfinished; published 1824). Drowned on July 8th when sailing back from Leghorn to Lerici.

1824   *Posthumous Poems* published (includes *Julian and Maddalo, The Witch of Atlas, The Triumph of Life,* etc.).

ALASTOR;

OR,
THE SPIRIT OF SOLITUDE:
AND OTHER POEMS.

BY
PERCY BYSSHE SHELLEY.

———————

LONDON:
PRINTED FOR BALDWIN, CRADOCK, AND JOY, PATER-
NOSTER ROW; AND CARPENTER AND SON,
OLD BOND-STREET:
By S. Hamilton, Weybridge, Surrey.

———

1816.

Contents

PREFACE   17

ALASTOR   19

'O! THERE ARE SPIRITS OF THE AIR'   41

STANZAS—APRIL, 1814   42

MUTABILITY   43

'THE PALE, THE COLD, AND THE MOONY
    SMILE'   44

A SUMMER EVENING CHURCH-YARD   46

TO WORDSWORTH   47

ON THE FALL OF BONAPARTE   47

SUPERSTITION   48

SONNET FROM THE ITALIAN OF DANTE   49

TRANSLATED FROM THE GREEK OF MOSCHUS   50

THE DÆMON OF THE WORLD   51

PREFACE

The poem entitled 'Alastor' may be considered as allegorical of one of the most interesting situations of the human mind. It represents a youth of uncorrupted feelings and adventurous genius, led forth by an imagination inflamed and purified through familiarity 5 with all that is excellent and majestic to the contemplation of the universe. He drinks deep of the fountains of knowledge, and is still insatiate. The magnificence and beauty of the external world sinks profoundly into the frame of his conceptions, and affords to their modi- 10 fications a variety not to be exhausted. So long as it is possible for his desires to point towards objects thus infinite and unmeasured, he is joyous, and tranquil, and self-possessed. But the period arrives when these objects cease to suffice. His mind is at length suddenly 15 awakened and thirsts for intercourse with an intelligence similar to itself. He images to himself the Being whom he loves. Conversant with speculations of the sublimest and most perfect natures, the vision in which he embodies his own imaginations unites all of wonder- 20 ful, or wise, or beautiful, which the poet, the philosopher, or the lover could depicture. The intellectual faculties, the imagination, the functions of sense, have their respective requisitions on the sympathy of corresponding powers in other human beings. The Poet is 25 represented as uniting these requisitions, and attaching them to a single image. He seeks in vain for a prototype of his conception. Blasted by his disappointment, he descends to an untimely grave.

The picture is not barren of instruction to actual 30 men. The Poet's self-centred seclusion was avenged by the furies of an irresistible passion pursuing him to speedy ruin. But that Power which strikes the luminaries of the world with sudden darkness and extinction,

by awakening them to too exquisite a perception of its influences, dooms to a slow and poisonous decay those meaner spirits that dare to abjure its dominion. Their destiny is more abject and inglorious as their delin-
5 quency is more contemptible and pernicious. They who, deluded by no generous error, instigated by no sacred thirst of doubtful knowledge, duped by no illustrious superstition, loving nothing on this earth, and cherishing no hopes beyond, yet keep aloof from
10 sympathies with their kind, rejoicing neither in human joy nor mourning with human grief; these, and such as they, have their apportioned curse. They languish, because none feel with them their common nature. They are morally dead. They are neither friends, nor
15 lovers, nor fathers, nor citizens of the world, nor benefactors of their country. Among those who attempt to exist without human sympathy, the pure and tender-hearted perish through the intensity and passion of their search after its communities, when the vacancy
20 of their spirit suddenly makes itself felt. All else, selfish, blind, and torpid, are those unforeseeing multitudes who constitute, together with their own, the lasting misery and loneliness of the world. Those who love not their fellow-beings live unfruitful lives, and
25 prepare for their old age a miserable grave.

'The good die first,
And those whose hearts are dry as summer dust,
Burn to the socket!'

The Fragment, entitled 'The Dæmon of the World,'
30 is a detached part of a poem which the author does not intend for publication. The metre in which it is composed is that of *Samson Agonistes* and the Italian pastoral drama, and may be considered as the natural measure into which poetical conceptions, expressed in
35 harmonious language, necessarily fall.

December 14, 1815.

ALASTOR

OR

THE SPIRIT OF SOLITUDE

Nondum amabam, et amare amabam, quærebam quid amarem,
amans amare.

—Confess. St. August.

Earth, ocean, air, belovèd brotherhood!
If our great Mother has imbued my soul
With aught of natural piety to feel
Your love, and recompense the boon with mine;
If dewy morn, and odorous noon, and even,   5
With sunset and its gorgeous ministers,
And solemn midnight's tingling silentness;
If autumn's hollow sighs in the sere wood,
And winter robing with pure snow and crowns
Of starry ice the grey grass and bare boughs;   10
If spring's voluptuous pantings when she breathes
Her first sweet kisses, have been dear to me;
If no bright bird, insect, or gentle beast
I consciously have injured, but still loved
And cherished these my kindred; then forgive   15
This boast, belovèd brethren, and withdraw
No portion of your wonted favour now!

Mother of this unfathomable world!
Favour my solemn song, for I have loved
Thee ever, and thee only; I have watched   20
Thy shadow, and the darkness of thy steps,
And my heart ever gazes on the depth

Of thy deep mysteries. I have made my bed
In charnels and on coffins, where black death
Keeps record of the trophies won from thee,   25
Hoping to still these obstinate questionings
Of thee and thine, by forcing some lone ghost
Thy messenger, to render up the tale
Of what we are. In lone and silent hours,
When night makes a weird sound of its own stillness,   30
Like an inspired and desperate alchemist
Staking his very life on some dark hope,
Have I mixed awful talk and asking looks
With my most innocent love, until strange tears
Uniting with those breathless kisses, made   35
Such magic as compels the charmèd night
To render up thy charge: . . . and, though ne'er yet
Thou hast unveiled thy inmost sanctuary,
Enough from incommunicable dream,
And twilight phantasms, and deep noonday thought,   40
Has shone within me, that serenely now
And moveless, as a long-forgotten lyre
Suspended in the solitary dome
Of some mysterious and deserted fane,
I wait thy breath, Great Parent, that my strain   45
May modulate with murmurs of the air,
And motions of the forests and the sea,
And voice of living beings, and woven hymns
Of night and day, and the deep heart of man.

There was a Poet whose untimely tomb   50
No human hands with pious reverence reared,
But the charmed eddies of autumnal winds
Built o'er his mouldering bones a pyramid
Of mouldering leaves in the waste wilderness:
A lovely youth—no mourning maiden decked   55
With weeping flowers, or votive cypress wreath,
The lone couch of his everlasting sleep:

Gentle, and brave, and generous—no lorn bard
Breathed o'er his dark fate one melodious sigh:
He lived, he died, he sung, in solitude.   60
Strangers have wept to hear his passionate notes,
And virgins, as unknown he passed, have pined
And wasted for fond love of his wild eyes.
The fire of those soft orbs has ceased to burn,
And Silence, too enamoured of that voice,   65
Locks its mute music in her rugged cell.

    By solemn vision, and bright silver dream,
His infancy was nurtured. Every sight
And sound from the vast earth and ambient air,
Sent to his heart its choicest impulses.   70
The fountains of divine philosophy
Fled not his thirsting lips, and all of great,
Or good, or lovely, which the sacred past
In truth or fable consecrates, he felt
And knew. When early youth had passed, he left   75
His cold fireside and alienated home
To seek strange truths in undiscovered lands.
Many a wide waste and tangled wilderness
Has lured his fearless steps; and he has bought
With his sweet voice and eyes, from savage men   80
His rest and food. Nature's most secret steps
He like her shadow has pursued, where'er
The red volcano overcanopies
Its fields of snow and pinnacles of ice
With burning smoke, or where bitumen lakes   85
On black, bare, pointed islets ever beat
With sluggish surge, or where the secret caves
Rugged and dark, winding among the springs
Of fire and poison, inaccessible
To avarice or pride, their starry domes   90
Of diamond and of gold expand above
Numberless and immeasurable halls,

Frequent with crystal column, and clear shrines
Of pearl, and thrones radiant with chrysolite.
Nor had that scene of ampler majesty   95
Than gems or gold, the varying roof of heaven
And the green earth lost in his heart its claims
To love and wonder; he would linger long
In lonesome vales, making the wild his home,
Until the doves and squirrels would partake   100
From his innocuous hand his bloodless food,
Lured by the gentle meaning of his looks,
And the wild antelope, that starts whene'er
The dry leaf rustles in the brake, suspend
Her timid steps to gaze upon a form   105
More graceful than her own.

                His wandering step,
Obedient to high thoughts, has visited
The awful ruins of the days of old:
Athens, and Tyre, and Balbec, and the waste
Where stood Jerusalem, the fallen towers   110
Of Babylon, the eternal pyramids,
Memphis and Thebes, and whatsoe'er of strange
Sculptured on alabaster obelisk,
Or jasper tomb, or mutilated sphinx,
Dark Ethiopia in her desert hills   115
Conceals. Among the ruined temples there,
Stupendous columns, and wild images
Of more than man, where marble dæmons watch
The Zodiac's brazen mystery, and dead men
Hang their mute thoughts on the mute walls around, 120
He lingered, poring on memorials
Of the world's youth, through the long burning day
Gazed on those speechless shapes, nor when the moon
Filled the mysterious halls with floating shades
Suspended he that task, but ever gazed   125
And gazed, till meaning on his vacant mind

Flashed like strong inspiration, and he saw
The thrilling secrets of the birth of time.

Meanwhile an Arab maiden brought his food,
Her daily portion, from her father's tent,   130
And spread her matting for his couch, and stole
From duties and repose to tend his steps—
Enamoured, yet not daring for deep awe
To speak her love—and watched his nightly sleep.
Sleepless herself, to gaze upon his lips   135
Parted in slumber, whence the regular breath
Of innocent dreams arose: then, when red morn
Made paler the pale moon, to her cold home
Wildered, and wan, and panting, she returned.

The Poet wandering on, through Arabie   140
And Persia, and the wild Carmanian waste,
And o'er the aërial mountains which pour down
Indus and Oxus from their icy caves,
In joy and exultation held his way;
Till in the vale of Kashmir, far within   145
Its loneliest dell, where odorous plants entwine
Beneath the hollow rocks a natural bower,
Beside a sparkling rivulet he stretched
His languid limbs. A vision on his sleep
There came, a dream of hopes that never yet   150
Had flushed his cheek. He dreamed a veilèd maid
Sat near him, talking in low solemn tones.
Her voice was like the voice of his own soul
Heard in the calm of thought; its music long,
Like woven sounds of streams and breezes, held   155
His inmost sense suspended in its web
Of many-coloured woof and shifting hues.
Knowledge and truth and virtue were her theme,
And lofty hopes of divine liberty,
Thoughts the most dear to him, and poesy,   160

Herself a poet. Soon the solemn mood
Of her pure mind kindled through all her frame
A permeating fire: wild numbers then
She raised, with voice stifled in tremulous sobs
Subdued by its own pathos: her fair hands   165
Were bare alone, sweeping from some strange harp
Strange symphony, and in their branching veins
The eloquent blood told an ineffable tale.
The beating of her heart was heard to fill
The pauses of her music, and her breath   170
Tumultuously accorded with those fits
Of intermitted song. Sudden she rose,
As if her heart impatiently endured
Its bursting burden: at the sound he turned,
And saw by the warm light of their own life   175
Her glowing limbs beneath the sinuous veil
Of woven wind, her outspread arms now bare,
Her dark locks floating in the breath of night,
Her beamy bending eyes, her parted lips
Outstretched, and pale, and quivering eagerly.   180
His strong heart sunk and sickened with excess
Of love. He reared his shuddering limbs and quelled
His gasping breath, and spread his arms to meet
Her panting bosom: ... she drew back a while,
Then, yielding to the irresistible joy,   185
With frantic gesture and short breathless cry
Folded his frame in her dissolving arms.
Now blackness veiled his dizzy eyes, and night
Involved and swallowed up the vision; sleep,
Like a dark flood suspended in its course,   190
Rolled back its impulse on his vacant brain.

  Roused by the shock he started from his trance—
The cold white light of morning, the blue moon
Low in the west, the clear and garish hills,
The distinct valley and the vacant woods,   195

Spread round him where he stood. Whither have fled
The hues of heaven that canopied his bower
Of yesternight? The sounds that soothed his sleep.
The mystery and the majesty of Earth,
The joy, the exultation? His wan eyes   200
Gaze on the empty scene as vacantly
As ocean's moon looks on the moon in heaven.
The spirit of sweet human love has sent
A vision to the sleep of him who spurned
Her choicest gifts. He eagerly pursues   205
Beyond the realms of dream that fleeting shade;
He overleaps the bounds. Alas! alas!
Were limbs, and breath, and being intertwined
Thus treacherously? Lost, lost, for ever lost,
In the wide pathless desert of dim sleep,   210
That beautiful shape! Does the dark gate of death
Conduct to thy mysterious paradise,
O Sleep? Does the bright arch of rainbow clouds,
And pendent mountains seen in the calm lake,
Lead only to a black and watery depth,   215
While death's blue vault, with loathliest vapours hung,
Where every shade which the foul grave exhales
Hides its dead eye from the detested day,
Conduct, O Sleep, to thy delightful realms?
This doubt with sudden tide flowed on his heart;   220
The insatiate hope which it awakened, stung
His brain even like despair.

                      While daylight held
The sky, the Poet kept mute conference
With his still soul. At night the passion came,
Like the fierce fiend of a distempered dream,   225
And shook him from his rest, and led him forth
Into the darkness. As an eagle grasped
In folds of the green serpent, feels her breast
Burn with the poison, and precipitates

Through night and day, tempest, and calm, and cloud, 230
Frantic with dizzying anguish, her blind flight
O'er the wide aëry wilderness: thus driven
By the bright shadow of that lovely dream,
Beneath the cold glare of the desolate night,
Through tangled swamps and deep precipitous dells, 235
Startling with careless step the moonlight snake,
He fled. Red morning dawned upon his flight,
Shedding the mockery of its vital hues
Upon his cheek of death. He wandered on
Till vast Aornos seen from Petra's steep 240
Hung o'er the low horizon like a cloud;
Through Balk, and where the desolated tombs
Of Parthian kings scatter to every wind
Their wasting dust, wildly he wandered on,
Day after day, a weary waste of hours, 245
Bearing within his life the brooding care
That ever fed on its decaying flame.
And now his limbs were lean; his scattered hair
Sered by the autumn of strange suffering
Sung dirges in the wind; his listless hand 250
Hung like dead bone within its withered skin;
Life, and the lustre that consumed it, shone
As in a furnace burning secretly
From his dark eyes alone. The cottagers,
Who ministered with human charity 255
His human wants, beheld with wondering awe
Their fleeting visitant. The mountaineer,
Encountering on some dizzy precipice
That spectral form, deemed that the Spirit of wind
With lightning eyes, and eager breath, and feet 260
Disturbing not the drifted snow, had paused
In its career: the infant would conceal
His troubled visage in his mother's robe
In terror at the glare of those wild eyes,
To remember their strange light in many a dream 265

Of after-times; but youthful maidens, taught
By nature, would interpret half the woe
That wasted him, would call him with false names
Brother, and friend, would press his pallid hand
At parting, and watch, dim through tears, the path   270
Of his departure from their father's door.

   At length upon the lone Chorasmian shore
He paused, a wide and melancholy waste
Of putrid marshes. A strong impulse urged
His steps to the sea-shore. A swan was there,   275
Beside a sluggish stream among the reeds.
It rose as he approached, and with strong wings
Scaling the upward sky, bent its bright course
High over the immeasurable main.
His eyes pursued its flight.—'Thou hast a home,   280
Beautiful bird; thou voyagest to thine home,
Where thy sweet mate will twine her downy neck
With thine, and welcome thy return with eyes
Bright in the lustre of their own fond joy.
And what am I that I should linger here,   285
With voice far sweeter than thy dying notes,
Spirit more vast than thine, frame more attuned
To beauty, wasting these surpassing powers
In the deaf air, to the blind earth, and heaven
That echoes not my thoughts?' A gloomy smile   290
Of desperate hope wrinkled his quivering lips.
For sleep, he knew, kept most relentlessly
Its precious charge, and silent death exposed,
Faithless perhaps as sleep, a shadowy lure,
With doubtful smile mocking its own strange charms.   295

   Startled by his own thoughts he looked around.
There was no fair fiend near him, not a sight
Or sound of awe but in his own deep mind.
A little shallop floating near the shore

Caught the impatient wandering of his gaze.   300
It had been long abandoned, for its sides
Gaped wide with many a rift, and its frail joints
Swayed with the undulations of the tide.
A restless impulse urged him to embark
And meet lone Death on the drear ocean's waste;   305
For well he knew that mighty Shadow loves
The slimy caverns of the populous deep.

The day was fair and sunny, sea and sky
Drank its inspiring radiance, and the wind
Swept strongly from the shore, blackening the waves. 310
Following his eager soul, the wanderer
Leaped in the boat, he spread his cloak aloft
On the bare mast, and took his lonely seat,
And felt the boat speed o'er the tranquil sea
Like a torn cloud before the hurricane.   315

As one that in a silver vision floats
Obedient to the sweep of odorous winds
Upon resplendent clouds, so rapidly
Along the dark and ruffled waters fled
The straining boat. A whirlwind swept it on,   320
With fierce gusts and precipitating force,
Through the white ridges of the chafèd sea.
The waves arose. Higher and higher still
Their fierce necks writhed beneath the tempest's scourge
Like serpents struggling in a vulture's grasp.   325
Calm and rejoicing in the fearful war
Of wave ruining on wave, and blast on blast
Descending, and black flood on whirlpool driven
With dark obliterating course, he sat:
As if their genii were the ministers   330
Appointed to conduct him to the light
Of those belovèd eyes, the Poet sat
Holding the steady helm. Evening came on;

The beams of sunset hung their rainbow hues
High 'mid the shifting domes of sheeted spray   335
That canopied his path o'er the waste deep;
Twilight, ascending slowly from the east,
Entwined in duskier wreaths her braided locks
O'er the fair front and radiant eyes of day;
Night followed, clad with stars. On every side   340
More horribly the multitudinous streams
Of ocean's mountainous waste to mutual war
Rushed in dark tumult thundering, as to mock
The calm and spangled sky. The little boat
Still fled before the storm; still fled, like foam   345
Down the steep cataract of a wintry river;
Now pausing on the edge of the riven wave;
Now leaving far behind the bursting mass
That fell, convulsing ocean. Safely fled—
As if that frail and wasted human form   350
Had been an elemental god.

                        At midnight
The moon arose: and lo! the etherial cliffs
Of Caucasus, whose icy summits shone
Among the stars like sunlight, and around
Whose caverned base the whirlpools and the waves   355
Bursting and eddying irresistibly
Rage and resound for ever. Who shall save?
The boat fled on, the boiling torrent drove,
The crags closed round with black and jaggèd arms,
The shattered mountain overhung the sea,   360
And faster still, beyond all human speed,
Suspended on the sweep of the smooth wave,
The little boat was driven. A cavern there
Yawned, and amid its slant and winding depths
Engulfed the rushing sea. The boat fled on   365
With unrelaxing speed.—'Vision and Love!'
The Poet cried aloud, 'I have beheld
29

The path of thy departure. Sleep and death
Shall not divide us long! '

                  The boat pursued
The windings of the cavern. Daylight shone   370
At length upon that gloomy river's flow;
Now, where the fiercest war among the waves
Is calm, on the unfathomable stream
The boat moved slowly. Where the mountain, riven
Exposed those black depths to the azure sky,   375
Ere yet the flood's enormous volume fell
Even to the base of Caucasus, with sound
That shook the everlasting rocks, the mass
Filled with one whirlpool all that ample chasm;
Stair above stair the eddying waters rose,   380
Circling immeasurably fast, and laved
With alternating dash the gnarlèd roots
Of mighty trees, that stretched their giant arms
In darkness over it. I' the midst was left,
Reflecting yet distorting every cloud,   385
A pool of treacherous and tremendous calm.
Seized by the sway of the ascending stream,
With dizzy swiftness, round, and round, and round,
Ridge after ridge the straining boat arose,
Till on the verge of the extremest curve,   390
Where, through an opening of the rocky bank,
The waters overflow, and a smooth spot
Of glassy quiet mid those battling tides
Is left, the boat paused shuddering.—Shall it sink
Down the abyss? Shall the reverting stress   395
Of that resistless gulf embosom it?
Now shall it fall?—A wandering stream of wind,
Breathed from the west, has caught the expanded sail,
And, lo! with gentle motion, between banks
Of mossy slope, and on a placid stream,   400
Beneath a woven grove it sails, and, hark!

The ghastly torrent mingles its far roar,
With the breeze murmuring in the musical woods.
Where the embowering trees recede, and leave
A little space of green expanse, the cove   405
Is closed by meeting banks, whose yellow flowers
For ever gaze on their own drooping eyes,
Reflected in the crystal calm. The wave
Of the boat's motion marred their pensive task,
Which nought but vagrant bird, or wanton wind,   410
Or falling spear-grass, or their own decay
Had e'er disturbed before. The Poet longed
To deck with their bright hues his withered hair,
But on his heart its solitude returned,
And he forbore. Not the strong impulse hid   415
In those flushed cheeks, bent eyes, and shadowy frame
Had yet performed its ministry: it hung
Upon his life, as lightning in a cloud
Gleams, hovering ere it vanish, ere the floods
Of night close over it.

                      The noonday sun   420
Now shone upon the forest, one vast mass
Of mingling shade, whose brown magnificence
A narrow vale embosoms. There, huge caves,
Scooped in the dark base of their aëry rocks
Mocking its moans, respond and roar for ever.   425
The meeting boughs and implicated leaves
Wove twilight o'er the Poet's path, as led
By love, or dream, or god, or mightier Death,
He sought in Nature's dearest haunt, some bank,
Her cradle, and his sepulchre. More dark   430
And dark the shades accumulate. The oak,
Expanding its immense and knotty arms,
Embraces the light beech. The pyramids
Of the tall cedar overarching, frame
Most solemn domes within, and far below,   435

Like clouds suspended in an emerald sky,
The ash and the acacia floating hang
Tremulous and pale. Like restless serpents, clothed
In rainbow and in fire, the parasites,
Starred with ten thousand blossoms, flow around   440
The grey trunks, and, as gamesome infants' eyes,
With gentle meanings, and most innocent wiles,
Fold their beams round the hearts of those that love,
These twine their tendrils with the wedded boughs
Uniting their close union; the woven leaves   445
Make network of the dark blue light of day,
And the night's noontide clearness, mutable
As shapes in the weird clouds. Soft mossy lawns
Beneath these canopies extend their swells,
Fragrant with perfumed herbs, and eyed with blooms   450
Minute yet beautiful. One darkest glen
Sends from its woods of musk-rose, twined with jasmine,
A soul-dissolving odour, to invite
To some more lovely mystery. Through the dell,
Silence and Twilight here, twin-sisters, keep   455
Their noonday watch, and sail among the shades,
Like vaporous shapes half seen; beyond, a well,
Dark, gleaming, and of most translucent wave,
Images all the woven boughs above,
And each depending leaf, and every speck   460
Of azure sky, darting between their chasms;
Nor aught else in the liquid mirror laves
Its portraiture, but some inconstant star
Between one foliaged lattice twinkling fair,
Or painted bird, sleeping beneath the moon,   465
Or gorgeous insect floating motionless,
Unconscious of the day, ere yet his wings
Have spread their glories to the gaze of noon.

Hither the Poet came. His eyes beheld
Their own wan light through the reflected lines   470

Of his thin hair, distinct in the dark depth
Of that still fountain; as the human heart.
Gazing in dreams over the gloomy grave,
Sees its own treacherous likeness there. He heard
The motion of the leaves, the grass that sprung   475
Startled and glanced and trembled even to feel
An unaccustomed presence, and the sound
Of the sweet brook that from the secret springs
Of that dark fountain rose. A Spirit seemed
To stand beside him—clothed in no bright robes   480
Of shadowy silver or enshrining light,
Borrowed from aught the visible world affords
Of grace, or majesty, or mystery;
But, undulating woods, and silent well,
And leaping rivulet, and evening gloom   485
Now deepening the dark shades, for speech assuming,
Held commune with him, as if he and it
Were all that was—only . . . when his regard
Was raised by intense pensiveness, . . . two eyes.
Two starry eyes, hung in the gloom of thought,   490
And seemed with their serene and azure smiles
To beckon him.

         Obedient to the light
That shone within his soul, he went, pursuing
The windings of the dell. The rivulet
Wanton and wild, through many a green ravine   495
Beneath the forest flowed. Sometimes it fell
Among the moss with hollow harmony
Dark and profound. Now on the polished stones
It danced, like childhood laughing as it went;
Then, through the plain in tranquil wanderings crept, 500
Reflecting every herb and drooping bud
That overhung its quietness.—'O stream!
Whose source is inaccessibly profound,
Whither do thy mysterious waters tend?

Thou imagest my life. Thy darksome stillness,   505
Thy dazzling waves, thy loud and hollow gulfs,
Thy searchless fountain, and invisible course
Have each their type in me: and the wide sky,
And measureless ocean may declare as soon
What oozy cavern or what wandering cloud   510
Contains thy waters, as the universe
Tell where these living thoughts reside, when stretched
Upon thy flowers my bloodless limbs shall waste
I' the passing wind!'

                 Beside the grassy shore
Of the small stream he went; he did impress   515
On the green moss his tremulous step, that caught
Strong shuddering from his burning limbs. As one
Roused by some joyous madness from the couch
Of fever, he did move; yet, not like him,
Forgetful of the grave, where, when the flame   520
Of his frail exultation shall be spent,
He must descend. With rapid steps he went
Beneath the shade of trees, beside the flow
Of the wild babbling rivulet; and now
The forest's solemn canopies were changed   525
For the uniform and lightsome evening sky.
Grey rocks did peep from the spare moss, and stemmed
The struggling brook: tall spires of windlestrae
Threw their thin shadows down the rugged slope,
And nought but gnarlèd roots of ancient pines   530
Branchless and blasted, clenched with grasping roots
The unwilling soil. A gradual change was here,
Yet ghastly. For, as fast years flow away,
The smooth brow gathers, and the hair grows thin
And white, and where irradiate dewy eyes   535
Had shone gleam stony orbs—so from his steps
Bright flowers departed, and the beautiful shade
Of the green groves, with all their odorous winds

And musical motions. Calm, he still pursued
The stream, that with a larger volume now   540
Rolled through the labyrinthine dell; and there
Fretted a path through its descending curves
With its wintry speed. On every side now rose
Rocks, which, in unimaginable forms,
Lifted their black and barren pinnacles   545
In the light of evening, and, its precipice
Obscuring the ravine, disclosed above,
Mid toppling stones, black gulfs and yawning caves,
Whose windings gave ten thousand various tongues
To the loud stream. Lo! where the pass expands   550
Its stony jaws, the abrupt mountain breaks,
And seems, with its accumulated crags,
To overhang the world: for wide expand
Beneath the wan stars and descending moon
Islanded seas, blue mountains, mighty streams,   555
Dim tracts and vast, robed in the lustrous gloom
Of leaden-coloured even, and fiery hills
Mingling their flames with twilight, on the verge
Of the remote horizon. The near scene,
In naked and severe simplicity,   560
Made contrast with the universe. A pine,
Rock-rooted, stretched athwart the vacancy
Its swinging boughs, to each inconstant blast
Yielding one only response, at each pause
In most familiar cadence, with the howl   565
The thunder and the hiss of homeless streams
Mingling its solemn song, whilst the broad river,
Foaming and hurrying o'er its rugged path,
Fell into that immeasurable void
Scattering its waters to the passing winds.   570

    Yet the grey precipice and solemn pine
And torrent, were not all; one silent nook
Was there. Even on the edge of that vast mountain,

Upheld by knotty roots and fallen rocks,
It overlooked in its serenity   575
The dark earth, and the bending vault of stars.
It was a tranquil spot, that seemed to smile
Even in the lap of horror. Ivy clasped
The fissured stones with its entwining arms,
And did embower with leaves for ever green,   580
And berries dark, the smooth and even space
Of its inviolated floor, and here
The children of the autumnal whirlwind bore,
In wanton sport, those bright leaves, whose decay,
Red, yellow, or etherially pale,   585
Rivals the pride of summer. 'Tis the haunt
Of every gentle wind, whose breath can teach
The wilds to love tranquillity. One step,
One human step alone, has ever broken
The stillness of its solitude; one voice   590
Alone inspired its echoes—even that voice
Which hither came, floating among the winds,
And led the loveliest among human forms
To make their wild haunts the depository
Of all the grace and beauty that endued   595
Its motions, render up its majesty,
Scatter its music on the unfeeling storm,
And to the damp leaves and blue cavern mould,
Nurses of rainbow flowers and branching moss,
Commit the colours of that varying cheek,   600
That snowy breast, those dark and drooping eyes.

The dim and hornèd moon hung low, and poured
A sea of lustre on the horizon's verge
That overflowed its mountains. Yellow mist
Filled the unbounded atmosphere, and drank   605
Wan moonlight even to fulness; not a star
Shone, not a sound was heard; the very winds,
Danger's grim playmates, on that precipice

Slept, clasped in this embrace.—'O, storm of death!
Whose sightless speed divides this sullen night: 610
And thou, colossal Skeleton, that, still
Guiding its irresistible career
In thy devastating omnipotence,
Art king of this frail world, from the red field
Of slaughter, from the reeking hospital,   615
The patriot's sacred couch, the snowy bed
Of innocence, the scaffold and the throne,
A mighty voice invokes thee! Ruin calls
His brother Death. A rare and regal prey
He hath prepared, prowling around the world;   620
Glutted with which thou mayst repose, and men
Go to their graves like flowers or creeping worms.
Nor ever more offer at thy dark shrine
The unheeded tribute of a broken heart.'

When on the threshold of the green recess   625
The wanderer's footsteps fell, he knew that death
Was on him. Yet a little, ere it fled,
Did he resign his high and holy soul
To images of the majestic past,
That paused within his passive being now,   630
Like winds that bear sweet music, when they breathe
Through some dim latticed chamber. He did place
His pale lean hand upon the rugged trunk
Of the old pine. Upon an ivied stone
Reclined his languid head, his limbs did rest,   635
Diffused and motionless, on the smooth brink
Of that obscurest chasm; and thus he lay,
Surrendering to their final impulses
The hovering powers of life. Hope and despair
The torturers, slept; no mortal pain or fear   640
Marred his repose; the influxes of sense,
And his own being unalloyed by pain,
Yet feebler and more feeble, calmly fed

The stream of thought, till he lay breathing there
At peace, and faintly smiling; his last sight   645
Was the great moon, which o'er the western line
Of the wide world her mighty horn suspended,
With whose dun beams inwoven darkness seemed
To mingle. Now upon the jaggèd hills
It rests, and still as the divided frame   650
Of the vast meteor sunk, the Poet's blood,
That ever beat in mystic sympathy
With nature's ebb and flow, grew feebler still:
And when two lessening points of light alone
Gleamed through the darkness, the alternate gasp   655
Of his faint respiration scarce did stir
The stagnate night—till the minutest ray
Was quenched, the pulse yet lingered in his heart.
It paused—it fluttered. But when heaven remained
Utterly black, the murky shades involved   660
An image, silent, cold, and motionless,
As their own voiceless earth and vacant air.
Even as a vapour fed with golden beams
That ministered on sunlight, ere the west
Eclipses it, was now that wondrous frame—   665
No sense, no motion, no divinity—
A fragile lute, on whose harmonious strings
The breath of heaven did wander—a bright stream
Once fed with many-voicèd waves—a dream
Of youth, which night and time have quenched for   670
     ever,
Still, dark, and dry, and unremembered now.

     O, for Medea's wondrous alchemy,
Which wheresoe'er it fell made the earth gleam
With bright flowers, and the wintry boughs exhale
From vernal blooms fresh fragrance! O, that God,   675
Profuse of poisons, would concede the chalice
Which but one living man has drained, who now,

Vessel of deathless wrath, a slave that feels
No proud exemption in the blighting curse
He bears, over the world wanders for ever,   680
Lone as incarnate death! O, that the dream
Of dark magician in his visioned cave,
Raking the cinders of a crucible
For life and power, even when his feeble hand
Shakes in its last decay, were the true law   685
Of this so lovely world! But thou art fled
Like some frail exhalation, which the dawn
Robes in its golden beams—ah! thou hast fled!
The brave, the gentle, and the beautiful,
The child of grace and genius. Heartless things   690
Are done and said i' the world, and many worms
And beasts and men live on, and mighty Earth
From sea and mountain, city and wilderness,
In vesper low or joyous orison,
Lifts still its solemn voice: but thou art fled—   695
Thou canst no longer know or love the shapes
Of this phantasmal scene, who have to thee
Been purest ministers, who are, alas!
Now thou art not. Upon those pallid lips
So sweet even in their silence, on those eyes   700
That image sleep in death, upon that form
Yet safe from the worm's outrage, let no tear
Be shed—not even in thought. Nor, when those hues
Are gone, and those divinest lineaments,
Worn by the senseless wind, shall live alone   705
In the frail pauses of this simple strain,
Let not high verse, mourning the memory
Of that which is no more, or painting's woe
Or sculpture, speak in feeble imagery
Their own cold powers. Art and eloquence,   710
And all the shows o' the world are frail and vain
To weep a loss that turns their lights to shade.
It is a woe too 'deep for tears,' when all

Is reft at once, when some surpassing Spirit,
Whose light adorned the world around it, leaves   715
Those who remain behind, not sobs or groans,
The passionate tumult of a clinging hope;
But pale despair and cold tranquillity,
Nature's vast frame, the web of human things,
Birth and the grave, that are not as they were.   720

POEMS

'O! THERE ARE SPIRITS OF THE AIR'

Δάκρυσι διοίσω πότμον ἄποτμον

O! there are spirits of the air,
  And genii of the evening breeze,
And gentle ghosts, with eyes as fair
  As star-beams among twilight trees;
Such lovely ministers to meet   5
Oft hast thou turned from men thy lonely feet.

With mountain winds, and babbling springs,
  And moonlight seas, that are the voice
Of these inexplicable things,
  Thou didst hold commune, and rejoice   10
When they did answer thee; but they
Cast, like a worthless boon, thy love away.

And thou hast sought in starry eyes
  Beams that were never meant for thine,
Another's wealth—tame sacrifice   15
  To a fond faith! Still dost thou pine?
Still dost thou hope that greeting hands,
Voice, looks, or lips, may answer thy demands?

Ah! wherefore didst thou build thine hope
  On the false earth's inconstancy?   20
Did thine own mind afford no scope
  Of love, or moving thoughts to thee,
That natural scenes or human smiles
Could steal the power to wind thee in their wiles?

Yes, all the faithless smiles are fled　　　　25
　　Whose falsehood left thee broken-hearted;
The glory of the moon is dead;
　　Night's ghosts and dreams have now departed;
Thine own soul still is true to thee,
But changed to a foul fiend through misery.　　30

This fiend, whose ghastly presence ever
　　Beside thee like thy shadow hangs,
Dream not to chase—the mad endeavour
　　Would scourge thee to severer pangs.
Be as thou art. Thy settled fate,　　　　35
Dark as it is, all change would aggravate.

STANZAS—April, 1814

Away! the moor is dark beneath the moon,
　　Rapid clouds have drank the last pale beam of even:
Away! the gathering winds will call the darkness soon,
　　And profoundest midnight shroud the serene lights of
　　　　heaven.
Pause not! The time is past! Every voice cries, Away!　5
　　Tempt not with one last tear thy friend's ungentle
　　　　mood:
Thy lover's eye, so glazed and cold, dares not entreat thy
　　　　stay:
　　Duty and dereliction guide thee back to solitude.

Away, away! to thy sad and silent home;
　　Pour bitter tears on its desolated hearth;　　　10
Watch the dim shades as like ghosts they go and come,
　　And complicate strange webs of melancholy mirth.

42

The leaves of wasted autumn woods shall float around
    thine head;
  The blooms of dewy spring shall gleam beneath thy
    feet;
But thy soul or this world must fade in the frost that   15
    binds the dead,
  Ere midnight's frown and morning's smile, ere thou
    and peace may meet.

The cloud shadows of midnight possess their own repose,
  For the weary winds are silent, or the moon is in the
    deep;
Some respite to its turbulence unresting ocean knows;
  Whatever moves, or toils, or grieves, hath its
    appointed sleep.   20
Thou in the grave shalt rest—yet till the phantoms flee
  Which that house and heath and garden made dear to
    thee erewhile,
Thy remembrance, and repentance, and deep musings are
    not free
  From the music of two voices and the light of one
    sweet smile.

MUTABILITY

We are as clouds that veil the midnight moon;
  How restlessly they speed, and gleam, and quiver
Streaking the darkness radiantly!—yet soon
  Night closes round, and they are lost for ever;

Or like forgotten lyres, whose dissonant strings   5
  Give various response to each varying blast,
To whose frail frame no second motion brings
  One mood or modulation like the last.

We rest—a dream has power to poison sleep;
   We rise—one wandering thought pollutes the day; 10
We feel, conceive or reason, laugh or weep;
   Embrace fond woe, or cast our cares away:

It is the same!—For, be it joy or sorrow,
   The path of its departure still is free:
Man's yesterday may ne'er be like his morrow; 15
   Nought may endure but Mutability.

'THE PALE, THE COLD, AND THE MOONY SMILE'

There is no work, nor device, nor knowledge, nor wisdom,
in the grave, whither thou goest. *Ecclesiastes*

The pale, the cold, and the moony smile
   Which the meteor beam of a starless night
Sheds on a lonely and sea-girt isle,
   Ere the dawning of morn's undoubted light,
Is the flame of life so fickle and wan 5
That flits round our steps till their strength is gone.

O man! hold thee on in courage of soul
   Through the stormy shades of thy worldly way,
And the billows of cloud that around thee roll
   Shall sleep in the light of a wondrous day, 10
Where hell and heaven shall leave thee free
To the universe of destiny.

This world is the nurse of all we know,
   This world is the mother of all we feel,
And the coming of death is a fearful blow 15
   To a brain unencompassed with nerves of steel;
When all that we know, or feel, or see,
Shall pass like an unreal mystery.

The secret things of the grave are there,
   Where all but this frame must surely be,   20
Though the fine-wrought eye and the wondrous ear
   No longer will live to hear or to see
All that is great and all that is strange
In the boundless realm of unending change.

Who telleth a tale of unspeaking death?   25
   Who lifteth the veil of what is to come?
Who painteth the shadows that are beneath
   The wide-winding caves of the peopled tomb?
Or uniteth the hopes of what shall be
With the fears and the love for that which we see? 30

A SUMMER EVENING CHURCH-YARD,
LECHLADE, GLOUCESTERSHIRE

The wind has swept from the wide atmosphere
Each vapour that obscured the sunset's ray;
And pallid evening twines its beaming hair
In duskier braids around the languid eyes of day:
Silence and twilight, unbeloved of men,   5
Creep hand in hand from yon obscurest glen.

They breathe their spells towards the departing day,
Encompassing the earth, air, stars, and sea;
Light, sound, and motion own the potent sway,
Responding to the charm with its own mystery.   10
The winds are still, or the dry church-tower grass
Knows not their gentle motions as they pass.

Thou too, aërial Pile! whose pinnacles
Point from one shrine like pyramids of fire,
Obeyest in silence their sweet solemn spells,   15
Clothing in hues of heaven thy dim and distant spire,
Around whose lessening and invisible height
Gather among the stars the clouds of night.

The dead are sleeping in their sepulchres:
And, mouldering as they sleep, a thrilling sound   20
Half sense, half thought, among the darkness stirs,
Breathed from their wormy beds all living things around,
And mingling with the still night and mute sky
Its awful hush is felt inaudibly.

Thus solemnized and softened, death is mild   25
And terrorless as this serenest night:
Here could I hope, like some enquiring child
Sporting on graves, that death did hide from human sight
Sweet secrets, or beside its breathless sleep
That loveliest dreams perpetual watch did keep.   30

TO WORDSWORTH

Poet of Nature, thou hast wept to know
That things depart which never may return:
Childhood and youth, friendship and love's first glow,
Have fled like sweet dreams, leaving thee to mourn.
These common woes I feel. One loss is mine   5
Which thou too feel'st, yet I alone deplore.
Thou wert as a lone star, whose light did shine
On some frail bark in winter's midnight roar:
Thou hast like to a rock-built refuge stood
Above the blind and battling multitude: 10
In honoured poverty thy voice did weave
Songs consecrate to truth and liberty—
Deserting these, thou leavest me to grieve,
Thus having been, that thou shouldst cease to be.

FEELINGS OF A REPUBLICAN

ON THE FALL OF BONAPARTE

I hated thee, fallen tyrant! I did groan
To think that a most unambitious slave,
Like thou, shouldst dance and revel on the grave
Of Liberty. Thou might'st have built thy throne
Where it had stood even now: thou didst prefer   5
A frail and bloody pomp which time has swept
In fragments towards oblivion. Massacre,
For this I prayed, would on thy sleep have crept,
Treason and Slavery, Rapine, Fear, and Lust,
And stifled thee, their minister. I know   10
Too late, since thou and France are in the dust,
That Virtue owns a more eternal foe
Than Force or Fraud: old Custom, legal Crime
And bloody Faith the foulest birth of time.

SUPERSTITION

Thou taintest all thou look'st upon! The stars,
Which on thy cradle beamed so brightly sweet,
Were gods to the distempered playfulness
Of thy untutored infancy; the trees,
The grass, the clouds, the mountains, and the sea,   5
All living things that walk, swim, creep, or fly,
Were gods: the sun had homage, and the moon
Her worshipper. Then thou becam'st, a boy,
More daring in thy frenzies: every shape,
Monstrous or vast, or beautifully wild,   10
Which, from sensation's relics, fancy culls;
The spirits of the air, the shuddering ghost,
The genii of the elements, the powers
That give a shape to nature's varied works,
Had life and place in the corrupt belief   15
Of thy blind heart: yet still thy youthful hands
Were pure of human blood. Then manhood gave
Its strength and ardour to thy frenzied brain;
Thine eager gaze scanned the stupendous scene,
Whose wonders mocked the knowledge of thy pride: 20
Their everlasting and unchanging laws
Reproached thine ignorance. Awhile thou stood'st
Baffled and gloomy; then thou didst sum up
The elements of all that thou didst know;
The changing seasons, winter's leafless reign,   25
The budding of the heaven-breathing trees,
The eternal orbs that beautify the night
The sun-rise, and the setting of the moon,
Earthquakes and wars, and poisons and disease,
And all their causes, to an abstract point   30
Converging thou didst give it name, and form,
Intelligence, and unity, and power.

SONNET

FROM THE ITALIAN OF DANTE

Dante Alighieri to Guido Cavalcanti

Guido, I would that Lapo, thou, and I,
Led by some strong enchantment, might ascend
A magic ship, whose charmèd sails should fly
With winds at will where'er our thoughts might wend:
And that no change, nor any evil chance   5
Should mar our joyous voyage; but it might be,
That even satiety should still enhance
Between our hearts their strict community:
And that the bounteous wizard then would place
Vanna and Bice and my gentle love,   10
Companions of our wandering, and would grace
With passionate talk wherever we might rove
Our time, and each were as content and free
As I believe that thou and I should be.

TRANSLATED FROM THE GREEK OF MOSCHUS

Τὰν ἅλα τὰν γλαυκὰν ὅταν ὤνεμος ἀτρέμα βάλλῃ, κ.τ.λ.

When winds that move not its calm surface sweep
The azure sea, I love the land no more;
The smiles of the serene and tranquil deep
Tempt my unquiet mind. But when the roar
Of ocean's grey abyss resounds, and foam   5
Gathers upon the sea, and vast waves burst
I turn from the drear aspect to the home
Of earth and its deep woods, where interspersed,
When winds blow loud, pines make sweet melody.
Whose house is some lone bark, whose toil the sea,   10
Whose prey the wandering fish, an evil lot
Has chosen. But I my languid limbs will fling
Beneath the plane, where the brook's murmuring
Moves the calm spirit, but disturbs it not.

THE DÆMON OF THE WORLD
A FRAGMENT

Nec tantum prodere vati,
Quantum scire licet. Venit ætas omnis in unam
Congeriem, miserumque premunt tot sæcula pectus.

Lucan Phars. v. 176

How wonderful is Death,
Death and his brother Sleep!
One pale as yonder wan and hornèd moon,
With lips of lurid blue,
The other glowing like the vital morn,   5
When throned on ocean's wave
It breathes over the world:
Yet both so passing strange and wonderful!

Hath then the iron-sceptred Skeleton,
Whose reign is in the tainted sepulchres,   10
To the hell-dogs that couch beneath his throne
Cast that fair prey? Must that divinest form,
Which love and admiration cannot view
Without a beating heart, whose azure veins
Steal like dark streams along a field of snow,   15
Whose outline is as fair as marble clothed
In light of some sublimest mind, decay?
Nor putrefaction's breath
Leave aught of this pure spectacle
But loathsomeness and ruin,   20
Spare aught but a dark theme,
On which the lightest heart might moralize?
Or is it but that downy-wingèd slumbers
Have charmed their nurse coy Silence near her lids
To watch their own repose?   25
Will they, when morning's beam
Flows through those wells of light,

Seek far from noise and day some western cave,
Where woods and streams with soft and pausing winds
    A lulling murmur weave?   30

    Ianthe doth not sleep
    The dreamless sleep of death;
Nor in her moonlight chamber silently
Doth Henry hear her regular pulses throb,
    Or mark her delicate cheek   35
With interchange of hues mock the broad moon,
    Outwatching weary night,
    Without assured reward.
    Her dewy eyes are closed;
On their translucent lids, whose texture fine   40
Scarce hides the dark blue orbs that burn below
    With unapparent fire,
    The baby Sleep is pillowed.
    Her golden tresses shade
    The bosom's stainless pride,   45
Twining like tendrils of the parasite
    Around a marble column.

    Hark! whence that rushing sound?
    'Tis like a wondrous strain that sweeps
    Around a lonely ruin   50
When west winds sigh and evening waves respond
    In whispers from the shore:
'Tis wilder than the unmeasured notes
Which from the unseen lyres of dells and groves
    The genii of the breezes sweep.   55
Floating on waves of music and of light,
The chariot of the Dæmon of the World
    Descends in silent power:
Its shape reposed within: slight as some cloud
That catches but the palest tinge of day   60
    When evening yields to night,

Bright as that fibrous woof when stars indue
  Its transitory robe.
Four shapeless shadows bright and beautiful
Draw that strange car of glory; reins of light 65
Check their unearthly speed; they stop and fold
  Their wings of braided air.
The Dæmon leaning from the etherial car
  Gazed on the slumbering maid.
Human eye hath ne'er beheld 70
A shape so wild, so bright, so beautiful,
As that which o'er the maiden's charmèd sleep
  Waving a starry wand,
  Hung like a mist of light.
Such sounds as breathed around like odorous winds 75
  Of wakening spring arose,
Filling the chamber and the moonlight sky.

'Maiden, the world's supremest spirit
  Beneath the shadow of her wings
Folds all thy memory doth inherit 80
  From ruin of divinest things,
   Feelings that lure thee to betray,
   And light of thoughts that pass away.

For thou hast earned a mighty boon:
  The truths which wisest poets see 85
Dimly, thy mind may make its own,
  Rewarding its own majesty,
   Entranced in some diviner mood
   Of self-oblivious solitude.

Custom, and Faith, and Power thou spurnest; 90
  From hate and awe thy heart is free;
Ardent and pure as day thou burnest,
  For dark and cold mortality
   A living light, to cheer it long,
   The watch-fires of the world among. 95

Therefore from nature's inner shrine,
 Where gods and fiends in worship bend,
Majestic spirit, be it thine
 The flame to seize, the veil to rend,
  Where the vast snake Eternity   100
  In charmèd sleep doth ever lie.

All that inspires thy voice of love,
 Or speaks in thy unclosing eyes,
Or through thy frame doth burn or move,
 Or think or feel, awake, arise!   105
  Spirit, leave for mine and me
  Earth's unsubstantial mimicry!'

It ceased, and from the mute and moveless frame
 A radiant spirit arose,
All beautiful in naked purity.   110
Robed in its human hues it did ascend,
Disparting as it went the silver clouds
It moved towards the car, and took its seat
 Beside the Dæmon shape.

Obedient to the sweep of aëry song,   115
 The mighty ministers
Unfurled their prismy wings.
 The magic car moved on;
The night was fair, innumerable stars
 Studded heaven's dark blue vault;   120
 The eastern wave grew pale
 With the first smile of morn.

 The magic car moved on.
 From the swift sweep of wings
The atmosphere in flaming sparkles flew;   125
 And where the burning wheels
Eddied above the mountain's loftiest peak

Was traced a line of lightning.
Now far above a rock the utmost verge
    Of the wide earth it flew,   130
The rival of the Andes, whose dark brow
    Frowned o'er the silver sea.

Far, far below the chariot's stormy path,
    Calm as a slumbering babe,
    Tremendous ocean lay.   135
Its broad and silent mirror gave to view
    The pale and waning stars,
    The chariot's fiery track,
    And the grey light of morn
    Tingeing those fleecy clouds   140
That cradled in their folds the infant dawn.
    The chariot seemed to fly
Through the abyss of an immense concave,
Radiant with million constellations, tinged
    With shades of infinite colour,   145
    And semicircled with a belt
    Flashing incessant meteors.

As they approached their goal,
The wingèd shadows seemed to gather speed.
The sea no longer was distinguished; earth   150
Appeared a vast and shadowy sphere, suspended
    In the black concave of heaven
    With the sun's cloudless orb,
    Whose rays of rapid light
Parted around the chariot's swifter course,   155
And fell like ocean's feathery spray
    Dashed from the boiling surge
    Before a vessel's prow.

    The magic car moved on.
    Earth's distant orb appeared   160

The smallest light that twinkles in the heavens,
      Whilst round the chariot's way
Innumerable systems widely rolled,
      And countless spheres diffused
         An ever-varying glory.   165
It was a sight of wonder! Some were horned,
And, like the moon's argentine crescent, hung
In the dark dome of heaven; some did shed
A clear mild beam like Hesperus, while the sea
Yet glows with fading sunlight; others dashed   170
Athwart the night with trains of bickering fire,
Like spherèd worlds to death and ruin driven;
Some shone like stars, and as the chariot passed
      Bedimmed all other light.

      Spirit of Nature! here   175
In this interminable wilderness
Of worlds, at whose involved immensity
      Even soaring fancy staggers,
      Here is thy fitting temple.
      Yet not the lightest leaf   180
That quivers to the passing breeze
      Is less instinct with thee;
      Yet not the meanest worm,
That lurks in graves and fattens on the dead
      Less shares thy eternal breath.   185
      Spirit of Nature! thou
Imperishable as this glorious scene,
      Here is thy fitting temple.

If solitude hath ever led thy steps
To the shore of the immeasurable sea,   190
      And thou hast lingered there
      Until the sun's broad orb
Seemed resting on the fiery line of ocean,

Thou must have marked the braided webs of gold
    That without motion hang   195
    Over the sinking sphere:
Thou must have marked the billowy mountain clouds
Edged with intolerable radiancy,
    Towering like rocks of jet
    Above the burning deep: 200
    And yet there is a moment
    When the sun's highest point
Peers like a star o'er ocean's western edge,
When those far clouds of feathery purple gleam
Like fairy lands girt by some heavenly sea: 205
Then has thy rapt imagination soared
Where in the midst of all existing things
The temple of the mightiest Dæmon stands.

    Yet not the golden islands
That gleam amid yon flood of purple light,   210
    Nor the feathery curtains
That canopy the sun's resplendent couch
    Nor the burnished ocean waves
    Paving that gorgeous dome,
    So fair, so wonderful a sight   215
As the eternal temple could afford.
The elements of all that human thought
Can frame of lovely or sublime, did join
To rear the fabric of the fane, nor aught
Of earth may image forth its majesty.   220
Yet likest evening's vault that faëry hall,
As heaven low resting on the wave it spread
    Its floors of flashing light,
    Its vast and azure dome;
And on the verge of that obscure abyss,   225
Where crystal battlements o'erhang the gulf
Of the dark world, ten thousand spheres diffuse
Their lustre through its adamantine gates.

The magic car no longer moved;
The Dæmon and the Spirit   230
Entered the eternal gates.
Those clouds of aëry gold
That slept in glittering billows
Beneath the azure canopy,
With the etherial footsteps trembled not;   235
While slight and odorous mists
Floated to strains of thrilling melody
Through the vast columns and the pearly shrines.

The Dæmon and the Spirit
Approached the overhanging battlement.   240
Below lay stretched the boundless universe!
There, far as the remotest line
That limits swift imagination's flight,
Unending orbs mingled in mazy motion,
Immutably fulfilling   245
Eternal Nature's law.
Above, below, around,
The circling systems formed
A wilderness of harmony,
Each with undeviating aim   250
In eloquent silence through the depths of space
Pursued its wondrous way.

Awhile the Spirit paused in ecstasy.
Yet soon she saw, as the vast spheres swept by,
Strange things within their belted orbs appear.   255
Like animated frenzies dimly moved
Shadows, and skeletons, and fiendly shapes,
Thronging round human graves, and o'er the dead
Sculpturing records for each memory
In verse, such as malignant gods pronounce,   260
Blasting the hopes of men, when heaven and hell
Confounded burst in ruin o'er the world:

And they did build vast trophies, instruments
Of murder, human bones, barbaric gold,
Skin torn from living men, and towers of skulls   265
With sightless holes gazing on blinder heaven,
Mitres, and crowns, and brazen chariots stained
With blood, and scrolls of mystic wickedness,
The sanguine codes of venerable crime.
The likeness of a thronèd king came by,   270
When these had passed, bearing upon his brow
A threefold crown; his countenance was calm,
His eye severe and cold; but his right hand
Was charged with bloody coin, and he did gnaw
By fits, with secret smiles, a human heart   275
Concealed beneath his robe; and motley shapes,
A multitudinous throng, around him knelt,
With bosoms bare, and bowed heads, and false looks
Of true submission, as the sphere rolled by,
Brooking no eye to witness their foul shame,   280
Which human hearts must feel, while human tongues
Tremble to speak; they did rage horribly,
Breathing in self-contempt fierce blasphemies
Against the Dæmon of the World, and high
Hurling their armèd hands where the pure Spirit,   285
Serene and inaccessibly secure,
Stood on an isolated pinnacle,
The flood of ages combating below,
The depth of the unbounded universe
      Above, and all around   290
Necessity's unchanging harmony.

PROMETHEUS UNBOUND

A LYRICAL DRAMA
IN FOUR ACTS

WITH OTHER POEMS

BY

PERCY BYSSHE SHELLEY.

Audisne hæc, Amphiarae, sub terram abdite?

LONDON.
C. and J. Ollier Vere Street Bond Street
1820.

Contents

PREFACE	63
PROMETHEUS UNBOUND	69
THE SENSITIVE PLANT	168
A VISION OF THE SEA	180
ODE TO HEAVEN	185
AN EXHORTATION	187
ODE TO THE WEST WIND	188
AN ODE	191
THE CLOUD	192
TO A SKYLARK	195
ODE TO LIBERTY	200

PREFACE

The Greek tragic writers, in selecting as their subject any portion of their national history or mythology, employed in their treatment of it a certain arbitrary discretion. They by no means conceived themselves bound to adhere to the common interpretation, or to 5 imitate in story as in title their rivals and predecessors. Such a system would have amounted to a resignation of those claims to preference over their competitors which incited the composition. The Agamemnonian story was exhibited on the Athenian theatre with as 10 many variations as dramas.

I have presumed to employ a similar licence. The *Prometheus Unbound* of Aeschylus supposed the reconciliation of Jupiter with his victim as the price of the disclosure of the danger threatened to his empire by 15 the consummation of his marriage with Thetis. Thetis, according to this view of the subject, was given in marriage to Peleus, and Prometheus, by the permission of Jupiter, delivered from his captivity by Hercules. Had I framed my story on this model, I should have 20 done no more than have attempted to restore the lost drama of Aeschylus; an ambition which, if my preference to this mode of treating the subject had incited me to cherish, the recollection of the high comparison such an attempt would challenge might well abate. 25 But, in truth, I was averse from a catastrophe so feeble as that of reconciling the Champion with the Oppressor of mankind. The moral interest of the fable, which is so powerfully sustained by the sufferings and endurance of Prometheus, would be annihilated if we 30 could conceive of him as unsaying his high language and quailing before his successful and perfidious adversary. The only imaginary being resembling in any degree Prometheus is Satan; and Prometheus is, in my

judgment, a more poetical character than Satan, be-
cause, in addition to courage, and majesty, and firm
and patient opposition to omnipotent force, he is
susceptible of being described as exempt from the
5 taints of ambition, envy, revenge, and a desire for
personal aggrandisement, which in the Hero of
Paradise Lost interfere with the interest. The character
of Satan engenders in the mind a pernicious casuistry
which leads us to weigh his faults with his wrongs, and
10 to excuse the former because the latter exceed all
measure. In the minds of those who consider that
magnificent fiction with a religious feeling it engenders
something worse. But Prometheus is, as it were, the
type of the highest perfection of moral and intellectual
15 nature, impelled by the purest and the truest motives
to the best and noblest ends.

This poem was chiefly written upon the mountain-
ous ruins of the Baths of Caracalla, among the flowery
glades and thickets of odoriferous blossoming trees,
20 which are extended in ever-widening labyrinths upon
its immense platforms and dizzy arches suspended in
the air. The bright blue sky of Rome, and the effect
of the vigorous awakening of spring in that divinest
climate, and the new life with which it drenches the
25 spirits even to intoxication, were the inspiration of this
drama.

The imagery which I have employed will be found,
in many instances, to have been drawn from the
operations of the human mind, or from those external
30 actions by which they are expressed. This is unusual
in modern poetry, although Dante and Shakespeare
are full of instances of the same kind: Dante indeed
more than any other poet, and with greater success.
But the Greek poets, as writers to whom no resource
35 of awakening the sympathy of their contemporaries
was unknown, were in the habitual use of this power;

and it is the study of their works (since a higher merit would probably be denied me) to which I am willing that my readers should impute this singularity.

One word is due in candour to the degree in which the study of contemporary writings may have tinged 5 my composition; for such has been a topic of censure with regard to poems far more popular, and indeed more deservedly popular, than mine. It is impossible that any one who inhabits the same age with such writers as those who stand in the foremost ranks of our 10 own, can conscientiously assure himself that his language and tone of thought may not have been modified by the study of the productions of those extraordinary intellects. It is true that, not the spirit of their genius, but the forms in which it has mani- 15 fested itself, are due less to the peculiarities of their own minds than to the peculiarity of the moral and intellectual condition of the minds among which they have been produced. Thus a number of writers possess the form, whilst they want the spirit of those whom, 20 it is alleged, they imitate; because the former is the endowment of the age in which they live, and the latter must be the uncommunicated lightning of their own mind.

The peculiar style of intense and comprehensive 25 imagery which distinguishes the modern literature of England, has not been, as a general power, the product of the imitation of any particular writer. The mass of capabilities remains at every period materially the same; the circumstances which awaken it to action perpetually 30 change. If England were divided into forty republics, each equal in population and extent to Athens, there is no reason to suppose but that, under institutions not more perfect than those of Athens, each would produce philosophers and poets equal to those who (if we 35 except Shakespeare) have never been surpassed. We

owe the great writers of the golden age of our literature
to that fervid awakening of the public mind which
shook to dust the oldest and most oppressive form of
the Christian religion. We owe Milton to the progress
5 and development of the same spirit: the sacred Milton
was, let it ever be remembered, a republican, and a
bold inquirer into morals and religion. The great
writers of our own age are, we have reason to suppose,
the companions or fore-runners of some unimagined
10 change in our social condition or the opinions which
cement it. The cloud of mind is discharging its collected
lightning, and the equilibrium between institutions
and opinions is now restoring, or is about to be
restored.

15   As to imitation, poetry is a mimetic art. It creates,
but it creates by combination and representation.
Poetical abstractions are beautiful and new, not be-
cause the portions of which they are composed had no
previous existence in the mind of man or in nature,
20 but because the whole produced by their combination
has some intelligible and beautiful analogy with those
sources of emotion and thought, and with the con-
temporary condition of them: one great poet is a
masterpiece of nature which another not only ought
25 to study, but must study. He might as wisely and as
easily determine that his mind should no longer be the
mirror of all that is lovely in the visible universe, as
exclude from his contemplation the beautiful which
exists in the writings of a great contemporary. The
30 pretence of doing it would be a presumption in any
but the greatest; the effect, even in him, would be
strained, unnatural and ineffectual. A poet is the
combined product of such internal powers as modify
the nature of others, and of such external influences as
35 excite and sustain these powers; he is not one, but
both. Every man's mind is, in this respect, modified

by all the objects of nature and art; by every word and every suggestion which he ever admitted to act upon his consciousness; it is the mirror upon which all forms are reflected, and in which they compose one form. Poets, not otherwise than philosophers, painters, 5 sculptors and musicians, are, in one sense, the creators, and, in another, the creations, of their age. From this subjection the loftiest do not escape. There is a similarity between Homer and Hesiod, between Aeschylus and Euripides, between Virgil and Horace, 10 between Dante and Petrarch, between Shakespeare and Fletcher, between Dryden and Pope; each has a generic resemblance under which their specific distinctions are arranged. If this similarity be the result of imitation, I am willing to confess that I have imitated. 15

Let this opportunity be conceded to me of acknowledging that I have what a Scotch philosopher characteristically terms 'a passion for reforming the world': what passion incited him to write and publish his book, he omits to explain. For my part I had rather 20 be damned with Plato and Lord Bacon than go to Heaven with Paley and Malthus. But it is a mistake to suppose that I dedicate my poetical compositions solely to the direct enforcement of reform, or that I consider them in any degree as containing a reasoned system on 25 the theory of human life. Didactic poetry is my abhorrence; nothing can be equally well expressed in prose that is not tedious and supererogatory in verse. My purpose has hitherto been simply to familiarize the highly refined imagination of the more select classes of 30 poetical readers with beautiful idealisms of moral excellence; aware that until the mind can love, and admire, and trust, and hope, and endure, reasoned principles of moral conduct are seeds cast upon the highway of life, which the unconscious passenger 35 tramples into the dust, although they would bear the

harvest of his happiness. Should I live to accomplish what I purpose, that is, produce a systematical history of what appear to me to be the genuine elements of human society, let not the advocates of injustice and
5 superstition flatter themselves that I should take Aeschylus rather than Plato as my model.

The having spoken of myself with unaffected freedom will need little apology with the candid; and let the uncandid consider that they injure me less than
10 their own hearts and minds by misrepresentation. Whatever talents a person may possess to amuse and instruct others, be they ever so inconsiderable, he is yet bound to exert them: if his attempt be ineffectual, let the punishment of an unaccomplished purpose have
15 been sufficient; let none trouble themselves to heap the dust of oblivion upon his efforts; the pile they raise will betray his grave, which might otherwise have been unknown.

PROMETHEUS UNBOUND

DRAMATIS PERSONAE

PROMETHEUS	ASIA
DEMOGORGON	PANTHÈA } Oceanides
JUPITER	IONE
The EARTH	The PHANTASM of JUPITER
OCEAN	The SPIRIT of the EARTH
APOLLO	The SPIRIT of the MOON
MERCURY	SPIRITS of the HOURS
HERCULES	SPIRITS, ECHOES, FAUNS, FURIES

ACT I

SCENE.—*A ravine of icy rocks in the Indian Caucasus.*
PROMETHEUS *is discovered bound to the precipice.* PANTHEA
and IONE *are seated at his feet. Time, night. During the
Scene, morning slowly breaks.*

PROMETHEUS

Monarch of Gods and Dæmons, and all Spirits
But One, who throng those bright and rolling worlds
Which Thou and I alone of living things
Behold with sleepless eyes, regard this Earth
Made multitudinous with thy slaves, whom thou   5
Requitest for knee-worship, prayer, and praise,
And toil, and hecatombs of broken hearts,
With fear and self-contempt and barren hope;
Whilst me, who am thy foe, eyeless in hate,
Hast thou made reign and triumph, to thy scorn,   10
O'er mine own misery and thy vain revenge.
Three thousand years of sleep-unsheltered hours,
And moments aye divided by keen pangs

Till they seemed years, torture and solitude,
Scorn and despair—these are mine empire: 15
More glorious far than that which thou surveyest
From thine unenvied throne, O Mighty God!
Almighty, had I deigned to share the shame
Of thine ill tyranny, and hung not here
Nailed to this wall of eagle-baffling mountain,   20
Black, wintry, dead, unmeasured; without herb,
Insect, or beast, or shape or sound of life.
Ah me! alas, pain, pain ever, forever!

No change, no pause, no hope! Yet I endure.
I ask the Earth, have not the mountains felt?   25
I ask yon Heaven, the all-beholding Sun,
Has it not seen? The Sea, in storm or calm,
Heaven's ever-changing shadow, spread below,
Have its deaf waves not heard my agony?
Ah me! alas, pain, pain ever, forever!   30

The crawling glaciers pierce me with the spears
Of their moon-freezing crystals; the bright chains
Eat with their burning cold into my bones.
Heaven's wingèd hound, polluting from thy lips
His beak in poison not his own, tears up   35
My heart; and shapeless sights come wandering by,
The ghastly people of the realm of dream,
Mocking me; and the Earthquake-fiends are charged
To wrench the rivets from my quivering wounds
When the rocks split and close again behind;   40
While from their loud abysses howling throng
The genii of the storm, urging the rage
Of whirlwind, and afflict me with keen hail.
And yet to me welcome is day and night,
Whether one breaks the hoar-frost of the morn,   45
Or starry, dim, and slow, the other climbs
The leaden-coloured east; for then they lead

Their wingless, crawling Hours, one among whom—
As some dark priest hales the reluctant victim—
Shall drag thee, cruel King, to kiss the blood   50
From these pale feet, which then might trample thee
If they disdained not such a prostrate slave.
Disdain? Ah no! I pity thee. What Ruin
Will hunt thee undefended through wide Heaven!
How will thy soul, cloven to its depth with terror,   55
Gape like a hell within! I speak in grief,
Not exultation, for I hate no more,
As then, ere misery made me wise. The curse
Once breathed on thee I would recall. Ye Mountains,
Whose many-voicèd Echoes, through the mist   60
Of cataracts, flung the thunder of that spell!
Ye icy Springs, stagnant with wrinkling frost,
Which vibrated to hear me, and then crept
Shuddering through India! Thou serenest Air,
Through which the Sun walks burning without beams!   65
And ye swift Whirlwinds, who on poisèd wings
Hung mute and moveless o'er yon hushed abyss,
As thunder, louder than your own, made rock
The orbèd world! If then my words had power—
Though I am changed so that aught evil wish   70
Is dead within; although no memory be
Of what is hate—let them not lose it now!
What was that curse? for ye all heard me speak.

FIRST VOICE (*from the Mountains*)

Thrice three hundred thousand years
   O'er the Earthquake's couch we stood;   75
Oft, as men convulsed with fears,
   We trembled in our multitude.

SECOND VOICE (*from the Springs*)

Thunderbolts had parched our water,
   We had been stained with bitter blood,

And had run mute, 'mid shrieks of slaughter, 80
Through a city and a solitude.

THIRD VOICE (*from the Air*)

I had clothed, since Earth uprose,
    Its wastes in colours not their own,
And oft had my serene repose
    Been cloven by many a rending groan.   85

FOURTH VOICE (*from the Whirlwinds*)

We had soared beneath these mountains
    Unresting ages; nor had thunder,
Nor yon volcano's flaming fountains,
    Nor any power above or under
    Ever made us mute with wonder.   90

FIRST VOICE

But never bowed our snowy crest
As at the voice of thine unrest.

SECOND VOICE

Never such a sound before
To the Indian waves we bore.
A pilot asleep on the howling sea   95
Leaped up from the deck in agony,
And heard, and cried, 'Ah, woe is me!'
And died as mad as the wild waves be.

THIRD VOICE

By such dread words from Earth to Heaven
My still realm was never riven: 100
When its wound was closed, there stood
Darkness o'er the day like blood.

Fourth Voice

And we shrank back: for dreams of ruin
To frozen caves our flight pursuing
Made us keep silence—thus—and thus—   105
Though silence is a hell to us.

The Earth

The tongueless Caverns of the craggy hills
Cried 'Misery!' then; the hollow Heaven replied
'Misery!' and the Ocean's purple waves,
Climbing the land, howled to the lashing winds,   110
And the pale nations heard it—'Misery!'

Prometheus

I hear a sound of voices—not the voice
Which I gave forth. Mother, thy sons and thou
Scorn him, without whose all-enduring will
Beneath the fierce omnipotence of Jove,   115
Both they and thou had vanished, like thin mist
Unrolled on the morning wind. Know ye not me,
The Titan? he who made his agony
The barrier to your else all-conquering foe?
O rock-embosomed lawns and snow-fed streams,   120
Now seen athwart frore vapours, deep below,
Through whose o'ershadowing woods I wandered once
With Asia, drinking life from her loved eyes—
Why scorns the spirit which informs ye, now
To commune with me? me alone, who checked,   125
As one who checks a fiend-drawn charioteer,
The falsehood and the force of him who reigns
Supreme, and with the groans of pining slaves
Fills your dim glens and liquid wildernesses?
Why answer ye not, still? Brethren!

The Earth

            They dare not.   130

PROMETHEUS

Who dares? for I would hear that curse again . . .
Ha, what an awful whisper rises up!
'Tis scarce like sound: it tingles through the frame
As lightning tingles, hovering ere it strike.
Speak, Spirit! from thine inorganic voice   135
I only know that thou art moving near
And love. How cursed I him?

THE EARTH

          How canst thou hear,
Who knowest not the language of the dead?

PROMETHEUS

Thou art a living spirit; speak as they.

THE EARTH

I dare not speak like life, lest Heaven's fell King   140
Should hear, and link me to some wheel of pain
More torturing than the one whereon I roll.
Subtle thou art and good; and though the Gods
Hear not this voice, yet thou art more than God,
Being wise and kind; earnestly harken now.   145

PROMETHEUS

Obscurely through my brain, like shadows dim,
Sweep awful thoughts, rapid and thick. I feel
Faint, like one mingled in entwining love;
Yet 'tis not pleasure.

THE EARTH

          No, thou canst not hear;
Thou art immortal, and this tongue is known   150
Only to those who die.

PROMETHEUS

> And what art thou,
O melancholy Voice?

THE EARTH

> I am the Earth,
Thy mother; she within whose stony veins,
To the last fibre of the loftiest tree
Whose thin leaves trembled in the frozen air,   155
Joy ran, as blood within a living frame,
When thou didst from her bosom, like a cloud
Of glory, arise—a spirit of keen joy!
And at thy voice her pining sons uplifted
Their prostrate brows from the polluting dust,   160
And our almighty Tyrant with fierce dread
Grew pale—until his thunder chained thee here.
Then—see those million worlds which burn and roll
Around us: their inhabitants beheld
My spherèd light wane in wide heaven; the sea   165
Was lifted by strange tempest, and new fire
From earthquake-rifted mountains of bright snow
Shook its portentous hair beneath Heaven's frown;
Lightning and inundation vexed the plains;
Blue thistles bloomed in cities; foodless toads   170
Within voluptuous chambers panting crawled;
When plague had fallen on man and beast and worm,
And famine; and black blight on herb and tree;
And in the corn, and vines, and meadow-grass,
Teemed ineradicable poisonous weeds   175
Draining their growth—for my wan breast was dry
With grief; and the thin air, my breath, was stained
With the contagion of a mother's hate
Breathed on her child's destroyer. Ay, I heard
Thy curse, the which, if thou rememberest not,   180
Yet my innumerable seas and streams,

Mountains, and caves, and winds, and yon wide air,
And the inarticulate people of the dead,
Preserve, a treasured spell. We meditate
In secret joy and hope those dreadful words,   185
But dare not speak them.

PROMETHEUS

                    Venerable Mother!
All else who live and suffer take from thee
Some comfort—flowers, and fruit, and happy sounds,
And love, though fleeting; these may not be mine,
But mine own words, I pray, deny me not.   190

THE EARTH

They shall be told. Ere Babylon was dust,
The Magus Zoroaster, my dead child,
Met his own image walking in the garden.
That apparition, sole of men, he saw.
For know, there are two worlds of life and death: 195
One, that which thou beholdest; but the other
Is underneath the grave, where do inhabit
The shadows of all forms that think and live,
Till death unite them and they part no more—
Dreams and the light imaginings of men,   200
And all that faith creates, or love desires,
Terrible, strange, sublime and beauteous shapes.
There thou art, and dost hang, a writhing shade,
'Mid whirlwind-shaken mountains; all the Gods
Are there, and all the Powers of nameless worlds,   205
Vast, sceptred Phantoms; heroes, men, and beasts;
And Demogorgon, a tremendous Gloom;
And he, the Supreme Tyrant, on his throne
Of burning gold. Son, one of these shall utter
The curse which all remember. Call at will   210
Thine own ghost, or the ghost of Jupiter,

Hades or Typhon, or what mightier Gods
From all-prolific Evil since thy ruin
Have sprung, and trampled on my prostrate sons.
Ask, and they must reply: so the revenge   215
Of the Supreme may sweep through vacant shades,
As rainy wind through the abandoned gate
Of a fallen palace.

PROMETHEUS

           Mother, let not aught
Of that which may be evil, pass again
My lips, or those of aught resembling me.   220
Phantasm of Jupiter, arise, appear!

IONE

  My wings are folded o'er mine ears;
    My wings are crossed over mine eyes;
  Yet through their silver shade appears,
    And through their lulling plumes arise,   225
      A Shape, a throng of sounds:
    May it be no ill to thee
      O thou of many wounds!
  Near whom, for our sweet sister's sake,
  Ever thus we watch and wake.   230

PANTHEA

The sound is of whirlwind underground,
  Earthquake, and fire, and mountains cloven;
The Shape is awful like the sound,
  Clothed in dark purple, star-inwoven.
    A sceptre of pale gold,   235
  To stay steps proud o'er the slow cloud,
    His veinèd hand doth hold.
Cruel he looks, but calm and strong,
Like one who does, not suffers wrong.

PHANTASM OF JUPITER

Why have the secret powers of this strange world 240
Driven me, a frail and empty phantom, hither
On direst storms? What unaccustomed sounds
Are hovering on my lips, unlike the voice
With which our pallid race hold ghastly talk
In darkness? And, proud Sufferer, who art thou? 245

PROMETHEUS

Tremendous Image, as thou art must be
He whom thou shadowest forth. I am his foe,
The Titan. Speak the words which I would hear,
Although no thought inform thine empty voice.

THE EARTH

Listen! And though your echoes must be mute, 250
Grey mountains, and old woods, and haunted springs,
Prophetic caves, and isle-surrounded streams,
Rejoice to hear what yet ye cannot speak.

PHANTASM

A spirit seizes me and speaks within:
It tears me as fire tears a thunder-cloud. 255

PANTHEA

See, how he lifts his mighty looks! the Heaven
Darkens above.

IONE

He speaks! Oh shelter me!

PROMETHEUS

I see the curse on gestures proud and cold,
And looks of firm defiance, and calm hate,
And such despair as mocks itself with smiles, 260
Written as on a scroll . . . yet speak—oh speak!

PHANTASM

Fiend, I defy thee! with a calm, fixed mind,
  All that thou canst inflict I bid thee do.
Foul Tyrant both of Gods and Humankind,
  One only being shalt thou not subdue.   265
    Rain then thy plagues upon me here,
    Ghastly disease, and frenzying fear;
    And let alternate frost and fire
    Eat into me, and be thine ire
Lightning, and cutting hail, and legioned forms   270
Of Furies, driving by upon the wounding storms.

Ay, do thy worst. Thou art omnipotent.
  O'er all things but thyself I gave thee power,
And my own will. Be thy swift mischiefs sent
  To blast mankind, from yon ætherial tower.   275
    Let thy malignant spirit move
    Its darkness over those I love:
    On me and mine I imprecate
    The utmost torture of thy hate,
And thus devote to sleepless agony   280
This undeclining head while thou must reign on high.

But thou, who art the God and Lord—O thou
  Who fillest with thy soul this world of woe,
To whom all things of Earth and Heaven do bow
  In fear and worship—all-prevailing foe!   285
    I curse thee! let a sufferer's curse
    Clasp thee, his torturer, like remorse,
    Till thine Infinity shall be
    A robe of envenomed agony;
And thine Omnipotence a crown of pain   290
To cling like burning gold round thy dissolving brain.

Heap on thy soul, by virtue of this curse,
  Ill deeds; then be thou damned, beholding good,

Both infinite as is the universe,
    And thou, and thy self-torturing solitude.   295
      An awful image of calm power
      Though now thou sittest, let the hour
      Come, when thou must appear to be
      That which thou art internally;
And after many a false and fruitless crime   300
Scorn track thy lagging fall through boundless space and
    time.

PROMETHEUS

Were these my words, O Parent?

THE EARTH

                They were thine.

PROMETHEUS

It doth repent me: words are quick and vain;
Grief for a while is blind, and so was mine.
I wish no living thing to suffer pain.   305

THE EARTH

    Misery, oh misery to me,
    That Jove at length should vanquish thee.
    Wail, howl aloud, Land and Sea;
    The Earth's rent heart shall answer ye.
    Howl, Spirits of the living and the dead;   310
Your refuge, your defence lies fallen and vanquishèd.

FIRST ECHO

Lies fallen and vanquishèd?

SECOND ECHO

Fallen and vanquishèd!

IONE

Fear not: 'tis but some passing spasm,
   The Titan is unvanquished still.   315
But see, where through the azure chasm
   Of yon forked and snowy hill,
Trampling the slant winds on high
   With golden-sandalled feet, that glow
Under plumes of purple dye,   320
Like rose-ensanguined ivory,
     A Shape comes now,
Stretching on high from his right hand
   A serpent-cinctured wand.

PANTHEA

'Tis Jove's world-wandering herald, Mercury.   325

IONE

And who are those with hydra tresses
   And iron wings that climb the wind,
Whom the frowning God represses,
   Like vapours steaming up behind,
Clanging loud, an endless crowd?   330

PANTHEA

These are Jove's tempest-walking hounds,
Whom he gluts with groans and blood,
When, charioted on sulphurous cloud,
   He bursts Heaven's bounds.

IONE

Are they now led from the thin dead,   335
   On new pangs to be fed?

PANTHEA

The Titan looks as ever, firm, not proud.

FIRST FURY

Ha! I scent life!

SECOND FURY

Let me but look into his eyes!

THIRD FURY

The hope of torturing him smells like a heap
Of corpses to a death-bird after battle.   340

FIRST FURY

Darest thou delay, O Herald? take cheer, Hounds
Of Hell: what if the Son of Maia soon
Should make us food and sport? Who can please long
The Omnipotent?

MERCURY

                    Back to your towers of iron,
And gnash, beside the streams of fire and wail,   345
Your foodless teeth! . . . Geryon, arise! and Gorgon,
Chimæra, and thou Sphinx, subtlest of fiends,
Who ministered to Thebes Heaven's poisoned wine—
Unnatural love and more unnatural hate:
These shall perform your task.

FIRST FURY

                    Oh, mercy! mercy!   350
We die with our desire: drive us not back!

MERCURY

Crouch then in silence.
                    Awful Sufferer!
To thee unwilling, most unwillingly
I come, by the great Father's will driven down,
To execute a doom of new revenge.   355

82

Alas! I pity thee, and hate myself
That I can do no more. Aye from thy sight
Returning, for a season, Heaven seems Hell,
So thy worn form pursues me night and day,
Smiling reproach. Wise art thou, firm and good,   360
But vainly wouldst stand forth alone in strife
Against the Omnipotent; as yon clear lamps
That measure and divide the weary years
From which there is no refuge, long have taught,
And long must teach. Even now thy torturer arms   365
With the strange might of unimagined pains
The powers who scheme slow agonies in Hell,
And my commission is to lead them here,
Or what more subtle, foul and savage fiends
People the abyss, and leave them to their task.   370
Be it not so! There is a secret known
To thee, and to none else of living things,
Which may transfer the sceptre of wide Heaven,
The fear of which perplexes the Supreme.
Clothe it in words, and bid it clasp his throne   375
In intercession; bend thy soul in prayer,
And like a suppliant in some gorgeous fane,
Let the will kneel within thy haughty heart:
For benefits and meek submission tame
The fiercest and the mightiest.

PROMETHEUS

                 Evil minds   380
Change good to their own nature. I gave all
He has; and in return he chains me here
Years, ages, night and day—whether the sun
Split my parched skin, or in the moony night
The crystal-wingèd snow cling round my hair—   385
Whilst my belovèd race is trampled down
By his thought-executing ministers.
Such is the tyrant's recompense—'tis just:

He who is evil can receive no good;
And for a world bestowed, or a friend lost, 390
He can feel hate, fear, shame—not gratitude:
He but requites me for his own misdeed.
Kindness to such is keen reproach, which breaks
With bitter stings the light sleep of Revenge.
Submission, thou dost know, I cannot try: 395
For what submission but that fatal word,
The death-seal of mankind's captivity,
Like the Sicilian's hair-suspended sword
Which trembles o'er his crown, would he accept,
Or could I yield?—Which yet I will not yield. 400
Let others flatter Crime, where it sits throned
In brief omnipotence; secure are they:
For Justice, when triumphant, will weep down
Pity, not punishment, on her own wrongs,
Too much avenged by those who err. I wait, 405
Enduring thus, the retributive hour
Which since we spake is even nearer now.
But hark, the hell-hounds clamour: fear delay:
Behold! Heaven lowers under thy Father's frown.

MERCURY

Oh, that we might be spared—I to inflict, 410
And thou to suffer! Once more answer me:
Thou knowest not the period of Jove's power?

PROMETHEUS

I know but this, that it must come.

MERCURY

Alas!
Thou canst not count thy years to come of pain?

PROMETHEUS

They last while Jove must reign; nor more, nor less 415
Do I desire or fear.

MERCURY

        Yet pause, and plunge
Into eternity, where recorded time,
Even all that we imagine, age on age,
Seems but a point, and the reluctant mind
Flags wearily in its unending flight,   420
Till it sink, dizzy, blind, lost, shelterless;
Perchance it has not numbered the slow years
Which thou must spend in torture, unreprieved.

PROMETHEUS

Perchance no thought can count them—yet they pass.

MERCURY

If thou might'st dwell among the Gods the while,   425
Lapped in voluptuous joy?

PROMETHEUS

        I would not quit
This bleak ravine, these unrepentant pains.

MERCURY

Alas! I wonder at, yet pity thee.

PROMETHEUS

Pity the self-despising slaves of Heaven,
Not me, within whose mind sits peace serene,   **430**
As light in the sun, throned ... How vain is talk!
Call up the fiends.

IONE

       O sister, look! White fire
Has cloven to the roots yon huge snow-loaded cedar;
How fearfully God's thunder howls behind!

MERCURY

I must obey his words and thine: alas!   435
Most heavily remorse hangs at my heart!

PANTHEA

See where the child of Heaven with wingèd feet
Runs down the slanted sunlight of the dawn.

IONE

Dear sister, close thy plumes over thine eyes
Lest thou behold and die: they come—they come   440
Blackening the birth of day with countless wings,
And hollow underneath, like death.

FIRST FURY

        Prometheus!

SECOND FURY

Immortal Titan!

THIRD FURY

    Champion of Heaven's slaves!

PROMETHEUS

He whom some dreadful voice invokes is here,
Prometheus, the chained Titan. Horrible forms,   445
What and who are ye? Never yet there came
Phantasms so foul through monster-teeming Hell
From the all-miscreative brain of Jove.
Whilst I behold such execrable shapes,
Methinks I grow like what I contemplate,   450
And laugh and stare in loathsome sympathy.

FIRST FURY

We are the ministers of pain, and fear,
And disappointment, and mistrust, and hate,

And clinging crime; and as lean dogs pursue
Through wood and lake some struck and sobbing
    fawn,   455
We track all things that weep, and bleed, and live
When the great King betrays them to our will.

PROMETHEUS

O many fearful natures in one name,
I know ye; and these lakes and echoes know
The darkness and the clangour of your wings.   460
But why more hideous than your loathèd selves
Gather ye up in legions from the deep?

SECOND FURY

We knew not that: Sisters, rejoice, rejoice!

PROMETHEUS

Can aught exult in its deformity?

SECOND FURY

The beauty of delight makes lovers glad,   465
Gazing on one another: so are we.
As from the rose which the pale priestess kneels
To gather for her festal crown of flowers
The aërial crimson falls, flushing her cheek—
So from our victim's destined agony   470
The shade which is our form invests us round;
Else are we shapeless as our mother Night.

PROMETHEUS

I laugh your power, and his who sent you here,
To lowest scorn. Pour forth the cup of pain.

FIRST FURY

Thou thinkest we will rend thee bone from bone,   475
And nerve from nerve, working like fire within?

87

PROMETHEUS

Pain is my element, as hate is thine;
Ye rend me now: I care not.

SECOND FURY

                        Dost imagine
We will but laugh into thy lidless eyes?

PROMETHEUS

I weigh not what ye do, but what ye suffer,   480
Being evil. Cruel was the Power which called
You, or aught else so wretched, into light.

THIRD FURY

Thou think'st we will live through thee, one by one,
Like animal life; and though we can obscure not
The soul which burns within, that we will dwell   485
Beside it, like a vain loud multitude
Vexing the self-content of wisest men;
That we will be dread thought beneath thy brain,
And foul desire round thine astonished heart,
And blood within thy labyrinthine veins   490
Crawling like agony?

PROMETHEUS

                Why, ye are thus now:
Yet am I king over myself, and rule
The torturing and conflicting throngs within,
As Jove rules you when Hell grows mutinous.

CHORUS OF FURIES

From the ends of the earth, from the ends of the earth, 495
Where the night has its grave and the morning its birth,
          Come, come, come!
O ye who shake hills with the scream of your mirth.
When cities sink howling in ruin; and ye

Who with wingless footsteps trample the sea,   500
And close upon Shipwreck and Famine's track
Sit chattering with joy on the foodless wreck;
      Come, come, come!
  Leave the bed, low, cold, and red,
  Strewed beneath a nation dead;   505
  Leave the hatred—as in ashes
    Fire is left for future burning—
  It will burst in bloodier flashes
    When ye stir it, soon returning;
  Leave the self-contempt implanted   510
  In young spirits, sense-enchanted,
    Misery's yet unkindled fuel;
  Leave Hell's secrets half unchanted
    To the maniac dreamer: cruel
  More than ye can be with hate   515
      Is he with fear.
      Come, come, come!
We are steaming up from Hell's wide gate,
  And we burden the blasts of the atmosphere,
  But vainly we toil till ye come here.   520

IONE

Sister, I hear the thunder of new wings.

PANTHEA

These solid mountains quiver with the sound
Even as the tremulous air: their shadows make
The space within my plumes more black than night.

FIRST FURY

    Your call was as a wingèd car,   525
    Driven on whirlwinds fast and far;
    It rapt us from red gulfs of war;

SECOND FURY

From wide cities, famine-wasted;

THIRD FURY

Groans half heard, and blood untasted;

FOURTH FURY

Kingly conclaves, stern and cold,   530
Where blood with gold is bought and sold;

FIFTH FURY

From the furnace, white and hot,
In which—

A FURY

       Speak not—whisper not:
I know all that ye would tell,
But to speak might break the spell   535
Which must bend the Invincible,
   The stern of thought;
He yet defies the deepest power of Hell.

FURY

Tear the veil!

ANOTHER FURY

  It is torn!

CHORUS

       The pale stars of the morn
Shine on a misery, dire to be borne,   540
Dost thou faint, mighty Titan? We laugh thee to scorn.
Dost thou boast the clear knowledge thou waken'dst for
    man?
Then was kindled within him a thirst which outran

Those perishing waters; a thirst of fierce fever,
Hope, love, doubt, desire—which consume him
    for ever.   545
        One came forth of gentle worth
        Smiling on the sanguine earth;
        His words outlived him, like swift poison
            Withering up truth, peace, and pity.
        Look where round the wide horizon   550
            Many a million-peopled city
        Vomits smoke in the bright air.
        Hark that outcry of despair!
        'Tis his mild and gentle ghost
        Wailing for the faith he kindled.   555
        Look again! the flames almost
            To a glow-worm's lamp have dwindled:
        The survivors round the embers
            Gather in dread.
                Joy, joy, joy!   560
Past ages crowd on thee, but each one remembers,
And the future is dark, and the present is spread
Like a pillow of thorns for thy slumberless head.

Semichorus I

        Drops of bloody agony flow
        From his white and quivering brow.   565
        Grant a little respite now.
        See! a disenchanted nation
        Springs like day from desolation;
        To Truth its state is dedicate,
        And Freedom leads it forth, her mate;   570
        A legioned band of linkèd brothers,
        Whom Love calls children—

Semichorus II

                 'Tis another's.
See how kindred murder kin!

'Tis the vintage-time for Death and Sin;
Blood, like new wine, bubbles within; 575
 Till Despair smothers
The struggling world—which slaves and tyrants win.
   [*All the* FURIES *vanish, except one.*

IONE

Hark, sister! what a low yet dreadful groan
Quite unsuppressed is tearing up the heart
Of the good Titan—as storms tear the deep, 580
And beasts hear the sea moan in inland caves.
Darest thou observe how the fiends torture him?

PANTHEA

Alas! I looked forth twice, but will no more.

IONE

What didst thou see?

PANTHEA

    A woeful sight: a youth
With patient looks nailed to a crucifix. 585

IONE

What next?

PANTHEA

    The heaven around, the earth below
Was peopled with thick shapes of human death,
All horrible, and wrought by human hands—
Though some appeared the work of human hearts,
For men were slowly killed by frowns and smiles; 590
And other sights too foul to speak and live
Were wandering by. Let us not tempt worse fear
By looking forth: those groans are grief enough.

FURY

Behold an emblem: those who do endure
Deep wrongs for man, and scorn, and chains, but heap 595
Thousandfold torment on themselves and him.

PROMETHEUS

Remit the anguish of that lighted stare;
Close those wan lips; let that thorn-wounded brow
Stream not with blood—it mingles with thy tears!
Fix, fix those tortured orbs in peace and death,   600
So thy sick throes shake not that crucifix,
So those pale fingers play not with thy gore.
Oh, horrible! Thy name I will not speak;
It hath become a curse. I see, I see
The wise, the mild, the lofty, and the just,   605
Whom thy slaves hate for being like to thee:
Some hunted by foul lies from their heart's home,
An early-chosen, late-lamented home,
As hooded ounces cling to the driven hind;
Some linked to corpses in unwholesome cells;   610
Some—hear I not the multitude laugh loud?—
Impaled in lingering fire: and mighty realms
Float by my feet, like sea-uprooted isles,
Whose sons are kneaded down in common blood
By the red light of their own burning homes.   615

FURY

Blood thou canst see, and fire; and canst hear groans:
Worse things unheard, unseen, remain behind.

PROMETHEUS

Worse?

FURY

In each human heart terror survives
The ravin it has gorged; the loftiest fear
All that they would disdain to think were true: 620

93

Hypocrisy and Custom make their minds
The fanes of many a worship, now outworn.
They dare not devise good for man's estate,
And yet they know not that they do not dare.
The good want power, but to weep barren tears;　　625
The powerful goodness want—worse need for them;
The wise want love; and those who love want wisdom;
And all best things are thus confused to ill.
Many are strong and rich, and would be just,
But live among their suffering fellow-men　　　　630
As if none felt: they know not what they do.

PROMETHEUS

Thy words are like a cloud of wingèd snakes;
And yet I pity those they torture not.

FURY

Thou pitiest them? I speak no more!　　　　[*Vanishes.*

PROMETHEUS

Ah woe!
Ah woe! Alas! pain, pain ever, for ever!　　　　635
I close my tearless eyes, but see more clear
Thy works within my woe-illumèd mind,
Thou subtle Tyrant! . . . Peace is in the grave—
The grave hides all things beautiful and good.
I am a God and cannot find it there;　　　　640
Nor would I seek it; for, though dread revenge,
This is defeat, fierce King, not victory!
The sights with which thou torturest gird my soul
With new endurance, till the hour arrives
When they shall be no types of things which are.　　645

PANTHEA

Alas! what sawest thou more?

94

PROMETHEUS

There are two woes:

To speak and to behold; thou spare me one.
Names are there, Nature's sacred watch-words: they
Were borne aloft in bright emblazonry.
The nations thronged around, and cried aloud,   650
As with one voice, 'Truth, Liberty, and Love!'
Suddenly fierce confusion fell from Heaven
Among them; there was strife, deceit, and fear;
Tyrants rushed in, and did divide the spoil.
This was the shadow of the truth I saw.   655

THE EARTH

I felt thy torture, Son, with such mixed joy
As pain and virtue give. To cheer thy state
I bid ascend those subtle and fair spirits,
Whose homes are the dim caves of human thought,
And who inhabit, as birds wing the wind,   660
Its world-surrounding æther; they behold
Beyond that twilight realm, as in a glass,
The future: may they speak comfort to thee!

PANTHEA

Look, sister, where a troop of spirits gather,
Like flocks of clouds in Spring's delightful weather,   665
Thronging in the blue air!

IONE

And see! more come,

Like fountain-vapours when the winds are dumb,
That climb up the ravine in scattered lines.
And hark! is it the music of the pines?
Is it the lake? is it the waterfall?   670

PANTHEA

'Tis something sadder, sweeter far than all.

CHORUS OF SPIRITS

From unremembered ages we
Gentle guides and guardians be
Of Heaven-oppressed mortality;
And we breathe, and sicken not,   675
The atmosphere of human thought:
Be it dim, and dank, and grey,
Like a storm-extinguished day,
Travelled o'er by dying gleams;
  Be it bright as all between   680
Cloudless skies and windless streams,
  Silent, liquid, and serene.
As the birds within the wind,
  As the fish within the wave,
As the thoughts of man's own mind   685
  Float through all above the grave,
We make there our liquid lair,
  Voyaging cloudlike and unpent
Through the boundless element:
Thence we bear the prophecy   690
Which begins and ends in thee!

IONE

More yet come, one by one: the air around them
Looks radiant as the air around a star.

FIRST SPIRIT

On a battle-trumpet's blast
I fled hither, fast, fast, fast,   695
'Mid the darkness upward cast.
From the dust of creeds outworn,
From the tyrant's banner torn,
Gathering round me, onward borne,
There was mingled many a cry—   700
'Freedom! Hope! Death! Victory!'

Till they faded through the sky;
And one sound above, around,
One sound beneath, around, above,
Was moving; 'twas the soul of love;   705
'Twas the hope, the prophecy,
Which begins and ends in thee.

SECOND SPIRIT

A rainbow's arch stood on the sea,
Which rocked beneath, immovably;
And the triumphant storm did flee,   710
Like a conqueror, swift and proud,
Between, with many a captive cloud,
A shapeless, dark and rapid crowd.
Each by lightning riven in half.
I heard the thunder hoarsely laugh.   715
Mighty fleets were strewn like chaff
And spread beneath a hell of death
O'er the white waters. I alit
On a great ship lightning-split,
And speeded hither on the sigh   720
Of one who gave an enemy
His plank—then plunged aside to die.

THIRD SPIRIT

I sat beside a sage's bed,
And the lamp was burning red
Near the book where he had fed;   725
When a Dream with plumes of flame
To his pillow hovering came,
And I knew it was the same
Which had kindled long ago
Pity, eloquence, and woe;   730
And the world awhile below
Wore the shade its lustre made.

It has borne me here as fleet
As Desire's lightning feet:
I must ride it back ere morrow,   735
Or the sage will wake in sorrow.

Fourth Spirit

On a poet's lips I slept
Dreaming like a love-adept
In the sound his breathing kept;
Nor seeks nor finds he mortal blisses,   740
But feeds on the aërial kisses
Of shapes that haunt thought's wildernesses.
He will watch from dawn to gloom
The lake-reflected sun illume
The yellow bees i' the ivy-bloom,   745
Nor heed nor see what things they be;
But from these create he can
Forms more real than living man,
Nurslings of immortality!
One of these awakened me.   750
And I sped to succour thee.

Ione

Behold'st thou not two shapes from the east and west
Come, as two doves to one belovèd nest,
Twin nurslings of the all-sustaining air,
On swift still wings glide down the atmosphere?   755
And hark! their sweet, sad voices! 'tis despair
Mingled with love and then dissolved in sound.

Panthea

Canst thou speak, sister? all my words are drowned.

Ione

Their beauty gives me voice. See how they float
On their sustaining wings of skiey grain.   760

Orange and azure deepening into gold:
Their soft smiles light the air like a star's fire.

CHORUS OF SPIRITS

Hast thou beheld the form of Love?

FIFTH SPIRIT

                      As over wide dominions
I sped, like some swift cloud that wings the wide air's
    wildernesses,
That planet-crested Shape swept by on lightning-
    braided pinions,   765
    Scattering the liquid joy of life from his ambrosial
    tresses:
His footsteps paved the world with light; but as I passed
    'twas fading,
    And hollow Ruin yawned behind: great sages bound in
    madness,
And headless patriots, and pale youths who perished,
    un-upbraiding,
    Gleamed in the night I wandered o'er—till thou, O
    King of sadness,   770
    Turned by thy smile the worst I saw to recollected
    gladness.

SIXTH SPIRIT

Ah, sister! Desolation is a delicate thing:
    It walks not on the earth, it floats not on the air,
But treads with lulling footstep, and fans with silent wing
    The tender hopes which in their hearts the best and
    gentlest bear,   775
Who, soothed to false repose by the fanning plumes above,
    And the music-stirring motion of its soft and busy feet,
Dream visions of aërial joy, and call the monster Love,
    And wake, and find the shadow Pain—as he whom now
    we greet.

Chorus

Though Ruin now Love's shadow be, 780
Following him destroyingly,
  On Death's white and wingèd steed,
Which the fleetest cannot flee—
  Trampling down both flower and weed,
Man and beast, and foul and fair, 785
Like a tempest through the air—
Thou shalt quell this Horseman grim,
Woundless though in heart or limb.

Prometheus

Spirits! how know ye this shall be?

Chorus

In the atmosphere we breathe— 790
  As buds grow red when snow-storms flee
  From spring gathering up beneath,
Whose mild winds shake the elder-brake,
  And the wandering herdsmen know
That the white-thorn soon will blow— 795
Wisdom, Justice, Love, and Peace,
When they struggle to increase,
Are to us as soft winds be
To shepherd-boys—the prophecy
Which begins and ends in thee. 800

Ione

Where are the Spirits fled?

Panthea

         Only a sense
Remains of them, like the omnipotence
Of music, when the inspired voice and lute
Languish, ere yet the responses are mute,

Which through the deep and labyrinthine soul,   805
Like echoes through long caverns, wind and roll.

PROMETHEUS

How fair these air-born shapes! and yet I feel
Most vain all hope but love; and thou art far,
Asia! who, when my being overflowed,
Wert like a golden chalice to bright wine   810
Which else had sunk into the thirsty dust.
All things are still. Alas! how heavily
This quiet morning weighs upon my heart.
Though I should dream, I could even sleep with grief,
If slumber were denied not . . . . I would fain   815
Be what it is my destiny to be,
The saviour and the strength of suffering man,
Or sink into the original gulf of things . . . .
There is no agony, and no solace left;
Earth can console, Heaven can torment no more.   820

PANTHEA

Hast thou forgotten one who watches thee
The cold dark night, and never sleeps but when
The shadow of thy spirit falls on her?

PROMETHEUS

I said all hope was vain but love: thou lovest.

PANTHEA

Deeply in truth; but the eastern star looks white,   825
And Asia waits in that far Indian vale
The scene of her sad exile—rugged once
And desolate and frozen, like this ravine,
But now invested with fair flowers and herbs,
And haunted by sweet airs and sounds, which flow   830
Among the woods and waters, from the æther
Of her transforming presence, which would fade
If it were mingled not with thine. Farewell!

ACT II

ASIA

From all the blasts of Heaven thou hast descended:
Yes, like a spirit, like a thought, which makes
Unwonted tears throng to the horny eyes,
And beatings haunt the desolated heart,
Which should have learnt repose; thou hast descended   5
Cradled in tempests; thou dost wake, O Spring!
O child of many winds! As suddenly
Thou comest as the memory of a dream,
Which now is sad because it hath been sweet;
Like genius, or like joy which riseth up   10
As from the earth, clothing with golden clouds
The desert of our life . . . .
This is the season, this the day, the hour;
At sunrise thou shouldst come, sweet sister mine;
Too long desired, too long delaying, come!   15
How like death-worms the wingless moments crawl!
The point of one white star is quivering still
Deep in the orange light of widening morn
Beyond the purple mountains; through a chasm
Of wind-divided mist the darker lake   20
Reflects it—now it wanes—it gleams again
As the waves fade, and as the burning threads
Of woven cloud unravel in pale air . . .
'Tis lost! and through yon peaks of cloud-like snow
The roseate sunlight quivers—hear I not   25
The Aeolian music of her sea-green plumes
Winnowing the crimson dawn?   [PANTHEA *enters.*
            I feel, I see
Those eyes which burn through smiles that fade in tears,
Like stars half quenched in mists of silver dew.

Belovèd and most beautiful, who wearest   30
The shadow of that soul by which I live,
How late thou art! the spherèd sun had climbed
The sea, my heart was sick with hope, before
The printless air felt thy belated plumes.

PANTHEA

Pardon, great sister! but my wings were faint   35
With the delight of a remembered dream,
As are the noontide plumes of summer winds
Satiate with sweet flowers. I was wont to sleep
Peacefully, and awake refreshed and calm,
Before the sacred Titan's fall and thy   40
Unhappy love had made, through use and pity,
Both love and woe familiar to my heart
As they had grown to thine. Erewhile I slept
Under the glaucous caverns of old Ocean
Within dim bowers of green and purple moss,   45
Our young Ione's soft and milky arms
Locked then, as now, behind my dark, moist hair,
While my shut eyes and cheek were pressed within
The folded depth of her life-breathing bosom:
But not as now, since I am made the wind   50
Which fails beneath the music that I bear
Of thy most wordless converse; since dissolved
Into the sense with which love talks, my rest
Was troubled and yet sweet, my waking hours
Too full of care and pain.

ASIA

                    Lift up thine eyes,   55
And let me read thy dream.

PANTHEA

                    As I have said,
With our sea-sister at his feet I slept.

The mountain mists, condensing at our voice
Under the moon, had spread their snowy flakes,
From the keen ice shielding our linkèd sleep.   60
Then two dreams came. One, I remember not.
But in the other, his pale, wound-worn limbs
Fell from Prometheus, and the azure night
Grew radiant with the glory of that form
Which lives unchanged within, and his voice fell   65
Like music which makes giddy the dim brain,
Faint with intoxication of keen joy:
'Sister of her whose footsteps pave the world
With loveliness—more fair than aught but her,
Whose shadow thou art—lift thine eyes on me.'   70
I lifted them: the overpowering light
Of that immortal shape was shadowed o'er
By love, which, from his soft and flowing limbs,
And passion-parted lips, and keen, faint eyes,
Steamed forth like vaporous fire, an atmosphere   75
Which wrapped me in its all-dissolving power,
As the warm æther of the morning sun
Wraps ere it drinks some cloud of wandering dew.
I saw not, heard not, moved not, only felt
His presence flow and mingle through my blood   80
Till it became his life, and his grew mine,
And I was thus absorbed—until it passed;
And like the vapours when the sun sinks down,
Gathering again in drops upon the pines,
And tremulous as they, in the deep night   85
My being was condensed; and as the rays
Of thought were slowly gathered, I could hear
His voice, whose accents lingered ere they died
Like footsteps of far melody. Thy name
Among the many sounds alone I heard   90
Of what might be articulate; though still
I listened through the night when sound was none.
Ione wakened then, and said to me:

'Canst thou divine what troubles me to-night?
I always knew what I desired before,   95
Nor ever found delight to wish in vain.
But now I cannot tell thee what I seek;
I know not; something sweet, since it is sweet
Even to desire. It is thy sport, false sister!
Thou hast discovered some enchantment old,   100
Whose spells have stolen my spirit as I slept
And mingled it with thine; for when just now
We kissed, I felt within thy parted lips
The sweet air that sustained me, and the warmth
Of the life-blood, for loss of which I faint,   105
Quivered between our intertwining arms.'
I answered not, for the eastern star grew pale,
But fled to thee.

ASIA

    Thou speakest, but thy words
Are as the air: I feel them not .... Oh, lift
Thine eyes, that I may read his written soul!   110

PANTHEA

I lift them, though they droop beneath the load
Of that they would express: what canst thou see
But thine own fairest shadow imaged there?

ASIA

Thine eyes are like the deep, blue, boundless heaven
Contracted to two circles underneath   115
Their long, fine lashes: dark, far, measureless,
Orb within orb, and line through line inwoven.

PANTHEA

Why lookest thou as if a spirit passed?

Asia

There is a change; beyond their inmost depth
I see a shade, a shape: 'tis He, arrayed   120
In the soft light of his own smiles, which spread
Like radiance from the cloud-surrounded moon.
Prometheus, it is thine! depart not yet!
Say not those smiles that we shall meet again
Within that bright pavilion which their beams   125
Shall build o'er the waste world? The dream is told.
What shape is that between us? Its rude hair
Roughens the wind that lifts it; its regard
Is wild and quick; yet 'tis a thing of air,
For through its grey robe gleams the golden dew   130
Whose stars the noon has quenched not.

Dream

Follow! Follow!

Panthea

It is mine other dream:—

Asia

It disappears.

Panthea

It passes now into my mind. Methought
As we sat here, the flower-infolding buds
Burst on yon lightning-blasted almond tree,   135
When swift from the white Scythian wilderness
A wind swept forth, wrinkling the earth with frost.
I looked, and all the blossoms were blown down;
But on each leaf was stamped—as the blue bells
Of Hyacinth tell Apollo's written grief—   140
Oh, follow, follow!

ASIA

As you speak, your words
Fill, pause by pause, my own forgotten sleep
With shapes. Methought among these lawns together
We wandered, underneath the young grey dawn,
And multitudes of dense, white, fleecy clouds   145
Were wandering in thick flocks along the mountains,
Shepherded by the slow, unwilling wind;
And the white dew on the new-bladed grass,
Just piercing the dark earth, hung silently:
And there was more which I remember not;   150
But on the shadows of the moving clouds
Athwart the purple mountain-slope, was written
FOLLOW, OH, FOLLOW! as they vanished by;
And on each herb, from which Heaven's dew had fallen,
The like was stamped, as with a withering fire.   155
A wind arose among the pines; it shook
The clinging music from their boughs, and then
Low, sweet, faint sounds, like the farewell of ghosts,
Were heard: OH, FOLLOW, FOLLOW, FOLLOW ME!
And then I said, 'Panthea, look on me:'   160
But in the depth of those belovèd eyes
Still I saw, FOLLOW, FOLLOW!

ECHO

Follow, follow!

PANTHEA

The crags, this clear spring morning, mock our voices,
As they were spirit-tongued.

ASIA

It is some being
Around the crags. What fine clear sounds! Oh list!   165

ECHOES (*unseen*)

Echoes we: listen!
We cannot stay:
As dew-stars glisten
Then fade away—
Child of Ocean!   170

ASIA

Hark! Spirits speak! The liquid responses
Of their aërial tongues yet sound.

PANTHEA   ●

I hear.

ECHOES

Oh, follow, follow,
As our voice recedeth
Through the caverns hollow,   175
Where the forest spreadeth;

(*More distant*)

Oh, follow, follow
Through the caverns hollow;
As the song floats, thou pursue,
Where the wild bee never flew,   180
Through the noontide darkness deep,
By the odour-breathing sleep
Of faint night-flowers, and the waves
At the fountain-lighted caves,
While our music, wild and sweet,   185
Mocks thy gently-falling feet,
Child of Ocean!

Asia

Shall we pursue the sound?—It grows more faint
And distant.

Panthea

List! the strain floats nearer now.

Echoes

In the world unknown 190
Sleeps a voice unspoken;
By thy step alone
Can its rest be broken,
Child of Ocean!

Asia

How the notes sink upon the ebbing wind! 195

Echoes

Oh, follow, follow
Through the caverns hollow;
As the song floats, thou pursue,
By the woodland noontide dew,
By the forests, lakes, and fountains, 200
Through the many-folded mountains,
To the rents, and gulfs, and chasms,
Where the Earth reposed from spasms,
On the day when he and thou
Parted—to commingle now, 205
Child of Ocean!

Asia

Come, sweet Panthea, link thy hand in mine,
And follow, ere the voices fade away.

SCENE II.— *A forest, intermingled with rocks and caverns.*
ASIA *and* PANTHEA *pass into it. Two young Fauns are
sitting on a rock, listening.*

SEMICHORUS I OF SPIRITS

The path through which that lovely twain
  Have passed, by cedar, pine, and yew,
  And each dark tree that ever grew,
  Is curtained out from heaven's wide blue;
Nor sun, nor moon, nor wind, nor rain,   5
    Can pierce its interwoven bowers;
  Nor aught, save where some cloud of dew,
Drifted along the earth-creeping breeze
Between the trunks of the hoar trees,
    Hangs each a pearl in the pale flowers   10
  Of the green laurel, blown anew,
And bends, and then fades silently,
One frail and fair anemone;
Or when some star of many a one
    That climbs and wanders through steep night, 15
Has found the cleft through which alone
Beams fall from high those depths upon,
Ere it is borne away, away,
By the swift heavens that cannot stay—
    It scatters drops of golden light,   20
    Like lines of rain that ne'er unite;
And the gloom divine is all around;
And underneath is the mossy ground.

SEMICHORUS II

There the voluptuous nightingales
    Are awake through all the broad noonday.   25
When one with bliss or sadness fails,
    And through the windless ivy-boughs,
  Sick with sweet love, droops dying away
On its mate's music-panting bosom,

Another from the swinging blossom, 30
    Watching to catch the languid close
Of the last strain, then lifts on high
The wings of the weak melody,
Till some new stream of feeling bear
    The song, and all the woods are mute; 35
When there is heard through the dim air
The rush of wings, and rising there
    Like many a lake-surrounded flute,
Sounds overflow the listener's brain
So sweet, that joy is almost pain. 40

Semichorus I

There those enchanted eddies play
    Of echoes, music-tongued, which draw,
    By Demogorgon's mighty law,
    With melting rapture or deep awe,
All spirits on that secret way, 45
    As inland boats are driven to ocean
Down streams made strong with mountain-thaw;
And first there comes a gentle sound
To those in talk or slumber bound,
    And wakes the destined; soft emotion 50
    Attracts, impels them. Those who saw
Say from the breathing earth behind
There streams a plume-uplifting wind
Which drives them on their path, while they
    Believe their own swift wings and feet 55
The sweet desires within obey;
And so they float upon their way,
Until, still sweet, but loud and strong,
The storm of sound is driven along,
    Sucked up and hurrying; as they fleet, 60
    Behind its gathering billows meet
And to the fatal mountain bear
Like clouds amid the yielding air.

FIRST FAUN

Canst thou imagine where those spirits live
Which make such delicate music in the woods? 65
We haunt within the least frequented caves
And closest coverts, and we know these wilds,
Yet never meet them, though we hear them oft:
Where may they hide themselves?

SECOND FAUN

'Tis hard to tell:
I have heard those more skilled in spirits say, 70
The bubbles, which the enchantment of the sun
Sucks from the pale faint water-flowers, that pave
The oozy bottom of clear lakes and pools,
Are the pavilions where such dwell and float
Under the green and golden atmosphere 75
Which noontide kindles through the woven leaves;
And when these burst, and the thin fiery air,
The which they breathed within those lucent domes,
Ascends to flow like meteors through the night,
They ride on them, and rein their headlong speed, 80
And bow their burning crests, and glide in fire
Under the waters of the earth again.

FIRST FAUN

If such live thus, have others other lives,
Under pink blossoms or within the bells
Of meadow-flowers, or folded violets deep, 85
Or on their dying odours, when they die,
Or in the sunlight of the spherèd dew?

SECOND FAUN

Ay, many more, which we may well divine.
But should we stay to speak, noontide would come,
And thwart Silenus find his goats undrawn, 90

And grudge to sing those wise and lovely songs
Of Fate, and Chance, and God, and Chaos old,
And Love, and the chained Titan's woeful doom,
And how he shall be loosed, and make the earth
One brotherhood: delightful strains which cheer   95
Our solitary twilights, and which charm
To silence the unenvying nightingales.

SCENE III.—*A pinnacle of rock among mountains.* ASIA *and*
PANTHEA.

PANTHEA

Hither the sound has borne us—to the realm
Of Demogorgon, and the mighty portal,
Like a volcano's meteor-breathing chasm,
Whence the oracular vapour is hurled up
Which lonely men drink wandering in their youth,   5
And call truth, virtue, love, genius, or joy—
That maddening wine of life, whose dregs they drain
To deep intoxication, and uplift,
Like Mænads who cry loud, Evoe! Evoe!
The voice which is contagion to the world.   10

ASIA

Fit throne for such a Power! Magnificent!
How glorious art thou, Earth! and if thou be
The shadow of some Spirit lovelier still,
Though evil stain its work, and it should be
Like its creation, weak yet beautiful,   15
I could fall down and worship that and thee.
Even now my heart adoreth. Wonderful!
Look, sister, ere the vapour dim thy brain:
Beneath is a wide plain of billowy mist,

As a lake, paving in the morning sky, 20
With azure waves which burst in silver light,
Some Indian vale. Behold it, rolling on
Under the curdling winds, and islanding
The peak whereon we stand—midway, around
Encinctured by the dark and blooming forests, 25
Dim twilight lawns and stream-illumèd caves,
And wind-enchanted shapes of wandering mist;
And far on high the keen sky-cleaving mountains
From icy spires of sunlike radiance fling
The dawn, as lifted ocean's dazzling spray, 30
From some Atlantic islet scattered up,
Spangles the wind with lamp-like water-drops.
The vale is girdled with their walls; a howl
Of cataracts from their thaw-cloven ravines
Satiates the listening wind, continuous, vast, 35
Awful as silence. Hark! the rushing snow!
The sun-awakened avalanche! whose mass,
Thrice sifted by the storm, had gathered there
Flake after flake, in Heaven-defying minds
As thought by thought is piled, till some great truth 40
Is ioosened, and the nations echo round,
Shaken to their roots, as do the mountains now.

PANTHEA

Look, how the gusty sea of mist is breaking
In crimson foam, even at our feet!—it rises
As ocean at the enchantment of the moon 45
Round foodless men wrecked on some oozy isle.

ASIA

The fragments of the cloud are scattered up—
The wind that lifts them disentwines my hair—
Its billows now sweep o'er mine eyes—my brain
Grows dizzy—seest thou shapes within the mist? 50

PANTHEA

A countenance with beckoning smiles: there burns
An azure fire within its golden locks!
Another and another: hark! they speak!

SONG OF SPIRITS

To the deep, to the deep,
    Down, down!   55
Through the shade of sleep,
Through the cloudy strife
Of Death and of Life;
Through the veil and the bar
Of things which seem and are,   60
Even to the steps of the remotest throne,
    Down, down!

While the sound swirls around,
    Down, down!
As the fawn draws the hound,   65
As the lightning the vapour,
As a weak moth the taper;
Death, Despair; Love, Sorrow;
Time both; to-day, to-morrow;
As steel obeys the spirit of the stone,   70
    Down, down!

Through the grey, void abysm,
    Down, down!
Where the air is no prism,
And the moon and stars are not,   75
And the cavern-crags wear not
The radiance of heaven,
Nor the gloom to earth given;
Where there is One pervading, One alone,
    Down, down!   80

In the depth of the deep,
Down, down!
Like veiled lightning asleep,
Like that spark nursed in embers,
The last look Love remembers,   85
Like a diamond, which shines
On the dark wealth of mines,
A spell is treasured but for thee alone.
Down, down!

We have bound thee, we guide thee,   90
Down, down!
With the bright form beside thee.
Resist not the weakness:
Such strength is in meekness
That the Eternal, the Immortal,   95
Must unloose through life's portal
The snake-like Doom coiled underneath his throne,
By that alone!

SCENE IV.—*The cave of* DEMOGORGON. ASIA *and* PANTHEA.

PANTHEA

What veilèd form sits on that ebon throne?

ASIA

The veil has fallen!

PANTHEA

        I see a mighty Darkness
Filling the seat of power; and rays of gloom
Dart round, as light from the meridian sun,
Ungazed upon and shapeless—neither limb,   5
Nor form, nor outline; yet we feel it is
A living Spirit.

DEMOGORGON

Ask what thou wouldst know.

ASIA

What canst thou tell?

DEMOGORGON

All things thou dar'st demand.

ASIA

Who made the living world?

DEMOGORGON

God.

ASIA

                Who made all
That it contains—thought, passion, reason, will,   10
Imagination?

DEMOGORGON

God: Almighty God.

ASIA

Who made that sense which, when the winds of spring
In rarest visitation, or the voice
Of one belovèd heard in youth alone,
Fills the faint eyes with falling tears which dim   15
The radiant looks of unbewailing flowers,
And leaves this peopled earth a solitude
When it returns no more?

DEMOGORGON

             Merciful God.

ASIA

And who made terror, madness, crime, remorse,
Which from the links of the great chain of things   20
To every thought within the mind of man
Sway and drag heavily, and each one reels
Under the load towards the pit of death;
Abandoned hope, and love that turns to hate;
And self-contempt, bitterer to drink than blood;   25
Pain, whose unheeded and familiar speech
Is howling, and keen shrieks, day after day;
And Hell, or the sharp fear of Hell?

DEMOGORGON

He reigns.

ASIA

Utter his name: a world pining in pain
Asks but his name: curses shall drag him down.   30

DEMOGORGON

He reigns.

ASIA

I feel, I know it: who?

DEMOGORGON

He reigns.

ASIA

Who reigns? There was the Heaven and Earth at first,
And Light and Love; then Saturn, from whose throne
Time fell, an envious shadow; such the state
Of the earth's primal spirits beneath his sway,   35
As the calm joy of flowers and living leaves
Before the wind or sun has withered them,

And semivital worms; but he refused
The birthrights of their being, knowledge, power,
The skill which wields the elements, the thought   40
Which pierces this dim universe like light,
Self-empire, and the majesty of love;
For thirst of which they fainted. Then Prometheus
Gave wisdom, which is strength, to Jupiter,
And with this law alone, 'Let man be free,'   45
Clothed him with the dominion of wide Heaven.
To know nor faith nor love nor law, to be
Omnipotent but friendless, is to reign;
And Jove now reigned; for on the race of man
First famine, and then toil, and then disease,   50
Strife, wounds, and ghastly death unseen before,
Fell; and the unseasonable seasons drove,
With alternating shafts of frost and fire,
Their shelterless, pale tribes to mountain caves;
And in their desert hearts fierce wants he sent,   55
And mad disquietudes, and shadows idle
Of unreal good, which levied mutual war,
So ruining the lair wherein they raged.
Prometheus saw, and waked the legioned hopes
Which sleep within folded Elysian flowers,   60
Nepenthe, Moly, Amaranth, fadeless blooms,
That they might hide with thin and rainbow wings
The shape of Death; and Love he sent to bind
The disunited tendrils of that vine
Which bears the wine of life, the human heart;   65
And he tamed fire, which like some beast of chase
Most terrible, but lovely, played beneath
The frown of man; and tortured to his will
Iron and gold, the slaves and signs of power,
And gems and poisons, and all subtlest forms   70
Hidden beneath the mountains and the waves.
He gave man speech, and speech created thought,
Which is the measure of the universe;

And Science struck the thrones of earth and heaven,
Which shook, but fell not; and the harmonious mind   75
Poured itself forth in all-prophetic song;
And music lifted up the listening spirit
Until it walked, exempt from mortal care,
Godlike, o'er the clear billows of sweet sound;
And human hands first mimicked and then mocked,   80
With moulded limbs more lovely than its own
The human form, till marble grew divine,
And mothers, gazing, drank the love men see
Reflected in their race—behold, and perish.
He told the hidden power of herbs and springs,   85
And Disease drank and slept. Death grew like sleep.
He taught the implicated orbits woven
Of the wide-wandering stars, and how the sun
Changes his lair, and by what secret spell
The pale moon is transformed, when her broad eye   90
Gazes not on the interlunar sea.
He taught to rule, as life directs the limbs,
The tempest-wingèd chariots of the ocean,
And the Celt knew the Indian. Cities then
Were built, and through their snow-like columns flowed 95
The warm winds, and the azure æther shone,
And the blue sea and shadowy hills were seen.
Such, the alleviations of his state,
Prometheus gave to man—for which he hangs
Withering in destined pain. But who rains down   100
Evil, the immedicable plague, which, while
Man looks on his creation like a God
And sees that it is glorious, drives him on,
The wreck of his own will, the scorn of earth,
The outcast, the abandoned, the alone?   105
Not Jove: while yet his frown shook heaven, ay, when
His adversary from adamantine chains
Cursed him, he trembled like a slave. Declare
Who is his master? Is he too a slave?

DEMOGORGON

All spirits are enslaved which serve things evil.   110
Thou knowest if Jupiter be such or no.

ASIA

Whom called'st thou God?

DEMOGORGON

    I spoke but as ye speak,
For Jove is the supreme of living things.

ASIA

Who is the master of the slave?

DEMOGORGON

    If the abysm
Could vomit forth its secrets—but a voice   115
Is wanting, the deep truth is imageless;
For what would it avail to bid thee gaze
On the revolving world? what to bid speak
Fate, Time, Occasion, Chance and Change? To these
All things are subject but eternal Love.   120

ASIA

So much I asked before, and my heart gave
The response thou hast given; and of such truths
Each to itself must be the oracle.
One more demand; and do thou answer me
As my own soul would answer, did it know   125
That which I ask. Prometheus shall arise
Henceforth the sun of this rejoicing world:
When shall the destined hour arrive?

DEMOGORGON

    Behold!

ASIA

The rocks are cloven, and through the purple night
I see cars drawn by rainbow-wingèd steeds   130
Which trample the dim winds: in each there stands
A wild-eyed charioteer, urging their flight.
Some look behind, as fiends pursued them there,
And yet I see no shapes but the keen stars;
Others, with burning eyes, lean forth, and drink   135
With eager lips the wind of their own speed,
As if the thing they loved fled on before,
And now, even now, they clasped it. Their bright locks
Stream like a comet's flashing hair: they all
Sweep onward.

DEMOGORGON

          These are the immortal Hours,   140
Of whom thou didst demand. One waits for thee.

ASIA

A Spirit with a dreadful countenance
Checks its dark chariot by the craggy gulf.
Unlike thy brethren, ghastly charioteer,
What art thou? Whither wouldst thou bear me?
    Speak!   145

SPIRIT

I am the shadow of a destiny
More dread than is my aspect: ere yon planet
Has set, the Darkness which ascends with me
Shall wrap in lasting night Heaven's kingless throne.

ASIA

What meanest thou?

PANTHEA

That terrible shadow floats   150
Up from its throne, as may the lurid smoke
Of earthquake-ruined cities o'er the sea.
Lo! it ascends the car . . . the coursers fly
Terrified. Watch its path among the stars
Blackening the night!

ASIA

Thus I am answered: strange!   155

PANTHEA

See, near the verge, another chariot stays—
An ivory shell inlaid with crimson fire,
Which comes and goes within its sculptured rim
Of delicate strange tracery. The young Spirit
That guides it has the dove-like eyes of hope;   160
How its soft smiles attract the soul!—as light
Lures wingèd insects through the lampless air.

SPIRIT

My coursers are fed with the lightning,
   They drink of the whirlwind's stream,
And when the red morning is bright'ning   165
   They bathe in the fresh sunbeam;
   They have strength for their swiftness I deem:
Then ascend with me, Daughter of Ocean.

I desire—and their speed makes night kindle;
   I fear—they outstrip the Typhoon;   170
Ere the cloud piled on Atlas can dwindle
   We encircle the earth and the moon;
   We shall rest from long labours at noon:
Then ascend with me, Daughter of Ocean.

SCENE V.—*The car pauses within a cloud on the top of a snowy mountain.* ASIA, PANTHEA, *and the* SPIRIT OF THE HOUR.

SPIRIT

On the brink of the night and the morning
  My coursers are wont to respire;
But the Earth has just whispered a warning
  That their flight must be swifter than fire:
  They shall drink the hot speed of desire!   5

ASIA

Thou breathest on their nostrils, but my breath
Would give them swifter speed.

SPIRIT

           Alas! it could not.

PANTHEA

O Spirit! pause, and tell whence is the light
Which fills this cloud—the sun is yet unrisen.

SPIRIT

The sun will rise not until noon. Apollo   10
Is held in Heaven by wonder; and the light
Which fills this vapour, as the aërial hue
Of fountain-gazing roses fills the water,
Flows from thy mighty sister.

PANTHEA

           Yes, I feel . . .

ASIA

What is it with thee, sister? Thou art pale.   15

PANTHEA

How thou art changed! I dare not look on thee;
I feel, but see thee not. I scarce endure

The radiance of thy beauty. Some good change
Is working in the elements, which suffer
Thy presence thus unveiled. The Nereids tell 20
That on the day when the clear hyaline
Was cloven at thine uprise, and thou didst stand
Within a veinèd shell, which floated on
Over the calm floor of the crystal sea,
Among the Aegean isles, and by the shores 25
Which bear thy name, love, like the atmosphere
Of the sun's fire filling the living world,
Burst from thee, and illumined earth and heaven
And the deep ocean and the sunless caves,
And all that dwells within them; till grief cast 30
Eclipse upon the soul from which it came:
Such art thou now; nor is it I alone,
Thy sister, thy companion, thine own chosen one,
But the whole world which seeks thy sympathy.
Hearest thou not sounds i' the air which speak the love 35
Of all articulate beings? Feelest thou not
The inanimate winds enamoured of thee?—List! [*Music.*

ASIA

Thy words are sweeter than aught else but his
Whose echoes they are: yet all love is sweet,
Given or returned. Common as light is love, 40
And its familiar voice wearies not ever.
Like the wide heaven, the all-sustaining air,
It makes the reptile equal to the God:
They who inspire it most are fortunate,
As I am now; but those who feel it most 45
Are happier still, after long sufferings,
As I shall soon become.

PANTHEA

List! Spirits speak.

VOICE (*in the air, singing*)

Life of life! thy lips enkindle
  With their love the breath between them;
And thy smiles before they dwindle   50
  Make the cold air fire; then screen them
In those looks, where whoso gazes
Faints, entangled in their mazes.

Child of Light! thy limbs are burning
  Through the vest which seems to hide them, 55
As the radiant lines of morning
  Through the clouds, ere they divide them;
And this atmosphere divinest
Shrouds thee wheresoe'er thou shinest.

Fair are others; none beholds thee,   60
  But thy voice sounds low and tender
Like the fairest, for it folds thee
  From the sight, that liquid splendour,
And all feel, yet see thee never,
As I feel now, lost forever!   65

Lamp of Earth! where'er thou movest,
  Its dim shapes are clad with brightness,
And the souls of whom thou lovest
  Walk upon the winds with lightness,
Till they fail, as I am failing,   70
Dizzy, lost . . . yet unbewailing!

ASIA

  My soul is an enchanted boat,
    Which, like a sleeping swan, doth float
  Upon the silver waves of thy sweet singing;
    And thine doth like an Angel sit   75
    Beside the helm conducting it,
  Whilst all the winds with melody are ringing.

It seems to float ever, for ever,
Upon that many-winding river,
Between mountains, woods, abysses,   80
A paradise of wildernesses!
Till, like one in slumber bound
Borne to the ocean, I float, down, around,
Into a sea profound of ever-spreading sound.

Meanwhile thy Spirit lifts its pinions   85
In Music's most serene dominions,
Catching the winds that fan that happy Heaven;
And we sail on, away, afar,
Without a course, without a star,
But by the instinct of sweet music driven;   90
Till, through Elysian garden islets
By thee, most beautiful of pilots,
Where never mortal pinnace glided,
The boat of my desire is guided:
Realms where the air we breathe is love,   95
Which in the winds and on the waves doth move,
Harmonizing this earth with what we feel above.

We have past Age's icy caves,
And Manhood's dark and tossing waves,
And Youth's smooth ocean, smiling to
        betray: 100
Beyond the glassy gulfs we flee
Of shadow-peopled Infancy,
Through Death and Birth, to a diviner day;
A paradise of vaulted bowers
Lit by downward-gazing flowers,   105
And watery paths that wind between
Wildernesses calm and green,
Peopled by shapes too bright to see,
And rest, having beheld—somewhat like thee—
Which walk upon the sea, and chant melodiously! 110

ACT III

SCENE I.—*Heaven.* JUPITER *on his throne*; THETIS *and the other Deities assembled.*

JUPITER

Ye congregated Powers of Heaven, who share
The glory and the strength of him ye serve,
Rejoice! henceforth I am omnipotent.
All else has been subdued to me; alone
The soul of man, like unextinguished fire,   5
Yet burns towards Heaven with fierce reproach, and doubt,
And lamentation, and reluctant prayer—
Hurling up insurrection, which might make
Our antique empire insecure, though built
On eldest faith, and Hell's coeval, fear;   10
And though my curses through the pendulous air,
Like snow on herbless peaks, fall flake by flake,
And cling to it; though under my wrath's night
It climb the crags of life, step after step,
Which wound it, as ice wounds unsandalled feet,   15
It yet remains supreme o'er misery,
Aspiring, unrepressed, yet soon to fall:
Even now have I begotten a strange wonder,
That fatal child, the terror of the earth,
Who waits but till the destined Hour arrive,   20
Bearing from Demogorgon's vacant throne
The dreadful might of ever-living limbs
Which clothed that awful spirit unbeheld,
To redescend, and trample out the spark.

Pour forth Heaven's wine, Idæan Ganymede   25
And let it fill the dædal cups like fire;
And from the flower-inwoven soil divine
Ye all-triumphant harmonies arise,

As dew from earth under the twilight stars.
Drink! be the nectar circling through your veins   30
The soul of joy, ye ever-living Gods,
Till exultation burst in one wide voice
Like music from Elysian winds.
                And thou
Ascend beside me, veilèd in the light
Of the desire which makes thee one with me,   35
Thetis, bright Image of Eternity!
When thou didst cry, 'Insufferable might!
God! Spare me! I sustain not the quick flames,
The penetrating presence; all my being,
Like him whom the Numidian seps did thaw   40
Into a dew with poison, is dissolved,
Sinking through its foundations'—even then
Two mighty spirits, mingling, made a third
Mightier than either, which, unbodied now,
Between us floats, felt, although unbeheld,   45
Waiting the incarnation, which ascends
(Hear ye the thunder of the fiery wheels
Griding the winds?) from Demogorgon's throne.
Victory! victory! Feel'st thou not, O world,
The earthquake of his chariot thundering up   50
Olympus?

[*The car of the* HOUR *arrives.* DEMOGORGON *descends, and
moves towards the throne of* JUPITER.]

        Awful Shape, what art thou? Speak!

DEMOGORGON

Eternity. Demand no direr name.
Descend, and follow me down the abyss.
I am thy child, as thou wert Saturn's child;
Mightier than thee: and we must dwell together   55

Henceforth in darkness. Lift thy lightnings not.
The tyranny of Heaven none may retain,
Or re-assume, or hold, succeeding thee:
Yet if thou wilt—as 'tis the destiny
Of trodden worms to writhe till they are dead— 60
Put forth thy might.

JUPITER

      Detested prodigy!
Even thus beneath the deep Titanian prisons
I trample thee! Thou lingerest?
           Mercy! mercy!
No pity, no release, no respite! . . . Oh,
That thou wouldst make mine enemy my judge, 65
Even where he hangs, seared by my long revenge,
On Caucasus! He would not doom me thus.
Gentle, and just, and dreadless, is he not
The monarch of the world? What then art thou?
No refuge! no appeal!
        Sink with me then— 70
We two will sink on the wide waves of ruin,
Even as a vulture and a snake outspent
Drop, twisted in inextricable fight,
Into a shoreless sea. Let Hell unlock
Its mounded oceans of tempestuous fire, 75
And whelm on them into the bottomless void
This desolated world, and thee, and me,
The conqueror and the conquered, and the wreck
Of that for which they combated.
           Ai! Ai!
The elements obey me not. . . . I sink . . . 80
Dizzily down—ever, for ever, down;
And, like a cloud, mine enemy above
Darkens my fall with victory! Ai, Ai!

SCENE II.—*The mouth of a great river in the island Atlantis.*
OCEAN is discovered reclining near the shore; APOLLO
stands beside him.

OCEAN

He fell, thou sayest, beneath his conqueror's frown?

APOLLO

Ay, when the strife was ended which made dim
The orb I rule, and shook the solid stars.
The terrors of his eye illumined Heaven
With sanguine light, through the thick ragged skirts   5
Of the victorious Darkness, as he fell—
Like the last glare of day's red agony,
Which, from a rent among the fiery clouds,
Burns far along the tempest-wrinkled deep.

OCEAN

He sunk to the abyss? to the dark void?   10

APOLLO

An eagle so, caught in some bursting cloud
On Caucasus, his thunder-baffled wings
Entangled in the whirlwind, and his eyes,
Which gazed on the undazzling sun, now blinded
By the white lightning, while the ponderous hail   15
Beats on his struggling form, which sinks at length
Prone, and the aërial ice clings over it.

OCEAN

Henceforth the fields of heaven-reflecting sea
Which are my realm, will heave, unstained with blood,
Beneath the uplifting winds, like plains of corn   20
Swayed by the summer air; my streams will flow
Round many-peopled continents, and round
Fortunate isles; and from their glassy thrones

Blue Proteus and his humid nymphs shall mark
The shadow of fair ships, as mortals see   25
The floating bark of the light-laden moon
With that white star, its sightless pilot's crest,
Borne down the rapid sunset's ebbing sea;
Tracking their path no more by blood and groans
And desolation, and the mingled voice   30
Of slavery and command, but by the light
Of wave-reflected flowers, and floating odours,
And music soft, and mild, free, gentle voices,
That sweetest music, such as spirits love.

APOLLO

And I shall gaze not on the deeds which make   35
My mind obscure with sorrow, as eclipse
Darkens the sphere I guide.—But list, I hear
The small, clear, silver lute of the young Spirit
That sits i' the Morning Star.

OCEAN

                      Thou must away;
Thy steeds will pause at even—till when, farewell.   40
The loud deep calls me home even now, to feed it
With azure calm out of the emerald urns
Which stand for ever full beside my throne.
Behold the Nereids under the green sea,
Their wavering limbs borne on the wind-like stream,   45
Their white arms lifted o'er their streaming hair,
With garlands pied and starry sea-flower crowns,
Hastening to grace their mighty sister's joy.
                  [A sound of waves is heard.
It is the unpastured Sea hungering for calm.
Peace, monster; I come now! Farewell.

APOLLO

                      Farewell!   50

SCENE III.—*Caucasus*. PROMETHEUS, HERCULES, IONE, *the* EARTH, SPIRITS. ASIA, *and* PANTHEA, *borne in the car with the* SPIRIT OF THE HOUR.

[HERCULES *unbinds* PROMETHEUS, *who descends*.]

HERCULES

Most glorious among Spirits, thus doth strength
To wisdom, courage, and long-suffering love,
And thee, who art the form they animate,
Minister, like a slave.

PROMETHEUS

        Thy gentle words
Are sweeter even than freedom long desired   5
And long delayed.
        Asia, thou light of life,
Shadow of beauty unbeheld; and ye,
Fair sister-nymphs, who made long years of pain
Sweet to remember, through your love and care;
Henceforth we will not part. There is a cave   10
All overgrown with trailing odorous plants,
Which curtain out the day with leaves and flowers,
And paved with veinèd emerald, and a fountain
Leaps in the midst with an awakening sound.
From its curved roof the mountain's frozen tears,   15
Like snow, or silver, or long diamond spires,
Hang downward, raining forth a doubtful light;
And there is heard the ever-moving air,
Whispering without from tree to tree, and birds,
And bees; and all around are mossy seats,   20
And the rough walls are clothed with long soft grass:
A simple dwelling, which shall be our own,
Where we will sit and talk of time and change,
As the world ebbs and flows, ourselves unchanged—
What can hide man from mutability?   25

And if ye sigh, then I will smile; and thou,
Ione, shalt chant fragments of sea-music,
Until I weep, when ye shall smile away
The tears she brought, which yet were sweet to shed.
We will entangle buds and flowers, and beams   30
Which twinkle on the fountain's brim, and make
Strange combinations out of common things,
Like human babes in their brief innocence;
And we will search, with looks and words of love,
For hidden thoughts, each lovelier than the last,   35
Our unexhausted spirits; and, like lutes
Touched by the skill of the enamoured wind,
Weave harmonies divine, yet ever new,
From difference sweet where discord cannot be.
And hither come—sped on the charmèd winds   40
Which meet from all the points of heaven, as bees
From every flower aërial Enna feeds
At their known island-homes in Himera—
The echoes of the human world, which tell
Of the low voice of love, almost unheard,   45
And dove-eyed pity's murmured pain, and music,
Itself the echo of the heart, and all
That tempers or improves man's life, now free;
And lovely apparitions, dim at first,
Then radiant—as the mind, arising bright   50
From the embrace of beauty, whence the forms
Of which these are the phantoms, casts on them
The gathered rays which are reality—
Shall visit us, the progeny immortal
Of Painting, Sculpture, and rapt Poesy,   55
And arts, though unimagined, yet to be.
The wandering voices and the shadows these
Of all that man becomes, the mediators
Of that best worship, love, by him and us
Given and returned; swift shapes and sounds, which
    grow   60

More fair and soft as man grows wise and kind,
And veil by veil evil and error fall:
Such virtue has the cave and place around.
                    [*Turning to the* SPIRIT OF THE HOUR.
For thee, fair Spirit, one toil remains. Ione,
Give her that curvèd shell, which Proteus old   65
Made Asia's nuptial boon, breathing within it
A voice to be accomplished, and which thou
Didst hide in grass under the hollow rock.

IONE

Thou most desired Hour, more loved and lovely
Than all thy sisters, this is the mystic shell;   70
See the pale azure fading into silver
Lining it with a soft yet glowing light:
Looks it not like lulled music sleeping there?

SPIRIT

It seems in truth the fairest shell of Ocean:
Its sound must be at once both sweet and strange.   75

PROMETHEUS

Go, borne over the cities of mankind
On whirlwind-footed coursers: once again
Outspeed the sun around the orbèd world;
And as thy chariot cleaves the kindling air,
Thou breathe into the many-folded shell,   80
Loosening its mighty music; it shall be
As thunder mingled with clear echoes. Then
Return; and thou shalt dwell beside our cave.
                              [*Kissing the ground.*
And thou, O Mother Earth!—

THE EARTH

                    I hear, I feel;
Thy lips are on me, and their touch runs down   85

135

Even to the adamantine central gloom
Along these marble nerves; 'tis life, 'tis joy,
And through my withered, old, and icy frame
The warmth of an immortal youth shoots down
Circling. Henceforth the many children fair   90
Folded in my sustaining arms—all plants,
And creeping forms, and insects rainbow-winged,
And birds, and beasts, and fish, and human shapes,
Which drew disease and pain from my wan bosom,
Draining the poison of despair—shall take   95
And interchange sweet nutriment; to me
Shall they become like sister-antelopes
By one fair dam, snow-white and swift as wind,
Nursed among lilies near a brimming stream.
The dew-mists of my sunless sleep shall float   100
Under the stars like balm; night-folded flowers
Shall suck unwithering hues in their repose;
And men and beasts in happy dreams shall gather
Strength for the coming day and all its joy;
And death shall be the last embrace of her   105
Who takes the life she gave, even as a mother,
Folding her child, says, 'Leave me not again.'

ASIA

O mother! wherefore speak the name of death?
Cease they to love, and move, and breathe, and speak,
Who die?

THE EARTH

       It would avail not to reply: 110
Thou art immortal, and this tongue is known
But to the uncommunicating dead.
Death is the veil which those who live call life:
They sleep, and it is lifted. And meanwhile
In mild variety the seasons mild—   115
With rainbow-skirted showers, and odorous winds,

And long blue meteors cleansing the dull night,
And the life-kindling shafts of the keen sun's
All-piercing bow, and the dew-mingled rain
Of the calm moonbeams, a soft influence mild—   120
Shall clothe the forests and the fields—ay, even
The crag-built deserts of the barren deep—
With ever-living leaves, and fruit, and flowers.
And Thou! There is a cavern where my spirit
Was panted forth in anguish whilst thy pain   125
Made my heart mad, and those who did inhale it
Became mad too, and built a temple there,
And spoke, and were oracular, and lured
The erring nations round to mutual war,
And faithless faith, such as Jove kept with thee—   130
Which breath now rises, as among tall weeds
A violet's exhalation, and it fills
With a serener light and crimson air
Intense, yet soft, the rocks and woods around;
It feeds the quick growth of the serpent vine,   135
And the dark linkèd ivy tangling wild,
And budding, blown, or odour-faded blooms
Which star the winds with points of coloured light
As they rain through them, and bright, golden globes
Of fruit, suspended in their own green heaven,   140
And, through their veinèd leaves and amber stems,
The flowers whose purple and translucid bowls
Stand ever mantling with aërial dew,
The drink of spirits; and it circles round,
Like the soft-waving wings of noonday dreams,   145
Inspiring calm and happy thoughts, like mine,
Now thou art thus restored. That cave is thine.
Arise! Appear!
                    [*A* SPIRIT *rises in the likeness of a winged child.*
                    This is my torch-bearer,
Who let his lamp out in old time with gazing
On eyes from which he kindled it anew   150

With love, which is as fire, sweet daughter mine,
For such is that within thine own. Run, wayward,
And guide this company beyond the peak
Of Bacchic Nysa, Mænad-haunted mountain,
And beyond Indus, and its tribute rivers,   155
Trampling the torrent streams and glassy lakes
With feet unwet, unwearied, undelaying;
And up the green ravine, across the vale,
Beside the windless and crystàlline pool,
Where ever lies, on unerasing waves,   160
The image of a temple, built above,
Distinct with column, arch, and architrave,
And palm-like capital, and over-wrought,
And populous with most living imagery—
Praxitelean shapes, whose marble smiles   165
Fill the hushed air with everlasting love.
It is deserted now, but once it bore
Thy name, Prometheus; there the emulous youths
Bore to thy honour through the divine gloom
The lamp which was thine emblem—even as those   170
Who bear the untransmitted torch of hope
Into the grave, across the night of life,
As thou hast borne it most triumphantly
To this far goal of time. Depart, farewell.
Beside that temple is the destined cave.   175

SCENE IV.—*A forest. In the background a cave.* PRO-
METHEUS, ASIA, PANTHEA, IONE, *and the* SPIRIT OF THE
EARTH.

IONE

Sister, it is not earthly ... How it glides
Under the leaves! how on its head there burns
A light, like a green star, whose emerald beams
Are twined with its fair hair! how, as it moves,

138

The splendour drops in flakes upon the grass!   5
Knowest thou it?

PANTHEA

        It is the delicate spirit
That guides the earth through heaven. From afar
The populous constellations call that light
The loveliest of the planets; and sometimes
It floats along the spray of the salt sea,   10
Or makes its chariot of a foggy cloud,
Or walks through fields or cities while men sleep,
Or o'er the mountain-tops, or down the rivers,
Or through the green waste wilderness, as now,
Wondering at all it sees. Before Jove reigned   15
It loved our sister Asia, and it came
Each leisure hour to drink the liquid light
Out of her eyes, for which it said it thirsted
As one bit by a dipsas; and with her
It made its childish confidence, and told her   20
All it had known or seen, for it saw much,
Yet idly reasoned what it saw; and called her—
For whence it sprung it knew not, nor do I—
'Mother, dear Mother.'

SPIRIT OF THE EARTH (*running to Asia*)

        Mother, dearest mother;
May I then talk with thee as I was wont?   25
May I then hide my eyes in thy soft arms,
After thy looks have made them tired of joy?
May I then play beside thee the long noons,
When work is none in the bright silent air?

ASIA

I love thee, gentlest being, and henceforth   30
Can cherish thee unenvied. Speak, I pray:
Thy simple talk once solaced, now delights.

Spirit of the Earth

Mother, I am grown wiser, though a child
Cannot be wise like thee, within this day;
And happier too; happier and wiser both.   35
Thou knowest that toads, and snakes, and loathly worms,
And venomous and malicious beasts, and boughs
That bore ill berries in the woods, were ever
An hindrance to my walks o'er the green world;
And that, among the haunts of humankind,   40
Hard-featured men, or with proud, angry looks,
Or cold, staid gait, or false and hollow smiles,
Or the dull sneer of self-loved ignorance,
Or other such foul masks, with which ill thoughts
Hide that fair being whom we spirits call man;   45
And women too, ugliest of all things evil,
(Though fair, even in a world where thou art fair,
When good and kind, free and sincere like thee),
When false or frowning made me sick at heart
To pass them, though they slept, and I unseen.   50
Well, my path lately lay through a great city
Into the woody hills surrounding it.
A sentinel was sleeping at the gate—
When there was heard a sound, so loud, it shook
The towers amid the moonlight, yet more sweet   55
Than any voice but thine, sweetest of all,
A long, long sound, as it would never end;
And all the inhabitants leapt suddenly
Out of their rest, and gathered in the streets,
Looking in wonder up to heaven, while yet   60
The music pealed along. I hid myself
Within a fountain in the public square,
Where I lay like the reflex of the moon
Seen in a wave under green leaves; and soon
Those ugly human shapes and visages   65
Of which I spoke as having wrought me pain,
Passed floating through the air, and fading still

Into the winds that scattered them; and those
From whom they passed seemed mild and lovely forms
After some foul disguise had fallen; and all   70
Were somewhat changed; and after brief surprise
And greetings of delighted wonder, all
Went to their sleep again; and when the dawn
Came—wouldst thou think that toads, and snakes, and efts,
Could e'er be beautiful? yet so they were,   75
And that with little change of shape or hue:
All things had put their evil nature off.
I cannot tell my joy, when o'er a lake,
Upon a drooping bough with nightshade twined,
I saw two azure halcyons clinging downward   80
And thinning one bright bunch of amber berries,
With quick, long beaks, and in the deep there lay
Those lovely forms imaged as in a sky.
So with my thoughts full of these happy changes,
We meet again, the happiest change of all.   85

ASIA

And never will we part, till thy chaste sister,
Who guides the frozen and inconstant moon,
Will look on thy more warm and equal light
Till her heart thaw like flakes of April snow,
And love thee.

SPIRIT OF THE EARTH

What! as Asia loves Prometheus?   90

ASIA

Peace, wanton! thou art yet not old enough.
Think ye by gazing on each other's eyes
To multiply your lovely selves, and fill
With spherèd fires the interlunar air?

141

SPIRIT OF THE EARTH

Nay, Mother, while my sister trims her lamp   95
'Tis hard I should go darkling.

ASIA

Listen! look!
[*The* SPIRIT OF THE HOUR *enters.*

PROMETHEUS

We feel what thou hast heard and seen: yet speak.

SPIRIT OF THE HOUR

Soon as the sound had ceased whose thunder filled
The abysses of the sky and the wide earth,
There was a change . . . the impalpable thin air   100
And the all-circling sunlight were transformed,
As if the sense of love, dissolved in them,
Had folded itself round the spherèd world.
My vision then grew clear, and I could see
Into the mysteries of the universe.   105
Dizzy as with delight I floated down,
Winnowing the lightsome air with languid plumes,
My coursers sought their birthplace in the sun,
Where they henceforth will live exempt from toil,
Pasturing flowers of vegetable fire;   110
And where my moonlike car will stand within
A temple—gazed upon by Phidian forms
Of thee, and Asia, and the Earth, and me,
And you fair nymphs, looking the love we feel,
In memory of the tidings it has borne—   115
Beneath a dome fretted with graven flowers,
Poised on twelve columns of resplendent stone,
And open to the bright and liquid sky.
Yoked to it by an amphisbænic snake
The likeness of those wingèd steeds will mock   120

The flight from which they find repose. Alas,
Whither has wandered now my partial tongue
When all remains untold which ye would hear?
As I have said, I floated to the earth:
It was, as it is still, the pain of bliss   125
To move, to breathe, to be; I wandering went
Among the haunts and dwellings of mankind,
And first was disappointed not to see
Such mighty change as I had felt within
Expressed in outward things; but soon I looked,   130
And behold! thrones were kingless, and men walked
One with the other even as spirits do:
None fawned, none trampled; hate, disdain, or fear,
Self-love or self-contempt, on human brows
No more inscribed, as o'er the gate of Hell,   135
'All hope abandon, ye who enter here';
None frowned, none trembled, none with eager fear
Gazed on another's eye of cold command,
Until the subject of a tyrant's will
Became, worse fate, the abject of his own,   140
Which spurred him, like an outspent horse, to death;
None wrought his lips in truth-entangling lines
Which smiled the lie his tongue disdained to speak;
None, with firm sneer, trod out in his own heart
The sparks of love and hope, till there remained   145
Those bitter ashes, a soul self-consumed,
And the wretch crept a vampire among men,
Infecting all with his own hideous ill;
None talked that common, false, cold, hollow talk
Which makes the heart deny the *yes* it breathes,   150
Yet question that unmeant hypocrisy
With such a self-mistrust as has no name.
And women, too, frank, beautiful, and kind
As the free heaven which rains fresh light and dew
On the wide earth, passed—gentle, radiant forms,   155
From custom's evil taint exempt and pure,

Speaking the wisdom once they could not think,
Looking emotions once they feared to feel,
And changed to all which once they dared not be,
Yet being now, made earth like Heaven; nor pride,   160
Nor jealousy, nor envy, nor ill shame,
The bitterest of those drops of treasured gall,
Spoilt the sweet taste of the nepenthe, love.

Thrones, altars, judgment-seats, and prisons—wherein
And beside which, by wretched men were borne   165
Sceptres, tiaras, swords, and chains, and tomes
Of reasoned wrong, glozed on by ignorance—
Were like those monstrous and barbaric shapes,
The ghosts of a no-more-remembered fame,
Which, from their unworn obelisks, look forth   170
In triumph o'er the palaces and tombs
Of those who were their conquerors, mouldering round.
These imaged to the pride of kings and priests
A dark yet mighty faith, a power as wide
As is the world it wasted, and are now   175
But an astonishment; even so the tools
And emblems of its last captivity,
Amid the dwellings of the peopled earth,
Stand, not o'erthrown, but unregarded now.
And those foul shapes, abhorred by God and man—   180
Which, under many a name and many a form,
Strange, savage, ghastly, dark and execrable,
Were Jupiter, the tyrant of the world;
And which the nations, panic-stricken, served
With blood, and hearts broken by long hope, and love 185
Dragged to his altars soiled and garlandless,
And slain amid men's unreclaiming tears,
Flattering the thing they feared, which fear was hate—
Frown, mouldering fast, o'er their abandoned shrines.
The painted veil, by those who were called life,   190
Which mimicked, as with colours idly spread,

All men believed or hoped, is torn aside;
The loathsome mask has fallen, the man remains
Sceptreless, free, uncircumscribed—but man:
Equal, unclassed, tribeless and nationless; 195
Exempt from awe, worship, degree; the king
Over himself; just, gentle, wise—but man:
Passionless? no—yet free from guilt or pain,
Which were, for his will made, or suffered them;
Nor yet exempt, though ruling them like slaves, 200
From chance, and death, and mutability,
The clogs of that which else might oversoar
The loftiest star of unascended Heaven,
Pinnacled dim in the intense inane.

ACT IV

SCENE.—*A part of the forest near the cave of* PROMETHEUS.
PANTHEA *and* IONE *are sleeping: they awaken gradually
during the first song.*

VOICE OF UNSEEN SPIRITS

The pale stars are gone!
For the sun, their swift shepherd,
To their folds them compelling,
In the depths of the dawn,
Hastes, in meteor-eclipsing array, and they flee 5
Beyond his blue dwelling,
As fawns flee the leopard—
But where are ye?

[*A train of dark Forms and Shadows passes by confusedly,
singing.*]

Here, oh, here!
We bear the bier 10

Of the Father of many a cancelled year!
   Spectres we
   Of the dead Hours be,
We bear Time to his tomb in eternity.

   Strew, oh strew   15
   Hair, not yew!
Wet the dusty pall with tears, not dew!
   Be the faded flowers
   Of Death's bare bowers
Spread on the corpse of the King of Hours! 20

   Haste, oh, haste!
   As shades are chased,
Trembling, by Day, from heaven's blue waste,
   We melt away,
   Like dissolving spray,   25
From the children of a diviner day,
   With the lullaby
   Of winds that die
On the bosom of their own harmony.

         [*They vanish.*

IONE

  What dark forms were they?   30

PANTHEA

  The past Hours weak and grey,
  With the spoil which their toil
   Raked together
  From the conquest but One could foil.

IONE

  Have they passed?

PANTHEA

They have passed;   35
They outspeeded the blast;
While 'tis said, they are fled—

IONE

Whither, oh, whither?

PANTHEA

To the dark, to the past, to the dead.

VOICE OF UNSEEN SPIRITS

Bright clouds float in heaven,   40
Dew-stars gleam on earth,
Waves assemble on ocean,
They are gathered and driven
By the storm of delight, by the panic of glee!
They shake with emotion,   45
They dance in their mirth—
But where are ye?

The pine-boughs are singing
Old songs with new gladness,
The billows and fountains   50
Fresh music are flinging,
Like the notes of a spirit, from land and from sea;
The storms mock the mountains
With the thunder of gladness—
But where are ye?   55

IONE

What charioteers are these?

PANTHEA

Where are their chariots?

SEMICHORUS OF HOURS I

The voice of the Spirits of Air and of Earth
  Have drawn back the figured curtain of sleep,
Which covered our being and darkened our birth
  In the deep—

A VOICE

In the deep?

SEMICHORUS II

Oh, below the deep.   60

SEMICHORUS I

An hundred ages we had been kept
  Cradled in visions of hate and care,
And each one who waked as his brother slept
  Found the truth—

SEMICHORUS II

Worse than his visions were!

SEMICHORUS I

We have heard the lute of Hope in sleep;   65
  We have known the voice of Love in dreams;
We have felt the wand of Power, and leap—

SEMICHORUS II

As the billows leap in the morning beams.

CHORUS

Weave the dance on the floor of the breeze,
  Pierce with song heaven's silent light,   70
Enchant the Day that too swiftly flees,
  To check its flight ere the cave of Night.

Once the hungry Hours were hounds
   Which chased the Day like a bleeding deer,
And it limped and stumbled with many wounds   75
   Through the nightly dells of the desert year.

But now—oh weave the mystic measure
   Of music, and dance, and shapes of light;
Let the Hours, and the Spirits of might and pleasure,
   Like the clouds and sunbeams, unite—

A VOICE

             Unite!   80

PANTHEA

See, where the Spirits of the human mind
Wrapped in sweet sounds, as in bright veils, approach.

CHORUS OF SPIRITS

   We join the throng
   Of the dance and the song,
By the whirlwind of gladness borne along;   85
   As the flying-fish leap
   From the Indian deep,
And mix with the sea-birds half asleep.

CHORUS OF HOURS

Whence come ye, so wild and so fleet,
For sandals of lightning are on your feet,   90
And your wings are soft and swift as thought,
And your eyes are as Love which is veilèd not?

CHORUS OF SPIRITS

   We come from the mind
   Of humankind,
Which was late so dusk, and obscene, and blind;   95

Now 'tis an ocean
Of clear emotion,
A heaven of serene and mighty motion;

From that deep abyss
Of wonder and bliss,   100
Whose caverns are crystal palaces;
From those skiey towers
Where Thought's crowned Powers
Sit watching your dance, ye happy Hours;

From the dim recesses   105
Of woven caresses,
Where lovers catch ye by your loose tresses;
From the azure isles,
Where sweet Wisdom smiles,
Delaying your ships with her siren wiles;   110

From the temples high
Of man's ear and eye,
Roofed over Sculpture and Poesy;
From the murmurings
Of the unsealed springs   115
Where Science bedews her dædal wings.

Years after years,
Through blood and tears,
And a thick hell of hatreds and hopes and fears
We waded and flew,   120
And the islets were few
Where the bud-blighted flowers of happiness grew.

Our feet now, every palm,
Are sandalled with calm,
And the dew of our wings is a rain of balm;   125
And, beyond our eyes,
The human love lies,
Which makes all it gazes on Paradise.

CHORUS OF SPIRITS AND HOURS

Then weave the web of the mystic measure;
  From the depths of the sky and the ends of the earth, 130
Come, swift Spirits of might and of pleasure,
  Fill the dance and the music of mirth,
As the waves of a thousand streams rush by
To an ocean of splendour and harmony!

CHORUS OF SPIRITS

      Our spoil is won, 135
      Our task is done,
We are free to dive, or soar, or run;
      Beyond and around,
      Or within the bound
Which clips the world with darkness round. 140

      We'll pass the eyes
      Of the starry skies
Into the hoar deep to colonize;
      Death, Chaos, and Night,
      From the sound of our flight 145
Shall flee, like mist from a tempest's might;

      And Earth, Air, and Light,
      And the Spirit of Might,
Which drives round the stars in their fiery flight;
      And love, Thought, and Breath, 150
      The powers that quell Death,
Wherever we soar shall assemble beneath;

      And our singing shall build
      In the void's loose field
A world for the Spirit of Wisdom to wield; 155
      We will take our plan
      From the new world of man,
And our work shall be called the Promethean.

Chorus of Hours

Break the dance, and scatter the song;
  Let some depart, and some remain.   160

Semichorus I

We, beyond heaven, are driven along—

Semichorus II

Us the enchantments of earth retain—

Semichorus I

Ceaseless, and rapid, and fierce, and free,
With the Spirits which build a new earth and sea,
And a Heaven where yet Heaven could never be—   165

Semichorus II

Solemn, and slow, and serene, and bright
Leading the Day, and outspeeding the Night,
With the Powers of a world of perfect light—

Semichorus I

We whirl, singing loud, round the gathering sphere,
Till the trees, and the beasts, and the clouds appear 170
From its chaos made calm by love, not fear—

Semichorus II

We encircle the oceans and mountains of earth,
And the happy forms of its death and birth
Change to the music of our sweet mirth.

Chorus of Hours and Spirits

Break the dance, and scatter the song;   175
  Let some depart, and some remain;
Wherever we fly we lead along
In leashes, like starbeams, soft yet strong,
  The clouds that are heavy with Love's sweet rain.

PANTHEA

Ha! they are gone!

IONE

                Yet feel you no delight   180
From the past sweetness?

PANTHEA

               As the bare green hill,
When some soft cloud vanishes into rain,
Laughs with a thousand drops of sunny water
To the unpavilioned sky!

IONE

             Even whilst we speak
New notes arise . . . . What is that awful sound?   185

PANTHEA

'Tis the deep music of the rolling world,
Kindling within the strings of the waved air
Aeolian modulations.

IONE

           Listen too,
How every pause is filled with under-notes,
Clear, silver, icy, keen, awakening tones,   190
Which pierce the sense, and live within the soul,
As the sharp stars pierce winter's crystal air
And gaze upon themselves within the sea.

PANTHEA

But see where, through two openings in the forest
Which hanging branches overcanopy,   195
And where two runnels of a rivulet,
Between the close moss, violet-inwoven,

Have made their path of melody—like sisters
Who part with sighs that they may meet in smiles,
Turning their dear disunion to an isle   200
Of lovely grief, a wood of sweet sad thoughts—
Two visions of strange radiance float upon
The ocean-like enchantment of strong sound,
Which flows intenser, keener, deeper yet
Under the ground and through the windless air.   205

IONE

I see a chariot—like that thinnest boat
In which the Mother of the Months is borne
By ebbing light into her western cave
When she upsprings from interlunar dreams—
O'er which is curved an orblike canopy   210
Of gentle darkness, and the hills and woods,
Distinctly seen through that dusk aëry veil,
Regard like shapes in an enchanter's glass;
Its wheels are solid clouds, azure and gold,
Such as the genii of the thunderstorm   215
Pile on the floor of the illumined sea
When the sun rushes under it; they roll
And move and grow as with an inward wind.
Within it sits a wingèd infant—white
Its countenance, like the whiteness of bright snow;   220
Its plumes are as feathers of sunny frost;
Its limbs gleam white, through the wind-flowing folds
Of its white robe, woof of ætherial pearl;
Its hair is white—the brightness of white light
Scattered in strings; yet its two eyes are heavens   225
Of liquid darkness, which the Deity
Within seems pouring, as a storm is poured
From jaggèd clouds, out of their arrowy lashes,
Tempering the cold and radiant air around
With fire that is not brightness; in its hand   230
It sways a quivering moonbeam, from whose point

A guiding power   ariot's prow
Over its wheelèd   n, as they roll
Over the grass a   d waves, wake sounds
Sweet as a sing   er dew.   235

                         THEA

And from th   in the wood
Rushes, wit   lwind harmony,
A sphere,   thousand spheres,
Solid as   gh all its mass
Flow, as   space, music and light: 240
Ten th   ving and involved,
Purple   and green and golden,
Sphe   and every space between
Peo   nable shapes,
Su   dwell in the lampless deep,   245
Y   picuous; and they whirl
C   th a thousand motions,
          sightless axles spinning,
          rce of self-destroying swiftness,
          y, solemnly roll on,   250
          mingled sounds, and many tones,
          words and music wild.
          ty whirl the multitudinous orb
          he bright brook into an azure mist
          ental subtlety, like light;   255
          he wild odour of the forest flowers,
          music of the living grass and air,
       emerald light of leaf-entangled beams,
       und its intense, yet self-conflicting speed,
       em kneaded into one aërial mass   260
Which drowns the sense. Within the orb itself,
Pillowed upon its alabaster arms,
Like to a child o'erwearied with sweet toil,
On its own folded wings and wavy hair,
The Spirit of the Earth is laid asleep;   265

And you can see its little lips are moving,
Amid the changing light of their own smiles,
Like one who talks of what he loves in dream.

IONE

'Tis only mocking the orb's harmony ....

PANTHEA

And from a star upon its forehead, shoot,   **270**
Like swords of azure fire, or golden spears
With tyrant-quelling myrtle overtwined,
Embleming Heaven and Earth united now,
Vast beams like spokes of some invisible wheel,
Which whirl as the orb whirls, swifter than thought,   **275**
Filling the abyss with sunlike lightenings,
And perpendicular now, and now transverse,
Pierce the dark soil, and, as they pierce and pass,
Make bare the secrets of the earth's deep heart—
Infinite mines of adamant and gold,   **280**
Valueless stones, and unimagined gems,
And caverns on crystàlline columns poised
With vegetable silver overspread;
Wells of unfathomed fire, and water-springs
Whence the great sea, even as a child, is fed,   **285**
Whose vapours clothe earth's monarch mountain-tops
With kingly, ermine snow. The beams flash on
And make appear the melancholy ruins
Of cancelled cycles—anchors, beaks of ships,
Planks turned to marble, quivers, helms, and spears,   **290**
And Gorgon-headed targes, and the wheels
Of scythèd chariots, and the emblazonry
Of trophies, standards, and armorial beasts,
Round which Death laughed, sepulchred emblems
Of dead Destruction, ruin within ruin!   **295**
The wrecks beside of many a city vast,

Whose population which the earth grew over
Was mortal, but not human—see, they lie,
Their monstrous works and uncouth skeletons,
Their statues, homes, and fanes; prodigious shapes　　300
Huddled in grey annihilation, split,
Jammed in the hard, black deep; and over these
The anatomies of unknown wingèd things,
And fishes which were isles of living scale,
And serpents, bony chains, twisted around　　305
The iron crags, or within heaps of dust
To which the tortuous strength of their last pangs
Had crushed the iron crags; and over these
The jaggèd alligator, and the might
Of earth-convulsing behemoth, which once　　310
Were monarch beasts, and on the slimy shores
And weed-overgrown continents of earth
Increased and multiplied like summer worms
On an abandoned corpse, till the blue globe
Wrapped deluge round it like a cloak, and they　　315
Yelled, gasped, and were abolished, or some God
Whose throne was in a comet, passed, and cried
'Be not!'—and like my words they were no more.

THE EARTH

The joy, the triumph, the delight, the madness!
The boundless, overflowing, bursting gladness!　　320
The vaporous exultation, not to be confined!
Ha! ha! the animation of delight
Which wraps me, like an atmosphere of light,
And bears me as a cloud is borne by its own wind!

THE MOON

Brother mine, calm wanderer,　　325
Happy globe of land and air,

157

Some spirit is darted like a beam from thee,
    Which penetrates my frozen frame,
    And passes with the warmth of flame,
With love, and odour, and deep melody   330
    Through me, through me!

THE EARTH

Ha! ha! the caverns of my hollow mountains,
My cloven fire-crags, sound-exulting fountains,
Laugh with a vast and inextinguishable laughter.
    The oceans, and the deserts, and the abysses   335
    Of the deep air's unmeasured wildernesses
Answer from all their clouds and billows, echoing after.

    They cry aloud as I do:—'Sceptred Curse,
    Who all our green and azure universe
Threatenedst to muffle round with black destruction,
        sending   340
    A solid cloud to rain hot thunderstones,
    And splinter and knead down my children's bones,
All I bring forth, to one void mass battering and blending;

    'Until each crag-like tower, and storied column,
    Palace, and obelisk, and temple solemn,   345
My imperial mountains crowned with cloud, and snow
        and fire,
    My sea-like forests, every blade and blossom
    Which finds a grave or cradle in my bosom,
Were stamped by thy strong hate into a lifeless mire:

    'How art thou sunk, withdrawn, covered—drunk up   350
    By thirsty nothing, as the brackish cup
Drained by a desert-troop, a little drop for all!
    And from beneath, around, within, above,
    Filling thy void annihilation, Love
Bursts in like light on caves cloven by the thunder-ball.' 355

The Moon

The snow upon my lifeless mountains
Is loosened into living fountains,
My solid oceans flow, and sing, and shine;
  A spirit from my heart bursts forth,
  It clothes with unexpected birth   360
My cold bare bosom: oh, it must be thine
      On mine, on mine!

  Gazing on thee I feel, I know
  Green stalks burst forth, and bright flowers grow,
And living shapes upon my bosom move;   365
  Music is in the sea and air,
  Wingèd clouds soar here and there,
Dark with the rain new buds are dreaming of:
      'Tis Love, all Love!

The Earth

It interpenetrates my granite mass,   370
  Through tangled roots and trodden clay doth pass
Into the utmost leaves and delicatest flowers;
  Upon the winds, among the clouds 'tis spread;
  It wakes a life in the forgotten dead—
They breathe a spirit up from their obscurest bowers—375

And like a storm, bursting its cloudy prison
  With thunder, and with whirlwind, has arisen
Out of the lampless caves of unimagined being,
  With earthquake shock and swiftness making shiver
  Thought's stagnant chaos, unremoved for ever,   380
Till Hate, and Fear, and Pain, light-vanquished shadows,
     fleeing,

  Leave Man—who was a many-sided mirror,
  Which could distort to many a shape of error
This true fair world of things—a sea reflecting Love;

159

Which over all his kind, as the sun's heaven   385
Gliding o'er ocean, smooth, serene, and even,
Darting from starry depths radiance and life, doth move:

Leave Man, even as a leprous child is left,
Who follows a sick beast to some warm cleft
Of rocks, through which the might of healing springs is
            poured;   390
Then when it wanders home with rosy smile,
Unconscious, and its mother fears awhile
It is a Spirit—then weeps on her child restored:

Man, oh, not men! a chain of linkèd thought,
Of love and might to be divided not,   395
Compelling the elements with adamantine stress,
As the sun rules, even with a tyrant's gaze,
The unquiet republic of the maze
Of planets, struggling fierce towards heaven's free wilder-
            ness:

Man, one harmonious soul of many a soul,   400
Whose nature is its own divine control,
Where all things flow to all, as rivers to the sea;
Familiar acts are beautiful through love;
Labour, and Pain, and Grief, in life's green grove
Sport like tame beasts—none knew how gentle they
            could be!   405

His will, with all mean passions, bad delights,
And selfish cares, its trembling satellites,
A spirit ill to guide, but mighty to obey,
Is as a tempest-wingèd ship, whose helm
Love rules, through waves which dare not over-
            whelm,   410
Forcing life's wildest shores to own its sovereign sway.

All things confess his strength. Through the cold mass
Of marble and of colour his dreams pass—
Bright threads whence mothers weave the robes their
      children wear;
  Language is a perpetual Orphic song,   415
  Which rules with dædal harmony a throng
Of thoughts and forms, which else senseless and shapeless
      were.

  The lightning is his slave; heaven's utmost deep
  Gives up her stars, and like a flock of sheep
They pass before his eye, are numbered, and roll on. 420
  The Tempest is his steed—he strides the air;
  And the abyss shouts from her depth laid bare,
'Heaven, hast thou secrets? Man unveils me; I have
      none.'

THE MOON

  The shadow of white Death has passed
  From my path in heaven at last,   425
A clinging shroud of solid frost and sleep;
  And through my newly-woven bowers
  Wander happy paramours,
Less mighty, but as mild as those who keep
    Thy vales more deep.   430

THE EARTH

As the dissolving warmth of dawn may fold
A half-unfrozen dew-globe, green and gold
And crystalline, till it becomes a wingèd mist,
  And wanders up the vault of the blue day,
  Outlives the noon, and on the sun's last ray   435
Hangs o'er the sea, a fleece of fire and amethyst—

The Moon

Thou art folded, thou art lying
In the light which is undying
Of thine own joy, and heaven's smile divine;
    All suns and constellations shower   440
    On thee a light, a life, a power
Which doth array thy sphere; thou pourest thine
    On mine, on mine!

The Earth

I spin beneath my pyramid of night,
Which points into the heavens, dreaming delight,   445
Murmuring victorious joy in my enchanted sleep;
    As a youth lulled in love-dreams, faintly sighing,
    Under the shadow of his beauty lying,
Which round his rest a watch of light and warmth doth
    keep.

The Moon

    As in the soft and sweet eclipse,   450
    When soul meets soul on lovers' lips,
High hearts are calm, and brightest eyes are dull;
    So, when thy shadow falls on me,
    Then am I mute and still, by thee
Covered; of thy love, Orb most beautiful,   455
    Full, oh, too full!

    Thou art speeding round the sun,
    Brightest world of many a one,
    Green and azure sphere, which shinest
    With a light which is divinest   460
    Among all the lamps of heaven
    To whom life and light is given.
    I, thy crystal paramour,
    Borne beside thee by a power

Like the polar paradise, 465
Magnet-like, of lovers' eyes;
I, a most enamoured maiden,
Whose weak brain is overladen
With the pleasure of her love,
Maniac-like around thee move, 470
Gazing, an insatiate bride,
On thy form from every side,
Like a Mænad round the cup
Which Agave lifted up
In the weird Cadmæan forest. 475
Brother, wheresoe'er thou soarest
I must hurry, whirl and follow
Through the heavens wide and hollow,
Sheltered by the warm embrace
Of thy soul from hungry space, 480
Drinking from thy sense and sight
Beauty, majesty, and might;
As a lover or chameleon
Grows like what it looks upon,
As a violet's gentle eye 485
Gazes on the azure sky
Until its hue grows like what it beholds.
As a grey and watery mist
Grows like solid amethyst
Athwart the western mountain it enfolds, 490
When the sunset sleeps
Upon its snow—

THE EARTH

And the weak day weeps
That it should be so.
O gentle Moon, the voice of thy delight 495
Falls on me like thy clear and tender light
Soothing the seaman, borne the summer night
Through isles forever calm;

163

O gentle Moon, thy crystal accents pierce
The caverns of my pride's deep universe,   500
Charming the tiger Joy, whose tramplings fierce
    Made wounds which need thy balm.

PANTHEA

I rise as from a bath of sparkling water,
A bath of azure light, among dark rocks,
Out of the stream of sound.

IONE

          Ah me! sweet sister,   505
The stream of sound has ebbed away from us,
And you pretend to rise out of its wave,
Because your words fall like the clear soft dew
Shaken from a bathing wood-nymph's limbs and hair.

PANTHEA

Peace! peace! a mighty Power, which is as darkness, 510
Is rising out of earth, and from the sky
Is showered like night, and from within the air
Bursts, like eclipse which had been gathered up
Into the pores of sunlight: the bright Visions,
Wherein the singing spirits rode and shone,   515
Gleam like pale meteors through a watery night.

IONE

There is a sense of words upon mine ear—

PANTHEA

A universal sound like words ... Oh, list!

DEMOGORGON

Thou Earth, calm empire of a happy soul,
    Sphere of divinest shapes and harmonies,   520
Beautiful Orb! gathering as thou dost roll
    The love which paves thy path along the skies:

The Earth

I hear: I am as a drop of dew that dies!

Demogorgon

Thou Moon, which gazest on the nightly Earth
  With wonder, as it gazes upon thee,   525
Whilst each to men, and beasts, and the swift birth
  Of birds, is beauty, love, calm, harmony:

The Moon

I hear: I am a leaf shaken by thee!

Demogorgon

Ye Kings of suns and stars, Dæmons and Gods,
  Ætherial Dominations, who possess   530
Elysian, windless, fortunate abodes
  Beyond heaven's constellated wilderness:

A Voice from Above

Our great Republic hears: we are blest, and bless.

Demogorgon

Ye happy dead, whom beams of brightest verse
  Are clouds to hide, not colours to portray,   535
Whether your nature is that universe
  Which once ye saw and suffered—

A Voice from Beneath

                   Or as they
Whom we have left, we change and pass away.

Demogorgon

Ye elemental Genii, who have homes
  From man's high mind even to the central stone 540
Of sullen lead; from heaven's star-fretted domes
  To the dull weed some sea-worm battens on:

A CONFUSED VOICE

We hear: thy words waken Oblivion.

DEMOGORGON

Spirits whose homes are flesh; ye beasts and birds;
   Ye worms and fish; ye living leaves and buds; 545
Lightning and wind; and ye untameable herds,
   Meteors and mists, which feed air's solitudes:

A VOICE

Thy voice to us is wind among still woods.

DEMOGORGON

Man, who wert once a despot and a slave;
   A dupe and a deceiver; a decay;   550
A traveller from the cradle to the grave
   Through the dim night of this immortal day:

ALL

Speak: thy strong words may never pass away.

DEMOGORGON

This is the day, which down the void abysm
At the Earth-born's spell yawns for Heaven's despotism, 555
   And Conquest is dragged captive through the deep;
Love, from its awful throne of patient power
In the wise heart, from the last giddy hour
   Of dread endurance, from the slippery, steep,
And narrow verge of crag-like agony, springs   560
And folds over the world its healing wings.

Gentleness, Virtue, Wisdom, and Endurance—
These are the seals of that most firm assurance
   Which bars the pit over Destruction's strength;

And if, with infirm hand, Eternity,   565
Mother of many acts and hours, should free
  The serpent that would clasp her with his length,
These are the spells by which to re-assume
An empire o'er the disentangled Doom.

To suffer woes which Hope thinks infinite;   570
To forgive wrongs darker than death or night;
  To defy Power, which seems omnipotent;
To love, and bear; to hope, till Hope creates
From its own wreck the thing it contemplates;
  Neither to change, nor falter, nor repent: 575
This, like thy glory, Titan, is to be
Good, great and joyous, beautiful and free;
This is alone Life, Joy, Empire, and Victory.

OTHER POEMS

THE SENSITIVE PLANT

PART I

A Sensitive Plant in a garden grew,
And the young winds fed it with silver dew,
And it opened its fan-like leaves to the light,
And closed them beneath the kisses of night.

And the spring arose on the garden fair,   5
Like the Spirit of Love felt everywhere;
And each flower and herb on Earth's dark breast
Rose from the dreams of its wintry rest.

But none ever trembled and panted with bliss
In the garden, the field, or the wilderness,   10
Like a doe in the noontide with love's sweet want,
As the companionless Sensitive Plant.

The snowdrop, and then the violet,
Arose from the ground with warm rain wet,
And their breath was mixed with fresh odour, sent   15
From the turf, like the voice and the instrument.

Then the pied wind-flowers and the tulip tall,
And narcissi, the fairest among them all,
Who gaze on their eyes in the stream's recess,
Till they die of their own dear loveliness;   20

And the Naiad-like lily of the vale,
Whom youth makes so fair and passion so pale,
That the light of its tremulous bells is seen
Through their pavilions of tender green;

And the hyacinth purple, and white, and blue, 25
Which flung from its bells a sweet peal anew
Of music so delicate, soft, and intense,
It was felt like an odour within the sense;

And the rose, like a nymph to the bath addressed,
Which unveiled the depth of her glowing breast, 30
Till, fold after fold, to the fainting air
The soul of her beauty and love lay bare;

And the wand-like lily, which lifted up,
As a Mænad, its moonlight-coloured cup,
Till the fiery star, which is its eye, 35
Gazed through clear dew on the tender sky;

And the jessamine faint, and the sweet tuberose,
The sweetest flower for scent that blows;
And all rare blossoms from every clime
Grew in that garden in perfect prime. 40

And on the stream whose inconstant bosom
Was pranked, under boughs of embowering blossom,
With golden and green lights, slanting through
Their heaven of many a tangled hue,

Broad water-lilies lay tremulously, 45
And starry river-buds glimmered by,
And around them the soft stream did glide and dance
With a motion of sweet sound and radiance.

And the sinuous paths of lawn and of moss,
Which led through the garden along and across, 50
Some open at once to the sun and the breeze,
Some lost among bowers of blossoming trees,

Were all paved with daisies and delicate bells
As fair as the fabulous asphodels,
And flowerets which, drooping as day drooped too,   55
Fell into pavilions, white, purple, and blue,
To roof the glow-worm from the evening dew.

And from this undefilèd Paradise
The flowers (as an infant's awakening eyes
Smile on its mother, whose singing sweet   60
Can first lull, and at last must awaken it),

When Heaven's blithe winds had unfolded them,
As mine-lamps enkindle a hidden gem,
Shone smiling to Heaven, and every one
Shared joy in the light of the gentle sun;   65

For each one was interpenetrated
With the light and the odour its neighbour shed,
Like young lovers whom youth and love make dear,
Wrapped and filled by their mutual atmosphere.

But the Sensitive Plant, which could give small fruit   70
Of the love which it felt from the leaf to the root,
Received more than all—it loved more than ever,
Where none wanted but it, could belong to the giver:

For the Sensitive Plant has no bright flower;
Radiance and odour are not its dower;   75
It loves, even like Love—its deep heart is full;
It desires what it has not, the beautiful!

The light winds which from unsustaining wings
Shed the music of many murmurings;
The beams which dart from many a star   80
Of the flowers whose hues they bear afar;

The plumèd insects swift and free,
Like golden boats on a sunny sea,
Laden with light and odour, which pass
Over the gleam of the living grass;   85

The unseen clouds of the dew, which lie
Like fire in the flowers till the sun rides high,
Then wander like spirits among the spheres,
Each cloud faint with the fragrance it bears;

The quivering vapours of dim noontide,   90
Which like a sea o'er the warm earth glide,
In which every sound, and odour, and beam,
Move, as reeds in a single stream;

Each and all like ministering angels were
For the Sensitive Plant sweet joy to bear,   95
Whilst the lagging hours of the day went by
Like windless clouds o'er a tender sky.

And when evening descended from heaven above,
And the Earth was all rest, and the air was all love,
And delight, though less bright, was far more deep,   100
And the day's veil fell from the world of sleep,

And the beasts, and the birds, and the insects were drowned
In an ocean of dreams without a sound;
Whose waves never mark, though they ever impress
The light sand which paves it, consciousness;   105

(Only overhead the sweet nightingale
Ever sang more sweet as the day might fail,
And snatches of its Elysian chant
Were mixed with the dreams of the Sensitive Plant.)

The Sensitive Plant was the earliest   110
Upgathered into the bosom of rest;
A sweet child weary of its delight,
The feeblest and yet the favourite,
Cradled within the embrace of night.

PART II

There was a Power in this sweet place,
An Eve in this Eden; a ruling grace
Which to the flowers, did they waken or dream,
Was as God is to the starry scheme.

A Lady, the wonder of her kind,   5
Whose form was upborne by a lovely mind
Which, dilating, had moulded her mien and motion
Like a sea-flower unfolded beneath the ocean,

Tended the garden from morn to even:
And the meteors of that sublunar heaven,   10
Like the lamps of the air when night walks forth,
Laughed round her footsteps up from the Earth!

She had no companion of mortal race,
But her tremulous breath and her flushing face
Told, whilst the morn kissed the sleep from her eyes,   15
That her dreams were less slumber than Paradise:

As if some bright Spirit for her sweet sake
Had deserted heaven while the stars were awake,
As if yet around her he lingering were,
Though the veil of daylight concealed him from her.   20

Her step seemed to pity the grass it pressed;
You might hear by the heaving of her breast,
That the coming and going of the wind
Brought pleasure there and left passion behind.

And wherever her airy footstep trod,   25
Her trailing hair from the grassy sod
Erased its light vestige, with shadowy sweep,
Like a sunny storm o'er the dark-green deep.

I doubt not the flowers of that garden sweet
Rejoiced in the sound of her gentle feet;   30
I doubt not they felt the spirit that came
From her glowing fingers through all their frame.

She sprinkled bright water from the stream
On those that were faint with the sunny beam;
And out of the cups of the heavy flowers   35
She emptied the rain of the thunder showers.

She lifted their heads with her tender hands,
And sustained them with rods and osier-bands;
If the flowers had been her own infants, she
Could never have nursed them more tenderly.   40

And all killing insects and gnawing worms,
And things of obscene and unlovely forms,
She bore in a basket of Indian woof,
Into the rough woods far aloof,

In a basket, of grass and wild flowers full,   45
The freshest her gentle hands could pull
For the poor banished insects, whose intent,
Although they did ill, was innocent.

173

But the bee and the beamlike ephemeris
Whose path is the lightning's, and soft moths that kiss 50
The sweet lips of the flowers, and harm not, did she
Make her attendant angels be.

And many an antenatal tomb,
Where butterflies dream of the life to come,
She left clinging round the smooth and dark 55
Edge of the odorous cedar-bark.

This fairest creature from earliest spring
Thus moved through the garden ministering
All the sweet season of summer-tide,
And ere the first leaf looked brown—she died! 60

PART III

Three days the flowers of the garden fair
Like stars when the moon is awakened were,
Or the waves of Baiæ, ere luminous
She floats up through the smoke of Vesuvius.

And on the fourth, the Sensitive Plant 5
Felt the sound of the funeral chant,
And the steps of the bearers, heavy and slow,
And the sobs of the mourners, deep and low;

The weary sound and the heavy breath,
And the silent motions of passing death, 10
And the smell, cold, oppressive, and dank,
Sent through the pores of the coffin plank.

The dark grass, and the flowers among the grass,
Were bright with tears as the crowd did pass;
From their sighs the wind caught a mournful tone, 15
And sat in the pines, and gave groan for groan.

The garden, once fair, became cold and foul,
Like the corpse of her who had been its soul,
Which at first was lovely as if in sleep,
Then slowly changed, till it grew a heap   20
To make men tremble who never weep.

Swift summer into the autumn flowed,
And frost in the mist of the morning rode,
Though the noonday sun looked clear and bright,
Mocking the spoil of the secret night.   25

The rose-leaves, like flakes of crimson snow,
Paved the turf and the moss below.
The lilies were drooping, and white, and wan,
Like the head and the skin of a dying man.

And Indian plants, of scent and hue   30
The sweetest that ever were fed on dew,
Leaf by leaf, day after day,
Were massed into the common clay.

And the leaves, brown, yellow, and grey, and red,
And white with the whiteness of what is dead,
Like troops of ghosts on the dry wind passed;   35
Their whistling noise made the birds aghast.

And the gusty winds waked the wingèd seeds
Out of their birthplace of ugly weeds,
Till they clung round many a sweet flower's stem,   40
Which rotted into the earth with them.

The water-blooms under the rivulet
Fell from the stalks on which they were set;
And the eddies drove them here and there,
As the winds did those of the upper air.   45

Then the rain came down, and the broken stalks
Were bent and tangled across the walks;
And the leafless net-work of parasite bowers
Massed into ruin, and all sweet flowers.

Between the time of the wind and the snow   50
All loathliest weeds began to grow,
Whose coarse leaves were splashed with many a speck,
Like the water-snake's belly and the toad's back.

And thistles, and nettles, and darnels rank,
And the dock, and henbane, and hemlock dank,   55
Stretched out its long and hollow shank,
And stifled the air till the dead wind stank.

And plants, at whose names the verse feels loath,
Filled the place with a monstrous undergrowth,
Prickly, and pulpous, and blistering, and blue,   60
Livid, and starred with a lurid dew.

And agarics and fungi, with mildew and mould,
Started like mist from the wet ground cold;
Pale, fleshy, as if the decaying dead
With a spirit of growth had been animated!   65

[Their moss rotted off them, flake by flake,
Till the thick stalk stuck like a murderer's stake,
Where rags of loose flesh yet tremble on high,
Infecting the winds that wander by.]

Spawn, weeds, and filth, a leprous scum,   70
Made the running rivulet thick and dumb,
And at its outlet flags huge as stakes
Dammed it up with roots knotted like water-snakes.

And hour by hour, when the air was still,
The vapours arose which have strength to kill;   75
At morn they were seen, at noon they were felt,
At night they were darkness no star could melt.

And unctuous meteors from spray to spray
Crept and flitted in broad noonday
Unseen; every branch on which they alit   80
By a venomous blight was burned and bit.

The Sensitive Plant, like one forbid,
Wept, and the tears within each lid
Of its folded leaves, which together grew,
Were changed to a blight of frozen glue.   85

For the leaves soon fell, and the branches soon
By the heavy axe of the blast were hewn;
The sap shrank to the root through every pore,
As blood to a heart that will beat no more.

For Winter came; the wind was his whip;   90
One choppy finger was on his lip;
He had torn the cataracts from the hills
And they clanked at his girdle like manacles;

His breath was a chain which without a sound
The earth, and the air, and the water bound;   95
He came, fiercely driven, in his chariot-throne
By the tenfold blasts of the Arctic zone.

Then the weeds which were forms of living death
Fled from the frost to the earth beneath.
Their decay and sudden flight from frost   100
Was but like the vanishing of a ghost!

And under the roots of the Sensitive Plant
The moles and the dormice died for want:
The birds dropped stiff from the frozen air
And were caught in the branches naked and bare.   105

First there came down a thawing rain,
And its dull drops froze on the boughs again;
Then there steamed up a freezing dew
Which to the drops of the thaw-rain grew;

And a northern whirlwind, wandering about   110
Like a wolf that had smelt a dead child out,
Shook the boughs thus laden and heavy and stiff,
And snapped them off with his rigid griff.

When winter had gone and spring came back,
The Sensitive Plant was a leafless wreck;   115
But the mandrakes, and toadstools, and docks, and darnels,
Rose like the dead from their ruined charnels.

CONCLUSION

Whether the Sensitive Plant, or that
Which within its boughs like a spirit sat
Ere its outward form had known decay.   120
Now felt this change, I cannot say.

Whether that Lady's gentle mind,
No longer with the form combined
Which scattered love, as stars do light,
Found sadness, where it left delight,   125

I dare not guess; but in this life
Of error, ignorance and strife,
Where nothing is, but all things seem,
And we the shadows of the dream,

It is a modest creed, and yet 130
Pleasant if one considers it,
To own that death itself must be,
Like all the rest, a mockery.

That garden sweet, that Lady fair,
And all sweet shapes and odours there, 135
In truth have never passed away:
'Tis we, 'tis ours, are changed; not they.

For love, and beauty, and delight,
There is no death nor change: their might
Exceeds our organs, which endure 140
No light, being themselves obscure.

A VISION OF THE SEA

'Tis the terror of tempest. The rags of the sail
Are flickering in ribbons within the fierce gale:
From the stark night of vapours the dim rain is driven,
And when lightning is loosed, like a deluge from heaven,
She sees the black trunks of the water-spouts spin,   5
And bend, as if heaven was ruining in,
Which they seemed to sustain with their terrible mass
As if ocean had sunk from beneath them: they pass
To their graves in the deep with an earthquake of sound,
And the waves and the thunders made silent around,   10
Leave the wind to its echo. The vessel, now tossed
Through the low-trailing rack of the tempest, is lost
In the skirts of the thunder-cloud; now down the sweep
Of the wind-cloven wave to the chasm of the deep
It sinks, and the walls of the watery vale,   15
Whose depths of dread calm are unmoved by the gale,
Dim mirrors of ruin, hang gleaming about;
While the surf, like a chaos of stars, like a rout
Of death-flames, like whirlpools of fire-flowing iron,
With splendour and terror the black ship environ,   20
Or, like sulphur-flakes hurled from a mine of pale fire,
In fountains spout o'er it. In many a spire
The pyramid-billows with white points of brine
In the cope of the lightning inconstantly shine,
As piercing the sky from the floor of the sea.   25

The great ship seems splitting! it cracks as a tree
While an earthquake is splintering its root, ere the blast
Of the whirlwind that stripped it of branches has passed.
The intense thunderballs which are raining from heaven
Have shattered its mast, and it stands black and riven.   30
The chinks suck destruction. The heavy dead hulk
On the living sea rolls, an inanimate bulk,
Like a corpse on the clay which is hungering to fold
Its corruption around it. Meanwhile, from the hold,

One deck is burst up by the waters below,   35
And it splits like the ice when the thaw-breezes blow
O'er the lakes of the desert! Who sits on the other?
Is that all the crew that lie burying each other,
Like the dead in a breach, round the foremast? Are those
Twin tigers, who burst, when the waters arose,   40
In the agony of terror their chains in the hold,
(What now makes them tame, is what then made them bold)
Who crouch side by side, and have driven, like a crank,
The deep grip of their claws through the vibrating plank—
Are these all?

             Nine weeks the tall vessel had lain   45
On the windless expanse of the watery plain,
Where the death-darting sun cast no shadow at noon,
And there seemed to be fire in the beams of the moon;
Till a lead-coloured fog gathered up from the deep,
Whose breath was quick pestilence; then, the cold sleep 50
Crept, like blight through the ears of a thick field of corn,
O'er the populous vessel. And even and morn,
With their hammocks for coffins, the seamen aghast
Like dead men the dead limbs of their comrades cast
Down the deep, which closed on them above and around, 55
And the sharks and the dogfish their grave-clothes
    unbound,
And were glutted like Jews with this manna rained down
From God on their wilderness. One after one
The mariners died; on the eve of this day,
When the tempest was gathering in cloudy array.   60
But seven remained. Six the thunder has smitten,
And they lie black as mummies on which Time has written
His scorn of the embalmer; the seventh, from the deck
An oak-splinter pierced through his breast and his back,
And hung out to the tempest, a wreck on the wreck.   65

No more? At the helm sits a woman more fair
Than heaven, when, unbinding its star-braided hair,

It sinks with the sun on the earth and the sea.
She clasps a bright child on her upgathered knee.
It laughs at the lightning; it mocks the mixed thunder 70
Of the air and the sea; with desire and with wonder
It is beckoning the tigers to rise and come near;
It would play with those eyes where the radiance of fear
Is outshining the meteors; its bosom beats high,
The heart-fire of pleasure has kindled its eye, 75
Whilst its mother's is lustreless. 'Smile not, my child,
But sleep deeply and sweetly, and so be beguiled
Of the pang that awaits us, whatever that be,
So dreadful since thou must divide it with me!
Dream, sleep! This pale bosom, thy cradle and bed, 80
Will it rock thee not, infant? 'Tis beating with dread!
Alas! what is life, what is death, what are we,
That when the ship sinks we no longer may be?
What! to see thee no more, and to feel thee no more?
To be after life what we have been before? 85
Not to touch those sweet hands? Not to look on those eyes,
Those lips, and that hair, all that smiling disguise
Thou yet wearest, sweet spirit, which I, day by day,
Have so long called my child, but which now fades away
Like a rainbow, and I the fall'n shower?'
                                                    Lo! the ship 90
Is settling, it topples, the leeward ports dip.
The tigers leap up when they feel the slow brine
Crawling inch by inch on them; hair, ears, limbs, and eyne,
Stand rigid with horror; a loud, long, hoarse cry
Bursts at once from their vitals tremendously, 95
And 'tis borne down the mountainous vale of the wave,
Rebounding, like thunder from crag to cave,
Mixed with the clash of the lashing rain,
Hurried on by the might of the hurricane.
The hurricane came from the west, and passed on 100
By the path of the gate of the eastern sun,
Transversely dividing the stream of the storm,

As an arrowy serpent, pursuing the form
Of an elephant, bursts through the brakes of the waste.
Black as a cormorant the screaming blast,   105
Between ocean and heaven, like an ocean, passed,
Till it came to the clouds on the verge of the world
Which, based on the sea and to heaven upcurled,
Like columns and walls did surround and sustain
The dome of the tempest. It rent them in twain,   110
As a flood rends its barriers of mountainous crag;
And the dense clouds in many a ruin and rag,
Like the stones of a temple ere earthquake has passed,
Like the dust of its fall, on the whirlwind are cast—
They are scattered like foam on the torrent; and where 115
The wind has burst out through the chasm, from the air
Of clear morning the beams of the sunrise flow in,
Unimpeded, keen, golden, and crystalline,
Banded armies of light and of air. At one gate
They encounter, but interpenetrate;   120
And that breach in the tempest is widening away,
And the caverns of cloud are torn up by the day,
And the fierce winds are sinking with weary wings
Lulled by the motion and murmurings,
And the long glassy heave of the rocking sea;   125
And overhead glorious, but dreadful to see,
The wrecks of the tempest, like vapours of gold,
Are consuming in sunrise. The heaped waves behold
The deep calm of blue heaven dilating above,
And, like passions made still by the presence of Love, 130
Beneath the clear surface reflecting it slide
Tremulous with soft influence; extending its tide
From the Andes to Atlas, round mountain and isle,
Round sea-birds and wrecks, paved with heaven's azure
     smile,
The wide world of waters is vibrating.
                                   Where   135
Is the ship? On the verge of the wave where it lay

One tiger is mingled in ghastly affray
With a sea-snake. The foam and the smoke of the battle
Stain the clear air with sunbows; the jar, and the rattle
Of solid bones crushed by the infinite stress   140
Of the snake's adamantine voluminousness;
And the hum of the hot blood that spouts and rains
Where the gripe of the tiger has wounded the veins
Swollen with rage, strength, and effort; the whirl and the
    splash
As of some hideous engine whose brazen teeth smash   145
The thin winds and soft waves into thunder; the screams
And hissings crawl fast o'er the smooth ocean-streams,
Each sound like a centipede. Near this commotion
A blue shark is hanging within the blue ocean,
The fin-wingèd tomb of the victor. The other   150
Is winning his way from the fate of his brother,
To his own with the speed of despair. Lo! a boat
Advances: twelve rowers with the impulse of thought
Urge on the keen keel; the brine foams. At the stern
Three marksmen stand levelling. Hot bullets burn   155
In the breast of the tiger, which yet bears him on
To his refuge and ruin. One fragment alone—
'Tis dwindling and sinking, 'tis now almost gone—
Of the wreck of the vessel peers out of the sea.
With her left hand she grasps it impetuously,   160
With her right she sustains her fair infant. Death, Fear,
Love, Beauty, are mixed in the atmosphere,
Which trembles and burns with the fervour of dread
Around her wild eyes, her bright hand, and her head,
Like a meteor of light o'er the waters! Her child   165
Is yet smiling, and playing, and murmuring; so smiled
The false deep ere the storm. Like a sister and brother
The child and the ocean still smile on each other,
Whilst—

ODE TO HEAVEN

FIRST SPIRIT

Palace-roof of cloudless nights!
Paradise of golden lights!
  Deep, immeasurable, vast,
Which art now, and which wert then;
  Of the present and the past,   5
Of the eternal where and when,
  Presence-chamber, temple, home;
  Ever-canopying dome
  Of acts and ages yet to come!

Glorious shapes have life in thee—   10
Earth, and all earth's company;
  Living globes which ever throng
Thy deep chasms and wildernesses;
  And green worlds that glide along;
And swift stars with flashing tresses;   15
  And icy moons most cold and bright,
  And mighty suns beyond the night,
  Atoms of intensest light.

Even thy name is as a god,
Heaven! for thou art the abode   20
  Of that Power which is the glass
Wherein man his nature sees.
  Generations as they pass
Worship thee with bended knees.
  Their unremaining gods and they   25
  Like a river roll away:
  Thou remainest such—alway.

SECOND SPIRIT

Thou art but the mind's first chamber,
Round which its young fancies clamber,
　　Like weak insects in a cave　　　　　　30
Lighted up by stalactites;
　　But the portal of the grave,
Where a world of new delights
　　Will make thy best glories seem
　　But a dim and noonday gleam　　　　　35
　　From the shadow of a dream!

THIRD SPIRIT

Peace! the abyss is wreathed with scorn
At your presumption, atom-born!
　　What is Heaven? and what are ye
Who its brief expanse inherit?　　　　　40
　　What are suns and spheres which flee
With the instinct of that Spirit
　　Of which ye are but a part?
　　Drops which Nature's mighty heart
　　Drives through thinnest veins. Depart!　45

What is Heaven? a globe of dew,
Filling in the morning new
　　Some eyed flower whose young leaves waken
On an unimagined world:
　　Constellated suns unshaken,　　　　　50
Orbits measureless, are furled
　　In that frail and fading sphere,
　　With ten millions gathered there,
　　To tremble, gleam, and disappear.

AN EXHORTATION

I

Chameleons feed on light and air:
  Poets' food is love and fame:
If in this wide world of care
  Poets could but find the same
With as little toil as they,   5
    Would they ever change their hue
    As the light chameleons do,
Suiting it to every ray
Twenty times a day?

II

Poets are on this cold earth,   10
    As chameleons might be,
Hidden from their early birth
    In a cave beneath the sea.
Where light is, chameleons change:
    Where love is not, poets do: 15
    Fame is love disguised: if few
Find either, never think it strange
That poets range.

III

Yet dare not stain with wealth or power
    A poet's free and heavenly mind: 20
If bright chameleons should devour
    Any food but beams and wind,
They would grow as earthly soon
    As their brother lizards are.
    Children of a sunnier star,   25
Spirits from beyond the moon,
Oh, refuse the boon!

ODE TO THE WEST WIND[1]

I

O Wild West Wind, thou breath of Autumn's being,
Thou, from whose unseen presence the leaves dead
Are driven, like ghosts from an enchanter fleeing,

Yellow, and black, and pale, and hectic red,
Pestilence-stricken multitudes: O thou,   5
Who chariotest to their dark wintry bed

The wingèd seeds, where they lie cold and low,
Each like a corpse within its grave, until
Thine azure sister of the Spring shall blow

Her clarion o'er the dreaming earth, and fill   10
(Driving sweet buds like flocks to feed in air)
With living hues and odours plain and hill:

Wild Spirit, which art moving everywhere;
Destroyer and preserver; hear, oh, hear!

[1]This poem was conceived and chiefly written in a wood that skirts the Arno, near Florence, and on a day when that tempestuous wind, whose temperature is at once mild and animating, was collecting the vapours which pour down the autumnal rains. They began, as I foresaw, at sunset with a violent tempest of hail and rain, attended by that magnificent thunder and lightning peculiar to the Cisalpine regions.
The phenomenon alluded to at the conclusion of the third stanza is well known to naturalists. The vegetation at the bottom of the sea, of rivers, and of lakes sympathizes with that of the land in the change of seasons, and is consequently influenced by the winds which announce it. [Shelley's Note]

II

Thou on whose stream, 'mid the steep sky's commotion, 15
Loose clouds like Earth's decaying leaves are shed,
Shook from the tangled boughs of Heaven and Ocean,

Angels of rain and lightning: there are spread
On the blue surface of thine airy surge,
Like the bright hair uplifted from the head   20

Of some fierce Mænad, even from the dim verge
Of the horizon to the zenith's height
The locks of the approaching storm. Thou dirge

Of the dying Year, to which this closing night
Will be the dome of a vast sepulchre,   25
Vaulted with all thy congregated might

Of vapours, from whose solid atmosphere
Black rain, and fire, and hail will burst: oh, hear!

III

Thou who didst waken from his summer dreams
The blue Mediterranean, where he lay,   30
Lulled by the coil of his crystàlline streams,

Beside a pumice-isle in Baiae's bay,
And saw in sleep old palaces and towers
Quivering within the wave's intenser day,

All overgrown with azure moss and flowers   35
So sweet, the sense faints picturing them! Thou
For whose path the Atlantic's level powers

Cleave themselves into chasms, while far below
The sea-blooms and the oozy woods which wear
The sapless foliage of the ocean, know   40

Thy voice, and suddenly grow grey with fear,
And tremble and despoil themselves: oh, hear!

IV

If I were a dead leaf thou mightest bear;
If I were a swift cloud to fly with thee;
A wave to pant beneath thy power, and share   45

The impulse of thy strength, only less free
Than thou, O uncontrollable! If even
I were as in my boyhood, and could be

The comrade of thy wanderings over Heaven
As then, when to outstrip thy skiey speed   50
Scarce seemed a vision; I would ne'er have striven

As thus with thee in prayer in my sore need.
Oh! lift me as a wave, a leaf, a cloud!
I fall upon the thorns of life! I bleed!

A heavy weight of hours has chained and bowed   55
One too like thee: tameless, and swift, and proud.

V

Make me thy lyre, even as the forest is:
What if my leaves are falling like its own!
The tumult of thy mighty harmonies

Will take from both a deep, autumnal tone,   60
Sweet though in sadness. Be thou, Spirit fierce,
My spirit! Be thou me, impetuous one!

Drive my dead thoughts over the universe
Like withered leaves to quicken a new birth!
And, by the incantation of this verse,   65

Scatter, as from an unextinguished hearth
Ashes and sparks, my words among mankind!
Be through my lips to unawakened Earth

The trumpet of a prophecy! O Wind,
If Winter comes, can Spring be far behind?   70

AN ODE

WRITTEN OCTOBER, 1819, BEFORE THE SPANIARDS HAD
RECOVERED THEIR LIBERTY.

   Arise, arise, arise!
 There is blood on the earth that denies ye bread;
   Be your wounds like eyes
 To weep for the dead, the dead, the dead.
What other grief were it just to pay?   5
Your sons, your wives, your brethren, were they;
Who said they were slain on the battle-day?

   Awaken, awaken, awaken!
 The slave and the tyrant are twin-born foes;
   Be the cold chains shaken   10
 To the dust where your kindred repose, repose:
Their bones in the grave will start and move,
When they hear the voices of those they love,
Most loud in the holy combat above.

   Wave, wave high the banner!   15
 When Freedom is riding to conquest by:
   Though the slaves that fan her
 Be Famine and Toil, giving sigh for sigh.
And ye who attend her imperial car,
Lift not your hands in the banded war,   20
But in her defence whose children ye are.

Glory, glory, glory,
To those who have greatly suffered and done!
Never name in story
Was greater than that which ye shall have won.   25
Conquerors have conquered their foes alone,
Whose revenge, pride, and power they have overthrown:
Ride ye, more victorious, over your own.

Bind, bind every brow
With crownals of violet, ivy, and pine: 30
Hide the blood-stains now
With hues which sweet Nature has made divine—
Green strength, azure hope, and eternity:
But let not the pansy among them be;
Ye were injured, and that means memory.   35

THE CLOUD

I bring fresh showers for the thirsting flowers,
From the seas and the streams;
I bear light shade for the leaves when laid
In their noonday dreams.
From my wings are shaken the dews that waken   5
The sweet buds every one,
When rocked to rest on their mother's breast,
As she dances about the sun.
I wield the flail of the lashing hail,
And whiten the green plains under,   10
And then again I dissolve it in rain,
And laugh as I pass in thunder.

I sift the snow on the mountains below,
And their great pines groan aghast;
And all the night 'tis my pillow white,   15
While I sleep in the arms of the blast.

Sublime on the towers of my skiey bowers,
    Lightning my pilot sits;
In a cavern under is fettered the thunder,
    It struggles and howls at fits;   20
Over earth and ocean, with gentle motion,
    This pilot is guiding me,
Lured by the love of the genii that move
    In the depths of the purple sea;
Over the rills, and the crags, and the hills,   25
    Over the lakes and the plains,
Wherever he dream under mountain or stream
    The Spirit he loves remains;
And I all the while bask in heaven's blue smile,
    Whilst he is dissolving in rains.   30

The sanguine sunrise, with his meteor eyes,
    And his burning plumes outspread,
Leaps on the back of my sailing rack,
    When the morning star shines dead,
As on the jag of a mountain crag,   35
    Which an earthquake rocks and swings.
An eagle alit one moment may sit
    In the light of its golden wings,
And when sunset may breathe, from the lit sea beneath,
    Its ardours of rest and of love,   40
And the crimson pall of eve may fall
    From the depth of heaven above,
With wings folded I rest, on mine airy nest,
    As still as a brooding dove.

That orbèd maiden with white fire laden,   45
    Whom mortals call the moon,
Glides glimmering o'er my fleece-like floor,
    By the midnight breezes strewn;
And wherever the beat of her unseen feet,
    Which only the angels hear,   50

May have broken the woof of my tent's thin roof,
   The stars peep behind her and peer;
And I laugh to see them whirl and flee,
   Like a swarm of golden bees,
When I widen the rent in my wind-built tent,   55
   Till the calm rivers, lakes, and seas,
Like strips of the sky fallen through me on high,
   Are each paved with the moon and these.

I bind the sun's throne with a burning zone,
   And the moon's with a girdle of pearl;   60
The volcanoes are dim, and the stars reel and swim,
   When the whirlwinds my banner unfurl.
From cape to cape, with a bridge-like shape,
   Over a torrent sea,
Sunbeam-proof, I hang like a roof—   65
   The mountains its columns be.
The triumphal arch through which I march
   With hurricane, fire, and snow,
When the Powers of the air are chained to my chair,
   Is the million-coloured bow;   70
The sphere-fire above its soft colours wove,
   While the moist earth was laughing below.

I am the daughter of earth and water,
   And the nursling of the sky;
I pass through the pores of the ocean and shores;   75
   I change, but I cannot die.
For after the rain, when with never a stain
   The pavilion of heaven is bare,
And the winds and sunbeams with their convex gleams
   Build up the blue dome of air,   80
I silently laugh at my own cenotaph,
   And out of the caverns of rain,
Like a child from the womb, like a ghost from the tomb,
   I arise, and unbuild it again.

TO A SKYLARK

I

Hail to thee, blithe Spirit!—
Bird thou never wert—
That from Heaven, or near it,
Pourest thy full heart
In profuse strains of unpremeditated art.　　　5

II

Higher still and higher
From the earth thou springest
Like a cloud of fire;
The blue deep thou wingest,
And singing still dost soar, and soaring ever singest.　　10

III

In the golden lightning
Of the sunken sun,
O'er which clouds are bright'ning,
Thou dost float and run;
Like an unbodied joy whose race is just begun.　　15

IV

The pale purple even
Melts around thy flight;
Like a star of Heaven,
In the broad daylight
Thou art unseen,—but yet I hear thy shrill delight,　　20

V

Keen as are the arrows
Of that silver sphere,
Whose intense lamp narrows
In the white dawn clear,
Until we hardly see—we feel that it is there.　　25

VI

All the earth and air
    With thy voice is loud,
As, when night is bare,
    From one lonely cloud
The moon rains out her beams, and Heaven is over-
    flowed.   30

VII

What thou art we know not;
    What is most like thee?
From rainbow clouds there flow not
    Drops so bright to see
As from thy presence showers a rain of melody.   35

VIII

Like a poet hidden
    In the light of thought,
Singing hymns unbidden
    Till the world is wrought
To sympathy with hopes and fears it heeded not: 40

IX

Like a high-born maiden
    In a palace-tower,
Soothing her love-laden
    Soul in secret hour
With music sweet as love, which overflows her bower: 45

X

Like a glow-worm golden
    In a dell of dew,
Scattering unbeholden
    Its aërial hue
Among the flowers and grass which screen it from the
    view: 50

XI

Like a rose embowered
        In its own green leaves,
By warm winds deflowered,
        Till the scent it gives
Makes faint with too much sweet those heavy-wingèd   55
        thieves:

XII

Sound of vernal showers
        On the twinkling grass,
Rain-awakened flowers,
        All that ever was
Joyous and clear and fresh, thy music doth surpass.   60

XIII

Teach us, Sprite or Bird,
        What sweet thoughts are thine:
I have never heard
        Praise of love or wine
That panted forth a flood of rapture so divine: 65

XIV

Chorus hymeneal
        Or triumphal chant,
Matched with thine, would be all
        But an empty vaunt,
A thing wherein we feel there is some hidden want.   70

XV

What objects are the fountains
        Of thy happy strain?
What fields or waves or mountains?
        What shapes of sky or plain?
What love of thine own kind? what ignorance of pain?   75

XVI

With thy clear keen joyance
    Languor cannot be:
Shadow of annoyance
    Never came near thee:
Thou lovest—but ne'er knew love's sad satiety.   80

XVII

Waking or asleep
    Thou of death must deem
Things more true and deep
    Than we mortals dream,
Or how could thy notes flow in such a crystal stream? 85

XVIII

We look before and after,
    And pine for what is not:
Our sincerest laughter
    With some pain is fraught;
Our sweetest songs are those that tell of saddest thought. 90

XIX

Yet if we could scorn
    Hate and pride and fear,
If we were things born
    Not to shed a tear,
I know not how thy joy we ever should come near.   95

XX

Better than all measures
    Of delightful sound,
Better than all treasures
    That in books are found,
Thy skill to poet were, thou scorner of the ground!   100

XXI

Teach me half the gladness
　　That thy brain must know,
Such harmonious madness
　　From my lips would flow
The world should listen then—as I am listening now. 105

ODE TO LIBERTY

Yet, Freedom, yet, thy banner, torn but flying,
Streams like a thunder-storm against the wind.

BYRON

I

A glorious people vibrated again
   The lightning of the nations: Liberty,
From heart to heart, from tower to tower, o'er Spain,
   Scattering contagious fire into the sky,
Gleamed. My soul spurned the chains of its dismay,   5
      And in the rapid plumes of song
      Clothed itself, sublime and strong,
As a young eagle soars the morning clouds among,
   Hovering in verse o'er its accustomed prey;
      Till from its station in the Heaven of fame   10
      The Spirit's whirlwind rapt it, and the ray
      Of the remotest sphere of living flame
Which paves the void was from behind it flung,
   As foam from a ship's swiftness, when there came
   A voice out of the deep: I will record the same.   15

II

The sun and the serenest moon sprang forth:
   The burning stars of the abyss were hurled
Into the depths of heaven. The dædal earth,
   That island in the ocean of the world,
Hung in its cloud of all-sustaining air: 20
      But this divinest universe
      Was yet a chaos and a curse,
For thou wert not: but, power from worst producing
      worse,

The spirit of the beasts was kindled there,
 And of the birds, and of the watery forms, 25
And there was war among them, and despair
 Within them, raging without truce or terms:
The bosom of their violated nurse
 Groaned, for beasts warred on beasts, and worms on
   worms,
And men on men; each heart was a hell of storms. 30

III

Man, the imperial shape, then multiplied
 His generations under the pavilion
Of the sun's throne: palace and pyramid,
 Temple and prison, to many a swarming million
Were as to mountain wolves their raggèd caves. 35
  This human living multitude
  Was savage, cunning, blind, and rude,
For thou wert not; but o'er the populous solitude,
 Like one fierce cloud over a waste of waves,
  Hung tyranny; beneath, sat deified 40
 The sister-pest, congregator of slaves;
  Into the shadow of her pinions wide
Anarchs and priests, who feed on gold and blood
  Till with the stain their inmost souls are dyed,
  Drove the astonished herds of men from every
   side. 45

IV

The nodding promontories, and blue isles,
 And cloud-like mountains, and dividuous waves
Of Greece, basked glorious in the open smiles
 Of favouring heaven: from their enchanted caves
Prophetic echoes flung dim melody 50
  On the unapprehensive wild.
  The vine, the corn, the olive mild,

Grew savage yet, to human use unreconciled;
    And, like unfolded flowers beneath the sea,
        Like the man's thought dark in the infant's brain, 55
    Like aught that is which wraps what is to be,
        Art's deathless dreams lay veiled by many a vein
Of Parian stone; and, yet a speechless child,
    Verse murmured, and Philosophy did strain
    Her lidless eyes for thee; when o'er the Aegean main 60

V

Athens arose: a city such as vision
    Builds from the purple crags and silver towers
Of battlemented cloud, as in derision
    Of kingliest masonry: the ocean floors
Pave it; the evening sky pavilions it;   65
        Its portals are inhabited
        By thunder-zonèd winds, each head
Within its cloudy wings with sunfire garlanded—
    A divine work! Athens, diviner yet,
        Gleamed with its crest of columns, on the will   70
    Of man, as on a mount of diamond, set;
        For thou wert, and thine all-creative skill
Peopled, with forms that mock the eternal dead
    In marble immortality, that hill
    Which was thine earliest throne and latest oracle.   75

VI

Within the surface of Time's fleeting river
    Its wrinkled image lies, as then it lay,
Immoveably unquiet, and forever
    It trembles, but it cannot pass away!
The voices of thy bards and sages thunder   80
        With an earth-awakening blast
        Through the caverns of the past:

(Religion veils her eyes; Oppression shrinks aghast:)
  A wingèd sound of joy, and love, and wonder,
    Which soars where Expectation never flew,   85
  Rending the veil of space and time asunder!
    One ocean feeds the clouds, and streams, and dew;
One sun illumines heaven; one Spirit vast
  With life and love makes chaos ever new,
  As Athens doth the world with thy delight renew.   90

VII

Then Rome was, and from thy deep bosom fairest,
  Like a wolf-cub from a Cadmæan Mænad,[1]
She drew the milk of greatness, though thy dearest
  From that Elysian food was yet unweanèd;
And many a deed of terrible uprightness   95
    By thy sweet love was sanctified;
    And in thy smile, and by thy side,
Saintly Camillus lived, and firm Atilius died.
  But when tears stained thy robe of vestal whiteness,
    And gold profaned thy Capitolian throne,   100
  Thou didst desert, with spirit-wingèd lightness,
    The senate of the tyrants: they sunk prone,
Slaves of one tyrant: Palatinus sighed
  Faint echoes of Ionian song; that tone
  Thou didst delay to hear, lamenting to disown.   105

VIII

From what Hyrcanian glen or frozen hill,
  Or piny promontory of the Arctic main,
Or utmost islet inaccessible,
  Didst thou lament the ruin of thy reign,

[1]See the *Bacchæ* of Euripides. [Shelley's Note]

Teaching the woods and waves, and desert rocks,   110
    And every Naiad's ice-cold urn,
    To talk in echoes sad and stern
Of that sublimest lore which man had dared unlearn?
  For neither didst thou watch the wizard flocks
    Of the Scald's dreams, nor haunt the Druid's
        sleep.   115
  What if the tears rained through thy shattered locks
    Were quickly dried? For thou didst groan, not weep,
When from its sea of death, to kill and burn,
  The Galilean serpent forth did creep,
  And made thy world an undistinguishable heap.   120

IX

A thousand years the Earth cried, 'Where art thou?'
  And then the shadow of thy coming fell
On Saxon Alfred's olive-cinctured brow:
  And many a warrior-peopled citadel,
Like rocks which fire lifts out of the flat deep,   125
    Arose in sacred Italy,
    Frowning o'er the tempestuous sea
Of kings, and priests, and slaves, in tower-crowned
      majesty;
    That multitudinous anarchy did sweep,
    And burst around their walls, like idle foam,   130
  Whilst from the human spirit's deepest deep
    Strange melody with love and awe struck dumb
Dissonant arms; and Art, which cannot die,
  With divine wand traced on our earthly home
  Fit imagery to pave heaven's everlasting dome.   135

X

Thou huntress swifter than the Moon! thou terror
  Of the world's wolves! thou bearer of the quiver,
Whose sunlike shafts pierce tempest-wingèd Error,

As light may pierce the clouds when they dissever
In the calm regions of the orient day! 140
    Luther caught thy wakening glance:
    Like lightning, from his leaden lance
Reflected, it dissolved the visions of the trance
    In which, as in a tomb, the nations lay:
       And England's prophets hailed thee as their
         queen, 145
    In songs whose music cannot pass away,
      Though it must flow forever: not unseen
Before the spirit-sighted countenance
    Of Milton didst thou pass, from the sad scene
    Beyond whose night he saw, with a dejected mien. 150

XI

The eager Hours and unreluctant Years
    As on a dawn-illumined mountain stood,
Trampling to silence their loud hopes and fears,
    Darkening each other with their multitude,
And cried aloud, 'Liberty!' Indignation 155
      Answered Pity from her cave;
      Death grew pale within the grave,
And Desolation howled to the Destroyer, 'Save!'
    When, like heaven's sun girt by the exhalation
      Of its own glorious light, thou didst arise, 160
    Chasing thy foes from nation unto nation
      Like shadows: as if day had cloven the skies
At dreaming midnight o'er the western wave,
    Men started, staggering with a glad surprise,
    Under the lightnings of thine unfamiliar eyes. 165

XII

Thou Heaven of earth! what spells could pall thee
        then,
    In ominous eclipse? A thousand years
Bred from the slime of deep Oppression's den,

Dyed all thy liquid light with blood and tears,
Till thy sweet stars could weep the stain away;   170
    How like Bacchanals of blood
    Round France, the ghastly vintage, stood
Destruction's sceptred slaves, and Folly's mitred brood!
  When one, like them, but mightier far than they,
    The Anarch of thine own bewildered powers,   175
  Rose: armies mingled in obscure array,
    Like clouds with clouds, darkening the sacred
       bowers
Of serene heaven. He, by the past pursued,
  Rests with those dead but unforgotten Hours,
  Whose ghosts scare victor kings in their ancestral
      towers.   180

XIII

England yet sleeps: was she not called of old?
  Spain calls her now, as with its thrilling thunder
Vesuvius wakens Etna, and the cold
  Snow-crags by its reply are cloven in sunder:
O'er the lit waves every Aeolian isle   185
    From Pithecusa to Pelorus
    Howls, and leaps, and glares in chorus:
They cry, 'Be dim, ye lamps of heaven suspended o'er us.'
  Her chains are threads of gold,—she need but smile
    And they dissolve; but Spain's were links of steel, 190
  Till bit to dust by Virtue's keenest file.
    Twins of a single destiny! appeal
To the eternal years enthroned before us
  In the dim West: impress, as from a seal,
  All ye have thought and done! Time cannot dare
      conceal.   195

XIV

Tomb of Arminius! render up thy dead
Till, like a standard from a watch-tower's staff,
206

His soul may stream over the tyrant's head;
  Thy victory shall be his epitaph,
Wild Bacchanal of truth's mysterious wine,   200
    King-deluded Germany,
    His dead spirit lives in thee.
Why do we fear or hope? thou art already free!
  And thou, lost Paradise of this divine
    And glorious world! thou flowery wilderness!   205
  Thou island of eternity! thou shrine
    Where Desolation, clothed with loveliness,
Worships the thing thou wert! O Italy,
  Gather thy blood into thy heart: repress
  The beasts who make their dens thy sacred palaces. 210

XV

Oh that the free would stamp the impious name
  Of KING into the dust! or write it there,
So that this blot upon the page of fame
  Were as a serpent's path, which the light air
Erases, and the flat sands close behind!   215
    Ye the oracle have heard;
    Lift the victory-flashing sword,
And cut the snaky knots of this foul gordian word,
  Which, weak itself as stubble, yet can bind
    Into a mass, irrefragably firm,   220
  The axes and the rods which awe mankind;
    The sound has poison in it; 'tis the sperm
Of what makes life foul, cankerous, and abhorred:
  Disdain not thou, at thine appointed term,
  To set thine armèd heel on this reluctant worm.   225

XVI

Oh that the wise from their bright minds would kindle
  Such lamps within the dome of this dim world,
That the pale name of PRIEST might shrink and dwindle
  Into the hell from which it first was hurled,

A scoff of impious pride from fiends impure; 230
    Till human thoughts might kneel alone
    Each before the judgment-throne
Of its own aweless soul, or of the Power unknown!
  Oh that the words which make the thoughts obscure
    From which they spring, as clouds of glimmering
      dew 235
  From a white lake blot heaven's blue portraiture,
    Were stripped of their thin masks and various hue
And frowns and smiles and splendours not their own,
    Till in the nakedness of false and true
    They stand before their Lord, each to receive its
      due. 240

XVII

He who taught man to vanquish whatsoever
  Can be between the cradle and the grave
Crowned him the King of Life: oh vain endeavour,
  If on his own high will, a willing slave,
He has enthroned the oppression and the oppressor! 245
    What if earth can clothe and feed
    Amplest millions at their need,
And power in thought be as the tree within the seed?
  Or what if Art, an ardent intercessor,
    Driving on fiery wings to Nature's throne, 250
  Checks the great Mother stooping to caress her,
    And cries, 'Give me, thy child, dominion
Over all height and depth', if Life can breed
  New wants, and Wealth from those who toil and groan
  Rend, of thy gifts and hers, a thousandfold for one? 255

XVIII

Come Thou, but lead out of the inmost cave
  Of man's deep spirit, as the morning-star
Beckons the Sun from the Eoan wave,
  Wisdom. I hear the pennons of her car

Self-moving, like cloud charioted by flame;   260
      Comes she not, and come ye not,
      Rulers of eternal thought,
To judge, with solemn truth, life's ill-apportioned lot,
  Blind Love, and equal Justice, and the Fame
    Of what has been, the Hope of what will be?   265
  O Liberty! if such could be thy name
    Wert thou disjoined from these, or they from thee:
If thine or theirs were treasures to be bought
  By blood or tears, have not the wise and free
  Wept tears, and blood like tears?—The solemn
      harmony   270

XIX

Paused, and the Spirit of that mighty singing
  To its abyss was suddenly withdrawn;
Then, as a wild swan, when sublimely winging
  Its path athwart the thunder-smoke of dawn,
Sinks headlong through the aërial golden light   275
      On the heavy-sounding plain,
      When the bolt has pierced its brain;
As summer clouds dissolve, unburdened of their rain;
  As a far taper fades with fading night,
    As a brief insect dies with dying day,   280
  My song, its pinions disarrayed of might,
    Drooped; o'er it closed the echoes far away
Of the great voice which did its flight sustain,
  As waves which lately paved his watery way
  Hiss round a drowner's head in their tempestuous
      play.   285

ADONAIS

AN ELEGY ON THE DEATH OF JOHN KEATS, AUTHOR OF ENDYMION, HYPERION ETC.

By

PERCY B. SHELLEY

Ἀστὴρ πρὶν μὲν ἔλαμπες ἐνὶ ζώοισιν ἑῷος.
Νῦν δὲ θανών, λάμπεις ἕσπερος ἐν φθιμένοις.
PLATO

PISA
WITH THE TYPES OF DIDOT
MDCCCXXI

PREFACE

Φάρμακον ἦλθε, Βίων, ποτὶ σὸν στόμα, φάρμακον εἶδες:
Πῶς τευ τοῖς χείλεσσι ποτέδραμε, κοὐκ ἐγλυκάνθη;
Τίς δὲ βροτὸς τοσσοῦτον ἀνάμερος, ἢ κεράσαι τοι,
Ἢ δοῦναι λαλέοντι τὸ φάρμακον; ἔκφυγεν ᾠδάν.

Moschus, *Epitaph. Bion.*

It is my intention to subjoin to the London edition of
this poem a criticism upon the claims of its lamented
object to be classed among the writers of the highest
genius who have adorned our age. My known repug-
5 nance to the narrow principles of taste on which several
of his earlier compositions were modelled proves at
least that I am an impartial judge. I consider the frag-
ment of *Hyperion* as second to nothing that was ever
produced by a writer of the same years.
10   John Keats died at Rome of a consumption, in his
twenty-fourth year, on the — of — 1821; and was
buried in the romantic and lonely cemetery of the
Protestants in that city, under the pyramid which is
the tomb of Cestius, and the massy walls and towers,
15 now mouldering and desolate, which formed the circuit
of ancient Rome. The cemetery is an open space among
the ruins, covered in winter with violets and daisies. It
might make one in love with death, to think that one
should be buried in so sweet a place.
20   The genius of the lamented person to whose memory
I have dedicated these unworthy verses was not less
delicate and fragile than it was beautiful; and where
canker-worms abound, what wonder if its young
flower was blighted in the bud? The savage criticism
25 on his *Endymion*, which appeared in the *Quarterly
Review*, produced the most violent effect on his sus-
ceptible mind; the agitation thus originated ended in
the rupture of a blood-vessel in the lungs; a rapid con-
sumption ensued; and the succeeding acknowledg-

212

ments, from more candid critics, of the true greatness of his powers were ineffectual to heal the wound thus wantonly inflicted.

It may be well said that these wretched men know not what they do. They scatter their insults and their slanders without heed as to whether the poisoned shaft lights on a heart made callous by many blows, or one, like Keats's, composed of more penetrable stuff. One of their associates is, to my knowledge, a most base and unprincipled calumniator. As to *Endymion*, was it a poem, whatever might be its defects, to be treated contemptuously by those who had celebrated with various degrees of complacency and panegyric *Paris*, and *Woman*, and a *Syrian Tale*, and Mrs. Lefanu, and Mr. Barrett, and Mr. Howard Payne, and a long list of the illustrious obscure? Are these the men who, in their venal good nature, presumed to draw a parallel between the Rev. Mr. Milman and Lord Byron? What gnat did they strain at here, after having swallowed all those camels? Against what woman taken in adultery dares the foremost of these literary prostitutes to cast his opprobrious stone? Miserable man! you, one of the meanest, have wantonly defaced one of the noblest specimens of the workmanship of God. Nor shall it be your excuse that, murderer as you are, you have spoken daggers, but used none.

The circumstances of the closing scene of poor Keats's life were not made known to me until the Elegy was ready for the press. I am given to understand that the wound which his sensitive spirit had received from the criticism of *Endymion* was exasperated by the bitter sense of unrequited benefits; the poor fellow seems to have been hooted from the stage of life no less by those on whom he had wasted the promise of his genius than those on whom he had

lavished his fortune and his care. He was accompanied
to Rome and attended in his last illness by Mr. Severn,
a young artist of the highest promise, who, I have been
informed, 'almost risked his own life, and sacrificed
5 every prospect to unwearied attendance upon his dying
friend.' Had I known these circumstances before the
completion of my poem, I should have been tempted
to add my feeble tribute of applause to the more solid
recompense which the virtuous man finds in the recol-
10 lection of his own motives. Mr. Severn can dispense
with a reward from 'such stuff as dreams are made of.'
His conduct is a golden augury of the success of his
future career. May the unextinguished spirit of his
illustrious friend animate the creations of his pencil,
15 and plead against oblivion for his name!

ADONAIS

I

I weep for Adonais—he is dead!
O, weep for Adonais! though our tears
Thaw not the frost which binds so dear a head!
And thou, sad Hour, selected from all years
To mourn our loss, rouse thy obscure compeers,   5
And teach them thine own sorrow, say: with me
Died Adonais; till the Future dares
Forget the Past, his fate and fame shall be
An echo and a light unto eternity!

II

Where wert thou, mighty Mother, when he lay,   10
When thy Son lay, pierced by the shaft which flies
In darkness? where was lorn Urania
When Adonais died? With veilèd eyes,
'Mid listening Echoes, in her Paradise
She sat, while one, with soft enamoured breath,   15
Rekindled all the fading melodies,
With which, like flowers that mock the corse beneath,
He had adorned and hid the coming bulk of death.

III

O, weep for Adonais—he is dead!
Wake, melancholy Mother, wake and weep!   20
Yet wherefore? Quench within their burning bed
Thy fiery tears, and let thy loud heart keep
Like his, a mute and uncomplaining sleep;
For he is gone, where all things wise and fair
Descend—oh, dream not that the amorous Deep   25
Will yet restore him to the vital air;
Death feeds on his mute voice, and laughs at our despair.

IV

Most musical of mourners, weep again!
Lament anew, Urania!—He died,
Who was the Sire of an immortal strain,   30
Blind, old, and lonely, when his country's pride,
The priest, the slave, and the liberticide
Trampled and mocked with many a loathèd rite
Of lust and blood; he went, unterrified,
Into the gulf of death; but his clear Sprite   35
Yet reigns o'er earth; the third among the sons of light.

V

Most musical of mourners, weep anew!
Not all to that bright station dared to climb;
And happier they their happiness who knew,
Whose tapers yet burn through that night of time   40
In which suns perish; others more sublime,
Struck by the envious wrath of man or God,
Have sunk, extinct in their refulgent prime;
And some yet live, treading the thorny road
Which leads, through toil and hate, to Fame's serene
    abode.   45

VI

But now, thy youngest, dearest one has perished,
The nursling of thy widowhood, who grew,
Like a pale flower by some sad maiden cherished,
And fed with true love tears, instead of dew;
Most musical of mourners, weep anew!   50
Thy extreme hope, the loveliest and the last,
The bloom, whose petals nipped before they blew
Died on the promise of the fruit, is waste;
The broken lily lies—the storm is overpast.

VII

To that high Capital, where kingly Death   55
Keeps his pale court in beauty and decay,
He came; and bought, with price of purest breath,
A grave among the eternal. Come away!
Haste, while the vault of blue Italian day
Is yet his fitting charnel-roof! while still   60
He lies, as if in dewy sleep he lay;
Awake him not! surely he takes his fill
Of deep and liquid rest, forgetful of all ill.

VIII

He will awake no more, oh, never more!
Within the twilight chamber spreads apace, 65
The shadow of white Death, and at the door
Invisible Corruption waits to trace
His extreme way to her dim dwelling-place;
The eternal Hunger sits, but pity and awe
Soothe her pale rage, nor dares she to deface 70
So fair a prey, till darkness, and the law
Of change, shall o'er his sleep the mortal curtain draw.

IX

O, weep for Adonais!—The quick Dreams,
The passion-wingèd Ministers of thought,
Who were his flocks, whom near the living streams 75
Of his young spirit he fed, and whom he taught
The love which was its music, wander not,
Wander no more, from kindling brain to brain,
But droop there, whence they sprung; and mourn their lot
Round the cold heart, where, after their sweet pain, 80
They ne'er will gather strength, or find a home again.

X

And one with trembling hand clasps his cold head,
And fans him with her moonlight wings, and cries,
'Our love, our hope, our sorrow, is not dead;
See, on the silken fringe of his faint eyes, 85
Like dew upon a sleeping flower, there lies
A tear some Dream has loosened from his brain.'
Lost Angel of a ruined Paradise!
She knew not 'twas her own; as with no stain
She faded, like a cloud which had outwept its rain. 90

XI

One from a lucid urn of starry dew
Washed his light limbs as if embalming them;
Another clipped her profuse locks, and threw
The wreath upon him, like an anadem,
Which frozen tears instead of pearls begem;   95
Another in her wilful grief would break
Her bow and wingèd reeds, as if to stem
A greater loss with one which was more weak;
And dull the barbèd fire against his frozen cheek.

XII

Another Splendour on his mouth alit,   100
That mouth, whence it was wont to draw the breath
Which gave it strength to pierce the guarded wit,
And pass into the panting heart beneath
With lightning and with music: the damp death
Quenched its caress upon his icy lips;   105
And, as a dying meteor stains a wreath
Of moonlight vapour, which the cold night clips,
It flushed through his pale limbs, and passed to its eclipse.

XIII

And others came . . . Desires and Adorations,
Wingèd Persuasions and veiled Destinies,   110
Splendours, and Glooms, and glimmering Incarnations
Of hopes and fears, and twilight Phantasies;
And Sorrow, with her family of Sighs,
And Pleasure, blind with tears, led by the gleam
Of her own dying smile instead of eyes,   115
Came in slow pomp; the moving pomp might seem
Like pageantry of mist on an autumnal stream.

XIV

All he had loved, and moulded into thought,
From shape, and hue, and odour, and sweet sound,
Lamented Adonais. Morning sought   120
Her eastern watch-tower, and her hair unbound,
Wet with the tears which should adorn the ground,
Dimmed the aërial eyes that kindle day;
Afar the melancholy thunder moaned,
Pale Ocean in unquiet slumber lay,   125
And the wild winds flew round, sobbing in their dismay.

XV

Lost Echo sits amid the voiceless mountains,
And feeds her grief with his remembered lay,
And will no more reply to winds or fountains,
Or amorous birds perched on the young green spray, 130
Or herdsman's horn, or bell at closing day,
Since she can mimic not his lips, more dear
Than those for whose disdain she pined away
Into a shadow of all sounds:—a drear
Murmur, between their songs, is all the woodmen hear. 135

XVI

Grief made the young Spring wild, and she threw down
Her kindling buds, as if she Autumn were,
Or they dead leaves; since her delight is flown,
For whom should she have waked the sullen year?
To Phoebus was not Hyacinth so dear   140
Nor to himself Narcissus, as to both
Thou, Adonais: wan they stand and sere
Amid the faint companions of their youth,
With dew all turned to tears; odour, to sighing ruth.

XVII

Thy spirit's sister, the lorn nightingale   145
Mourns not her mate with such melodious pain;
Not so the eagle, who like thee could scale
Heaven, and could nourish in the sun's domain
Her mighty youth with morning, doth complain,
Soaring and screaming round her empty nest,   150
As Albion wails for thee: the curse of Cain
Light on his head who pierced thy innocent breast,
And scared the angel soul that was its earthly guest!

XVIII

Ah, woe is me! Winter is come and gone,
But grief returns with the revolving year;   155
The airs and streams renew their joyous tone;
The ants, the bees, the swallows reappear;
Fresh leaves and flowers deck the dead Seasons' bier;
The amorous birds now pair in every brake,
And built their mossy homes in field and brere;   160
And the green lizard, and the golden snake,
Like unimprisoned flames, out of their trance awake.

XIX

Through wood and stream and field and hill and Ocean
A quickening life from the Earth's heart has burst
As it has ever done, with change and motion,   165
From the great morning of the world when first
God dawned on Chaos; in its steam immersed,
The lamps of Heaven flash with a softer light;
All baser things pant with life's sacred thirst;
Diffuse themselves; and spend in love's delight,   170
The beauty and the joy of their renewed might.

XX

The leprous corpse touched by this spirit tender
Exhales itself in flowers of gentle breath;
Like incarnations of the stars, when splendour
Is changed to fragrance, they illumine death   175
And mock the merry worm that wakes beneath;
Nought we know, dies. Shall that alone which knows
Be as a sword consumed before the sheath
By sightless lightning?—the intense atom glows
A moment, then is quenched in a most cold repose.   180

XXI

Alas! that all we loved of him should be,
But for our grief, as if it had not been,
And grief itself be mortal! Woe is me!
Whence are we, and why are we? of what scene
The actors or spectators? Great and mean   185
Meet massed in death, who lends what life must borrow.
As long as skies are blue, and fields are green,
Evenings must usher night, night urge the morrow,
Month follow month with woe, and year wake year to
    sorrow.

XXII

He will awake no more, oh, never more!   190
'Wake thou,' cried Misery, ' childless Mother, rise
Out of thy sleep, and slake, in thy heart's core,
A wound more fierce than his with tears and sighs.'
And all the Dreams that watched Urania's eyes,
And all the Echoes whom their sister's song   195
Had held in holy silence, cried: 'Arise!'
Swift as a Thought by the snake Memory stung,
From her ambrosial rest the fading Splendour sprung.

XXIII

She rose like an autumnal Night, that springs
Out of the East, and follows wild and drear   200
The golden Day, which, on eternal wings,
Even as a ghost abandoning a bier,
Has left the Earth a corpse. Sorrow and fear
So struck, so roused, so rapt Urania;
So saddened round her like an atmosphere   205
Of stormy mist; so swept her on her way
Even to the mournful place where Adonais lay.

XXIV

Out of her secret Paradise she sped,
Through camps and cities rough with stone, and steel,
And human hearts, which to her aery tread   210
Yielding not, wounded the invisible
Palms of her tender feet where'er they fell:
And barbèd tongues, and thoughts more sharp than they,
Rent the soft Form they never could repel,
Whose sacred blood, like the young tears of May,   215
Paved with eternal flowers that undeserving way.

XXV

In the death chamber for a moment Death,
Shamed by the presence of that living Might,
Blushed to annihilation, and the breath
Revisited those lips, and life's pale light   220
Flashed through those limbs, so late her dear delight.
'Leave me not wild and drear and comfortless,
As silent lightning leaves the starless night!
Leave me not!' cried Urania: her distress
Roused Death: Death rose and smiled, and met her vain
    caress.   225

XXVI

'Stay yet awhile! speak to me once again;
Kiss me, so long but as a kiss may live;
And in my heartless breast and burning brain
That word, that kiss shall all thoughts else survive,
With food of saddest memory kept alive,   230
Now thou art dead, as if it were a part
Of thee, my Adonais! I would give
All that I am to be as thou now art!
But I am chained to Time, and cannot thence depart!

XXVII

'Oh gentle child, beautiful as thou wert,   235
Why didst thou leave the trodden paths of men
Too soon, and with weak hands though mighty heart
Dare the unpastured dragon in his den?
Defenceless as thou wert, oh where was then
Wisdom the mirrored shield, or scorn the spear?   240
Or hadst thou waited the full cycle, when
Thy spirit should have filled its crescent sphere,
The monsters of life's waste had fled from thee like deer.

XXVIII

'The herded wolves, bold only to pursue;
The obscene ravens, clamorous o'er the dead;   245
The vultures to the conqueror's banner true
Who feed where Desolation first has fed,
And whose wings rain contagion;—how they fled,
When like Apollo, from his golden bow,
The Pythian of the age one arrow sped   250
And smiled!—The spoilers tempt no second blow,
They fawn on the proud feet that spurn them lying low.

XXIX

'The sun comes forth, and many reptiles spawn;
He sets, and each ephemeral insect then
Is gathered into death without a dawn,   255
And the immortal stars awake again;
So is it in the world of living men:
A godlike mind soars forth, in its delight
Making earth bare and veiling heaven, and when
It sinks, the swarms that dimmed or shared its light   260
Leave to its kindred lamps the spirit's awful night.'

XXX

Thus ceased she: and the mountain shepherds came,
Their garlands sere, their magic mantles rent;
The Pilgrim of Eternity, whose fame
Over his living head like Heaven is bent,   265
An early but enduring monument,
Came, veiling all the lightnings of his song
In sorrow; from her wilds Ierne sent
The sweetest lyrist of her saddest wrong,
And love taught grief to fall like music from his   270
        tongue.

XXXI

Midst others of less note, came one frail Form,
A phantom among men; companionless
As the last cloud of an expiring storm
Whose thunder is its knell; he, as I guess,
Had gazed on Nature's naked loveliness,   275
Actæon-like, and now he fled astray
With feeble steps o'er the world's wilderness,
And his own thoughts, along that rugged way,
Pursued, like raging hounds, their father and their prey.

XXXII

A pardlike Spirit beautiful and swift,   280
A Love in desolation masked, a Power
Girt round with weakness—it can scarce uplift
The weight of the superincumbent hour;
It is a dying lamp, a falling shower,
A breaking billow—even whilst we speak   285
Is it not broken? On the withering flower
The killing sun smiles brightly: on a cheek
The life can burn in blood, even while the heart may
    break.

XXXIII

His head was bound with pansies overblown,
And faded violets, white, and pied, and blue;   290
And a light spear topped with a cypress cone,
Round whose rude shaft dark ivy tresses grew
Yet dripping with the forest's noonday dew,
Vibrated, as the ever-beating heart
Shook the weak hand that grasped it; of that crew   295
He came the last, neglected and apart;
A herd-abandoned deer struck by the hunter's dart.

XXXIV

All stood aloof, and at his partial moan
Smiled through their tears; well knew that gentle band
Who in another's fate now wept his own—   300
As in the accents of an unknown land
He sang new sorrow; sad Urania scanned
The Stranger's mien, and murmured: 'Who art thou?'
He answered not, but with a sudden hand
Made bare his branded and ensanguined brow,   305
Which was like Cain's or Christ's—Oh! that it should
    be so!

XXXV

What softer voice is hushed over the dead?
Athwart what brow is that dark mantle thrown?
What form leans sadly o'er the white death-bed,
In mockery of monumental stone,   310
The heavy heart heaving without a moan?
If it be He, who, gentlest of the wise,
Taught, soothed, loved, honoured the departed one,
Let me not vex, with inharmonious sighs,
The silence of that heart's accepted sacrifice.   315

XXXVI

Our Adonais has drunk poison—oh!
What deaf and viperous murderer could crown
Life's early cup with such a draught of woe?
The nameless worm would now itself disown:
It felt, yet could escape, the magic tone   320
Whose prelude held all envy, hate, and wrong,
But what was howling in one breast alone,
Silent with expectation of the song,
Whose master's hand is cold, whose silver lyre unstrung.

XXXVII

Live thou, whose infamy is not thy fame!   325
Live! fear no heavier chastisement from me,
Thou noteless blot on a remembered name!
But be thyself, and know thyself to be!
And ever at thy season be thou free
To spill the venom when thy fangs o'erflow: 330
Remorse and Self-contempt shall cling to thee;
Hot Shame shall burn upon thy secret brow,
And like a beaten hound tremble thou shalt—as now.

XXXVIII

Nor let us weep that our delight is fled
Far from these carrion kites that scream below;   335
He wakes or sleeps with the enduring dead;
Thou canst not soar where he is sitting now.
Dust to the dust! but the pure spirit shall flow
Back to the burning fountain whence it came,
A portion of the Eternal, which must glow   340
Through time and change, unquenchably the same,
Whilst thy cold embers choke the sordid hearth of
    shame.

XXXIX

Peace, peace! he is not dead, he doth not sleep—
He hath awakened from the dream of life—
'Tis we, who lost in stormy visions, keep   345
With phantoms an unprofitable strife,
And in mad trance, strike with our spirit's knife
Invulnerable nothings.—*We* decay
Like corpses in a charnel; fear and grief
Convulse us and consume us day by day,   350
And cold hopes swarm like worms within our
    living clay.

XL

He has outsoared the shadow of our night;
Envy and calumny and hate and pain,
And that unrest which men miscall delight,
Can touch him not and torture not again;   355
From the contagion of the world's slow stain
He is secure, and now can never mourn
A heart grown cold, a head grown grey in vain;
Nor, when the spirit's self has ceased to burn,
With sparkless ashes load an unlamented urn.   360

XLI

He lives, he wakes—'tis Death is dead, not he;
Mourn not for Adonais.—Thou young Dawn
Turn all thy dew to splendour, for from thee
The spirit thou lamentest is not gone;
Ye caverns and ye forests, cease to moan! 365
Cease ye faint flowers and fountains, and thou Air
Which like a mourning veil thy scarf hadst thrown
O'er the abandoned Earth, now leave it bare
Even to the joyous stars which smile on its despair!

XLII

He is made one with Nature: there is heard 370
His voice in all her music, from the moan
Of thunder, to the song of night's sweet bird;
He is a presence to be felt and known
In darkness and in light, from herb and stone,
Spreading itself where'er that Power may move 375
Which has withdrawn his being to its own;
Which wields the world with never-wearied love,
Sustains it from beneath, and kindles it above.

XLIII

He is a portion of the loveliness
Which once he made more lovely: he doth bear 380
His part, while the one Spirit's plastic stress
Sweeps through the dull dense world, compelling there
All new successions to the forms they wear;
Torturing the unwilling dross that checks its flight
To its own likeness, as each mass may bear; 385
And bursting in its beauty and its might
From trees and beasts and men into the Heavens' light.

XLIV

The splendours of the firmament of time
May be eclipsed, but are extinguished not;
Like stars to their appointed height they climb,   390
And death is a low mist which cannot blot
The brightness it may veil. When lofty thought
Lifts a young heart above its mortal lair,
And love and life contend in it, for what
Shall be its earthly doom, the dead live there   395
And move like winds of light on dark and stormy
        air.

XLV

The inheritors of unfulfilled renown
Rose from their thrones, built beyond mortal
        thought,
Far in the Unapparent. Chatterton
Rose pale, his solemn agony had not   400
Yet faded from him; Sidney, as he fought
And as he fell and as he lived and loved
Sublimely mild, a Spirit without spot,
Arose; and Lucan, by his death approved:
Oblivion as they rose shrank like a thing reproved.   405

XLVI

And many more, whose names on Earth are dark,
But whose transmitted effluence cannot die
So long as fire outlives the parent spark,
Rose, robed in dazzling immortality.
'Thou art become as one of us,' they cry,   410
'It was for thee yon kingless sphere has long
Swung blind in unascended majesty,
Silent alone amid an Heaven of song.
Assume thy wingèd throne, thou Vesper of our throng!'

XLVII

Who mourns for Adonais? oh, come forth 415
Fond wretch! and know thyself and him aright.
Clasp with thy panting soul the pendulous Earth;
As from a centre, dart thy spirit's light
Beyond all worlds, until its spacious might
Satiate the void circumference: then shrink 420
Even to a point within our day and night;
And keep thy heart light lest it make thee sink
When hope has kindled hope, and lured thee to the
    brink;

XLVIII

Or go to Rome, which is the sepulchre,
Oh, not of him, but of our joy: 'tis naught 425
That ages, empires, and religions there
Lie buried in the ravage they have wrought;
For such as he can lend—they borrow not
Glory from those who made the world their prey;
And he is gathered to the kings of thought 430
Who waged contention with their time's decay,
And of the past are all that cannot pass away.

XLIX

Go thou to Rome—at once the Paradise,
The grave, the city, and the wilderness;
And where its wrecks like shattered mountains rise, 435
And flowering weeds, and fragrant copses dress
The bones of Desolation's nakedness,
Pass, till the Spirit of the spot shall lead
Thy footsteps to a slope of green access
Where, like an infant's smile, over the dead, 440
A light of laughing flowers along the grass is spread.

L

And grey walls moulder round, on which dull Time
Feeds, like slow fire upon a hoary brand;
And one keen pyramid with wedge sublime,
Pavilioning the dust of him who planned   445
This refuge for his memory, doth stand
Like flame transformed to marble; and beneath
A field is spread, on which a newer band
Have pitched in Heaven's smile their camp of death,
Welcoming him we lose with scarce extinguished
    breath.   450

LI

Here pause: these graves are all too young as yet
To have outgrown the sorrow which consigned
Its charge to each; and if the seal is set,
Here, on one fountain of a mourning mind,
Break it not thou! too surely shalt thou find   455
Thine own well full, if thou returnest home,
Of tears and gall. From the world's bitter wind
Seek shelter in the shadow of the tomb.
What Adonais is, why fear we to become?

LII

The One remains, the many change and pass;   460
Heaven's light forever shines, Earth's shadows fly;
Life, like a dome of many-coloured glass,
Stains the white radiance of Eternity,
Until Death tramples it to fragments.—Die,
If thou wouldst be with that which thou dost seek!   465
Follow where all is fled!—Rome's azure sky,
Flowers, ruins, statues, music, words, are weak
The glory they transfuse with fitting truth to speak.

LIII

Why linger, why turn back, why shrink, my Heart?
Thy hopes are gone before: from all things here   470
They have departed; thou shouldst now depart!
A light is passed from the revolving year,
And man, and woman; and what still is dear
Attracts to crush, repels to make thee wither.
The soft sky smiles, the low wind whispers near: 475
'Tis Adonais calls! oh, hasten thither,
No more let Life divide what Death can join together.

LIV

That Light whose smile kindles the Universe,
That Beauty in which all things work and move,
That Benediction which the eclipsing Curse   480
Of birth can quench not, that sustaining Love
Which through the web of being blindly wove
By man and beast and earth and air and sea,
Burns bright or dim, as each are mirrors of
The fire for which all thirst, now beams on me,   48
Consuming the last clouds of cold mortality.

LV

The breath whose might I have invoked in song
Descends on me; my spirit's bark is driven,
Far from the shore, far from the trembling throng
Whose sails were never to the tempest given;   490
The massy earth and spherèd skies are riven!
I am borne darkly, fearfully, afar;
Whilst burning through the inmost veil of Heaven,
The soul of Adonais, like a star,
Beacons from the abode where the Eternal are.   495

Notes

Notes

Editions of Shelley are referred to by the name of the editor, except that the Julian edition of his complete works is referred to as *Works*. Except when Shelley's own translations are used, translations from Plato are taken from *The Dialogues of Plato*, translated by B. Jowett (5 vols., O.U.P., 3rd ed., 1892); references are to the standard section numbers.

ALASTOR 15

Alastor was written in the autumn of 1815. During the previous two years Shelley had been through a time of great strain (his estrangement from Harriet, his elopement with Mary, financial difficulties, etc.), and had written very little. 'In the spring of 1815,' Mary Shelley wrote in her note on the poem, 'an eminent physician pronounced that he was dying rapidly of a consumption; abscesses were formed on his lungs, and he suffered acute spasms. Suddenly a complete change took place; and ... every symptom of pulmonary disease vanished .... In the summer ... he rented a house on Bishopsgate Heath, on the borders of Windsor Forest, where he enjoyed several months of comparative health and tranquil happiness. ... He spent his days under the oak-shades of Windsor Great Park; and the magnificent woodland was a fitting study to inspire the various descriptions of forest-scenery we find in the poem.' She tells also of his delight in boating on rivers—on the Reuss and Rhine during their visit to the Continent the year before, and on the Thames immediately before starting *Alastor*. A good deal of his own experience went into the poem—his search for truth and for love, his illness, scenes he had visited; but *Alastor* is not an autobiography. He was well and happy when he wrote it, and was able to view himself with some detachment, to *use* his experiences to create an imaginary character and a narrative. In comparison with

15 his earlier work *Alastor* shows an advance towards maturity in its greater detachment and control, as well as in its more assured handling of the verse.

It is interesting to compare *Alastor* with Keats's *Endymion*, written about two years later, after Keats had met Shelley and probably read his poem. The interest is not in speculating about possible influence, but in seeing how alike and how different are the two young poets' ways of handling similar themes.

Title. Shelley's friend Thomas Love Peacock wrote: 'He was at a loss for a title, and I proposed that which he adopted: Alastor, or the Spirit of Solitude. The Greek word ἀλάστωρ is an evil genius ... The poem treats the spirit of solitude as a spirit of evil. I mention the true meaning of the word because many have supposed Alastor to be the name of the hero of the poem.' In Greek it was, more specifically, an avenging power; and the word was used also for the victim of an avenging deity. But not too much significance should be attributed to the title, suggested probably after the poem was finished. The hero's fate is the consequence of his own nature; he is not driven to death by a supernatural power external to himself.

17 PREFACE

At a first reading it is best to skip the preface (and all notes, including these), approach the poem without preconceptions, and let it do its work. Later one may consider whether, as some critics say, the preface, especially the beginning of the second paragraph, misrepresents the poem, or whether it merely makes explicit what is implied in the poem.

3. *It represents a youth.* The protagonist is unnamed. Naturally Shelley makes use of his own experience and perhaps of that of other poets such as Wordsworth and Coleridge, but there is no reason to suppose he intended to represent any particular person. His own life had been

in some ways similar to, but in other ways very unlike, **17**
that of this youth. If he had been writing of himself he
might more justly have accused himself of over-hasty
and enthusiastic involvement with other people than of
'self-centred seclusion.' Cf. *The Revolt of Islam*, Dedic.,
stanzas V–VIII, in which he writes of his early pursuit of
knowledge, his awakening to the need for love, his lone-
liness, his search for love, his despair, and of his meeting
with Mary, with whom he journeys 'no more alone
through the world's wilderness.' In *The Revolt* itself,
Laon and Cythna give themselves not only to each other
but to the service of humanity. In I. XLI–IV, the lady
tells how she loved the morning star and dreamed of
union with him; waking, she walks by the sea and

> over my heart did creep
> A joy less soft, but more profound and strong
> Than my sweet dream; and it forbade
> To keep the path of the sea-shore . . . .

So she set out for the City, and 'braved death for liberty
and truth.' Shelley's ideal was expressed in characters
such as these and Prometheus rather than in the *Alastor*
poet, who does 'keep the path of the sea-shore.'
27–8. *He seeks . . . conception.* Does he ?
21. *All else:* utterly different. **18**
27–9. '*The good die first . . . socket !*' Wordsworth, *Excur-*
sion, I. 500–2. 'Those' should be 'they,' and there should
be no comma after 'dust.'
Epigraph. 'Nor yet was I in love, but I was in love **19**
with loving; I sought what I might love, being in love
with love.'

ALASTOR

1–49. The invocation is reminiscent of Wordsworth,
both in sentiment and phrasing—for instance 'natural
piety' (3), lines 13–5 (cf. *Excursion* II. 41–7), 'obstinate
questionings' (26) (cf. *Ode, Intimations of Immortality*
145), lines 45–9 (cf. *Tintern Abbey* 95–102). There are
other Wordsworthian echoes later in the poem—for
instance lines 196–7 (cf. *Ode, Intimations of Immortality*

19 56–7) and 'too deep for tears' (713) (*Ode, Intimations of Immortality* 204). Mary Shelley recorded in her journal (14 Sept. 1814) 'Shelley . . . brings home Wordsworth's *Excursion*, of which we read a part, much disappointed. He is a slave.' All this has led some to suppose that Wordsworth's poems were a major source for *Alastor*, and even that Shelley intended to display in his poet the decline of Wordsworth's genius as a result of his egotism, his seclusion. But Wordsworth's decline was attributed by Shelley to his having become 'a slave,' a renegade from his early liberal ideals. His situation was in many ways different from that of the *Alastor* poet. It has been maintained also, with no greater plausibility, that Shelley had Coleridge in mind when depicting his poet. See 'O! there are spirits of the air' (p. 41) and note. It is interesting to compare the *Alastor* poet with various real characters (Shelley himself, Wordsworth, Coleridge) and fictional ones (Wordsworth's Wanderer and Solitary in *The Excursion*, Coleridge's Ancient Mariner); but the poem should be read as an independent imaginative creation.

18–49. Compare the more mature statement of this theme in *Hymn to Intellectual Beauty*, written in 1816. Some of the imagery ('shadow') is Platonic, but Shelley's methods of trying to gain contact with the power which animates nature and the heart of man are more reminiscent of Gothic romance than of Plato. Earlier (*Queen Mab* VI. 198), in revulsion against Christianity, he had invoked the impersonal power of Necessity as the 'mother of the world.' But, whatever his intellectual beliefs, emotionally he needed to devote himself to a power which could be addressed with love and be prayed to. Compare also Urania in *Adonais*.

20 23–37. Hogg (*Life*, I. 33–4) says that Shelley, when a boy, 'sometimes watched the livelong nights for ghosts . . . . He even planned how he might gain access to the vault, or charnel-house, at Warnham Church, and might sit there all night, harrowed by fear, yet trembling with expectation, to see one of the spiritualized owners of the bones piled around him.' More recently he had sometimes sat up most of the night with his sister-in-law, Jane Clair-

mont, talking about 'unaccountable and mysterious feel- **20**
ings about supernatural things.' After several such nights
Mary recorded sardonically in her journal (18 Oct. 1814):
'I go to bed soon, but Shelley and Jane sit up, and, for a
wonder, do not frighten themselves.'

50–1. 'The too obtrusive alliteration is evidence of im-
maturity' (Locock).

93. *Frequent with:* crowded with; a Latinism.   **22**

101. *bloodless food.* Shelley was at this time a believer in
vegetarianism, and in 1813 had written his *Vindication of
Natural Diet.*

107–30. In Volney's *Les Ruines* (1791), a book Shelley
read more than once, the narrator tells how he visited
many ancient monuments in Egypt and Syria, and came
to Palmyra, where he was given hospitality by Arab
peasants, and where meditating in the moonlight over
the passing of ancient glories he was startled by the
appearance of a spectral, draped figure who rebuked him
for sentimentality, saying that man's destiny is in his own
hands. The narrator's soul is drawn out of his body and
transported to a vantage point from which the earth is
seen as a distant globe, and he is instructed in the secrets
of human history, shown how men became subject to
political tyranny and false religious ideas and how, in the
French Revolution, they are releasing themselves from
them. Shelley used the general plan of *Les Ruines* and
many of Volney's ideas in *Queen Mab*; and in this passage
he probably remembered Volney's journeys and his
speculations about the origins of science and religion.
Volney says that Ethiopia was 'the cradle of the sciences'
(*Les Ruines*, English translation (1841), p. 194), where the
movements of the stars were first plotted and the signs
of the zodiac devised. These latter were at first well
understood as convenient metaphors, but in time came
to be worshipped, and a false theological system was built
up. Our poet's 'strong inspiration' may have been that he,
too, was able to see through the impostures erected on
the basis of these symbols misunderstood.

109. *Tyre, and Ba[a]lbec:* ancient cities in what is now the
Lebanon.

22 112. *Memphis and Thebes:* ancient cities in Egypt.

23 140–5. The poet goes through Arabia and Persia (modern Iran), through the desert of Karmin in eastern Persia, over the Hindu Kush mountains (scene of Prometheus' ordeal in *P.U.* I) and into Kashmir in north-west India (scene of Asia's exile in *P.U.* II).

151. *veilèd maid.* Locock says: 'She is clearly the Alastor, or Spirit of Solitude, sent to avenge "the poet's self-centred seclusion." ' This interpretation may seem to be supported by lines 203–5. But the maid is not in herself evil. She is a vision of an ideal companion, a vision which is destructive only because the poet is unable to relate it to ordinary life. She is not a supernatural being, but a projection of the poet's own desires. 'He images to himself the Being whom he loves' (Preface).

153–4. Cf. Shelley's essay *On Love*: 'We dimly see within our intellectual nature a miniature as it were of our entire self, yet deprived of all that we condemn or despise, the ideal prototype of everything excellent or lovely that we are capable of conceiving as belonging to the nature of man' (*Works*, VI. 201–2).

158–82. In the essay *On Love* Shelley goes on to say that we desire to find the antitype of this 'soul within our soul,' to meet 'an understanding capable of clearly esti-mating our own,' an imagination able to sympathise with our inmost feelings, 'a frame whose nerves ... vibrate with the vibrations of our own.' In both the essay and the poem he descends, rather than ascends, the Platonic ladder—from intellect to feeling to sense; and in the poem he places an un-Platonic emphasis on the last.

24 163. *numbers:* verse, rhythmical utterance.

189. *Involved:* wrapped round.

192–8. Here the poet's experience diverges sharply from that written of in the essay *On Love*. In the essay our desire for love makes us 'love the flowers, the grass, and the waters, and the sky. In the motion of the very leaves of spring, in the blue air, there is then found a secret correspondence with our heart.' But the poet's awakening to the need for love causes him to find the natural world vacant and dead. His love is narcissistic, turned inwards

on to an ideal conceived in his own mind. Therefore his **24**
passion, finding no outlet, becomes a 'fierce fiend' (225),
pursuing him to death.

207. *the bounds:* ? between life and death. The vision is **25**
to be regained only in death, in eternity. Contrast *Epi-
psychidion* 233–49, where after a similar experience the
protagonist hears a voice saying 'The phantom is beside
thee whom thou seekest,' and so goes forth 'into the
wintry forest of our life.' The *Alastor* poet does not seek
a human counterpart of his vision in the actual world.
He wants the ideal he has imagined, and has no hope of
finding it except in sleep or death.

213–9. Does nature in all its beauty lead to nothing, and
death in its ugliness to the paradise revealed to the poet
in sleep? The question is not answered. 'Conduct' (219)
should be 'conducts'; probably Shelley was thinking of
this final clause as a question, still governed by 'does' (213).

220–2. Cf. *Adonais* 422–3. The poet has been lured to
the brink by hope, and is unable to keep his heart light.
He has been tantalised by a vision of the ideal, but has
no assurance of union with it, either in life or death.

239–75. The poet comes back from India, where the **26**
great rock Aornos stands by the Indus, through Balk(h),
an ancient city in what is now Afghanistan, and the area
south-east of the Caspian, where the Parthian kingdom
used to be, to the Caspian Sea, the east shore of which is
low-lying (272–4) and to the west of which rise the
Caucasus mountains (353). We need not be troubled by
the fact that, of the various cities called Petra ('rock-city'),
none is near Aornos.

249. *Sered:* properly 'withered, dried up'; here presum-
ably 'faded.'

250. *Sung dirges.* Shelley's fondness for certain images
leads him sometimes to use them inappropriately. Pre-
sumably the scattered hairs of the poet are imagined to
be strings of an instrument upon which the mind plays
dirges—a rather absurd variation on the Aeolian harp
theme. See note on *Mutability* 5, p. 247.

267. *half.* ? They guess that he is in love, but not that it is **27**
no mortal maiden that he loves.

27 272–80. The scene corresponds to the poet's state—the sluggish stream of his life nearing its end, the desolation of his spiritual condition, the hope of union elsewhere.

292–5. He has not experienced his vision again in sleep. The hope of union in death may be equally illusory.

297. *fiend:* death? or the tormenting vision he pursues?

299. *shallop:* small open boat.

28 308–15. This is an important turning-point. Instead of the stagnation of putrid marshes we now have the excitement of rushing over the sea. We read of the poet's 'eager soul' (311), of his seeming to be 'an elemental god' (351), whereas before the emphasis has been on his pallor, his despair. The change corresponds in some ways to that in Coleridge's *Ancient Mariner*, sections IV and V. Instead of just wandering about, the poet has made a decision (for death), and this, right or wrong, leads to a release of tension, an upsurge of life.

29 352. *etherial:* high in the air.

30 394–7. Will the boat be driven on and fall with the main mass of water 'to the base of Caucasus' (377) or will it be drawn back into the whirlpool? Neither: instead, a breeze guides it into a placid side-stream. Attempts to give detailed allegorical interpretations to these events are not convincing. (For instance, it has been suggested that the entrance to the cavern is the jaws of death, the whirlpool the possibility of oblivion after death, the quiet cove the possibility of survival. But the poet is not dead; the 'strong impulse' which drives him on has not yet 'performed its ministry.') Shelley was telling a story 'not barren of instruction'; but he was also enjoying the creation of impressive scenery, part imagined, part suggested by memories of his own journeys and of his reading, especially here of Robert Paltock's *Life and Adventures of Peter Wilkins* (1751). In *Peter Wilkins* we find a ship driven by a storm over the sea and attracted to a rock, a journey along a subterranean stream, a whirlpool, a quiet lake. Nevertheless the scenes are doubtless intended to correspond in a general way to psychological states. Perhaps we can say that after the tumult of desire (the whirlpool?) has subsided in the poet he is granted a short

period of comparative calm before death in which he may 30
review his past life.

409. *pensive:* a word found often in Wordsworth, but 31
only here in Shelley. 'Pensiveness' also appears in
Shelley's poems only in *Alastor* (line 489).

420–68. The poet enters the forest, a dark, shut-in place,
into which only a little light from sun or star enters and
in the midst of which is a well, from which flows the
stream which images the course of his (? of any) life.
He is travelling in imagination back to the source of life.
The imagery in lines 431–45 ('wedded boughs,' things
which flow round and embrace each other) has appro-
priately sexual associations. The poet's journey is similar
to that of Asia and Panthea in *P.U.* II. ii; but in *P.U.*
there is a much stronger suggestion that there is something
beyond this dark place full of sensuous life, this world of
generation, that light from eternity enters it, even if
fitfully. In *Alastor* the source and the end of life are left
equally mysterious; there is no assurance of anything
beyond this life.

455. Locock puts a comma before instead of after 'here.' 32
This would make good sense, but there is no textual
authority for it.

479–92. Shelley carefully avoids committing himself to 33
any doctrine. A Spirit (of Nature ?) *seemed* to stand beside
the poet, and for a moment he recovered the sense of
communion with nature that he had experienced in
youth. Then two eyes *seemed* to beckon him. This cor-
responds to his dream of the veilèd maid. He is beckoned
to seek communion beyond that which nature affords,
but there is no assurance that the hope of such ideal com-
munion is not an illusion. The eyes 'hung in the gloom of
thought.' The experience, like that of the veilèd maid,
takes place in the poet's mind, but that it is a *merely* sub-
jective one Shelley neither states nor denies.

507. *searchless:* unable to be found. 34

520. *Forgetful.* It is not the poet, but the sick man to
whom he is compared, who is 'forgetful of the grave.'

528. *windlestrae:* dry, withered stalks of grass.

546–8. A much disputed passage. I take 'its' to refer to 35

35 the ravine, and 'disclosed' to be the past tense of the
verb, not the past participle. The precipitous cliffs
darkened the ravine below, and disclosed above gulfs and
caves surrounded by toppling stones.

553–70. The waters of the stream are scattered; but
beyond the dark gulf another land is dimly seen. Alternative possibilities—dissolution, the entry into another
life after death—may be suggested. If so, the hint of the
possibility of another life is slight.

36 591. *voice.* Whose voice? The poet's, which is carried on
in front of his body, and so leads it? Of some avenging
spirit, leading him to death?

593. *loveliest among human forms.* The poet is praised in
a way which may seem hardly justified by what we have
been shown. He is 'a rare and regal prey' for death (619),
a 'child of grace and genius' (690), a 'surpassing Spirit'
(714). This has led some critics to say that the poem and
the preface are incompatible with each other; that
Shelley wrote a poem which is primarily a celebration of
his usual idealist-martyr figure and then, perhaps stimulated by Peacock's suggested title, imposed a moral on it
in the preface which he had not embodied in it. It may
be answered that it is a matter of differing emphasis rather
than of contradiction. Explicitly in the preface and implicitly in the narrative the poet is criticised because of
his neglect of human sympathies; in both he is preferred
to the man of the world incapable of any vision of the
ideal. In the poem the second theme is given greater,
perhaps too much, emphasis, especially at the end.

594. *their:* the winds'.

596–600. *render ... scatter ... commit.* To render, etc.,
following on from 'led.'

37 610. *sightless:* invisible.

38 651. *meteor:* used by Shelley for any luminous body,
here for the moon.

657. *stagnate:* obsolete form of 'stagnant.'

663–71. A loosely constructed sentence. The poet's
frame is like a cloud, once but no longer lit by the sun
[not what is said, but I presume it to be what is meant];
it has no sense, no motion, no divinity; it is a lute now

still, a stream (to be exact, the bed of a stream) now dark **38**
and dry, a dream now unremembered.

672. *Medea:* a magician in Greek mythology; was able
to restore Aeson, the father of her lover Jason, to the
vigour of youth.

677. *one living man:* the wandering Jew, Ahasuerus, sup-
posed to have been condemned, for striking or insulting
Christ before the crucifixion, to wander through the
world until Christ's second coming. Shelley seems aware
that it is odd to wish for the poet the immortality which
for Ahasuerus has been a cruel punishment.

682. *magician:* an alchemist, seeking for the elixir which **39**
would give immortality and convert all metals to gold.
visioned: peopled with visions.

697. *phantasmal scene:* the world of phenomena, of things
as they seem. The use of this phrase, if related to Platon-
ism, might be taken to imply belief in the existence of a
world of reality of which this phantasmal scene is the
shadow. But the context here suggests Berkeleian idealism
rather than Platonism. The senses give us knowledge
only of appearances. Nothing more positive than this is
being asserted here. What lies behind the appearances
we do not know.

705: *senseless:* unfeeling.

713. *too 'deep for tears.'* Wordsworth, *Ode, Intimations of
Immortality* 204.

'O! THERE ARE SPIRITS OF THE AIR'   41

Mrs Shelley wrote that this poem 'was addressed in idea
to Coleridge, whom [Shelley] never knew; and at whose
character he could only guess imperfectly, through his
writings, and accounts he heard of him from some who
knew him well.' Some critics question this, believing the
poem to be autobiographical; but it is not likely that Mrs
Shelley would write so positively without authority. The
situation of the protagonist is in some ways similar to
that of the *Alastor* poet. He has communed with nature,
then sought love (but among faithless human beings, as
the *Alastor* poet did not). Now he has apparently given

41 up the quest, and his soul has been changed to a foul
fiend. The conclusion, different from that of *Alastor*, is
that it is better to remain in numb insensitivity than to
rouse oneself to new pain. It is quite reasonable to
suppose the poem addressed to Coleridge. Compare espe-
cially *Dejection: An Ode*, in which Coleridge writes of the
loss of his delight in nature and of his poetic inspiration
owing to his loss of joy (due largely to his unhappy
marriage and too late love for Sara Hutchinson), of his
attempts to be 'still and patient,' and of how he was roused
from a state of numb despondency, but only into one of
more acute suffering. Probably Shelley felt, or imagined,
an affinity with Coleridge, and used his own experience
in interpreting the other's.

Epigraph. Euripides, *Hippolytus* 1143–4. 'I will endure in
tears an unhappy lot.'

13. *starry eyes*. Cf. *Alastor* 179 and 490, where there
is the same transition from nature to the search for
human love. But here nature rejects the love of the pro-
tagonist, whereas the *Alastor* poet turns from nature when
made aware of the need for a more reciprocal relationship.

16. *fond faith:* ? the foolish belief that it is possible to
find the complete sympathy he is looking for. He should
have relied on his own strength, not made himself de-
pendent on others.

20. *false earth's*. Contrast *Dejection: An Ode*, stanza IV,
in which the failure is entirely within the speaker.

42 25–8. Shelley wrote in a similar way of his own state
after the breach with his first wife and before his elope-
ment with Mary (*The Revolt of Islam*, Dedic., 46–52). If
the present poem is mainly autobiographical it was pre-
sumably written at that time (early 1814); but more
probably it was written at about the same time as *Alastor*,
when his situation was very different.

STANZAS—APRIL, 1814

In April 1814 Shelley was living in Bracknell in Berkshire.
His wife Harriet was unable fully to share his intellectual
interests, and he spent much time with neighbours—an

accomplished elderly lady named Mrs Boinville and her **42**
attractive married daughter Cornelia Turner, with whom
he was learning Italian. Probably Mrs Boinville ('thy
friend') felt the situation to be dangerous for her daughter
('thy lover'; lover only in a Platonic sense), and forbade
further visits. The poet is addressing himself.

Robert Bridges in *Milton's Prosody* (O.U.P. 1921),
pp. 103–4, discusses the metre, one of the most interesting
features of this poem. 'The scheme,' he writes, 'on which
this poem is written, is one of four main or double stresses
in the line; but, if read with due gravity, it will show
generally six accents, and sometimes five or seven.' The
first edition's arrangement in three sections is retained
here; but metrically the poem consists of six quatrains.

9. *silent home.* When Shelley went back to his own house
after his last visit to the Boinvilles Harriet was away in
London. But in any case his home was sad because their
relationship was no longer satisfying to him.

Again the elusive metre, based presumably on a norm of
four stresses to the line, is one of the most interesting
features.

5. *lyres.* Cf. *Alastor* 42, 667–8, *The Dæmon of the World*
48–55, and other similar passages. In early days a believer
in Necessity, Shelley writes here as if we were merely
passive receivers of impressions. Later he laid more
stress on the creative power of the mind. Cf. *Defence of
Poetry:* 'Man is an instrument over which a series of
external and internal impressions are driven, like the
alternations of an ever-changing wind over an Aeolian
lyre . . . But there is a principle within the human being,
and perhaps within all sentient beings, which acts other-
wise than in the lyre, and produces not melody, alone,
but harmony, by an internal adjustment of the sounds or
motions thus excited to the impressions which excite
them' (*Works*, VII. 109). Shelley presumably got the
idea of Aeolian music from the Aeolian harp, a stringed
instrument, quite common in his day, specifically de-

43 signed to produce harmonious sounds when exposed to the wind; but his own references are to the production of this effect without contrivance, as when the wind plays on forgotten lyres, on trees, wings (*P.U.* II. i. 26), or even on the *Alastor* poet's hair (*Alastor* 248-50). Aeolus was god of the winds.

44 13-16. Mrs Shelley printed this stanza at the head of Chapter XIII of Vol. III of her novel *Lodore* (183;), amending it to

> It is the same, for be it joy or sorrow,
> The path of its departure still is free;
> Man's yesterday can ne'er be like his morrow,
> Nor aught endure save mutability.

'THE PALE, THE COLD, AND THE MOONY SMILE'

Composed by 1813, when it was written into a notebook (the Esdaile Notebook, now in the Pforzheimer Library); revised, and much improved, for publication in the *Alastor* volume. Shelley may have thought of revising it after he had written *A Summer Evening Church-Yard*, to which it forms a fitting prelude. Mrs Shelley entitled it *On Death*.

Epigraph. Ecclesiastes 9: 10. This expresses only one side of what the poem says. For though our earthly senses will be gone, 'all but this frame' ('body' in the notebook) will continue to exist after death. Even thus early, Shelley was not, or not consistently, a materialist. But more than in similar later statements he here admits to an attachment to 'the fine-wrought eye and the wondrous ear.' Afterwards death, the lifting of the veil, is usually more desired than feared. Cf. *Adonais*, stanzas LI-LIII.

13-18. More concrete and clear, and rhythmically stronger, than the notebook version, which read:

All we behold, we feel that we know;

   All we perceive, we know that we feel;

And the coming of death is a fearful blow

   To a brain unencompassed by nervestrings of steel—

When all that we know, we feel and we see

Shall fleet by like an unreal mystery.

248

A SUMMER EVENING CHURCH-YARD   **46**

Written late in the summer of 1815, when Shelley went
on a boat trip up the Thames from Windsor and spent
two nights at Lechlade. Uneven in quality, derivative
(from eighteenth century 'graveyard' and meditative
poems) and yet showing, in places, direct observation and
having an individual accent, this is a typical product of an
immature poet of genius.

3–4. Cf. *Alastor* 337–8, *A Vision of the Sea* 67.

13. *aërial:* rising high in the air.

15. *their:* refers back to silence and twilight.

27–9. Cf. *Alastor* 23–9 and note.

TO WORDSWORTH   **47**

Perhaps prompted by Shelley's disappointment on read-
ing *The Excursion* (see note on *Alastor* 1–49). Shelley
connected Wordsworth's decline as a poet with his adop-
tion of increasingly conservative opinions in politics, and
with his acceptance of Government patronage (in 1813
Wordsworth had been appointed Distributor of Stamps
for Westmorland at the quite high salary for those days
of £400 a year).

The arrangement of rhymes, with a couplet in lines
9–10, is unusual in a sonnet.

1–4. Refers to Wordsworth's *Ode, Intimations of Im-
mortality*.

ON THE FALL OF BONAPARTE

Written presumably in the summer of 1815 after the battle
of Waterloo. Cf. *Ode to Liberty* 170–80. Shelley preferred
Napoleon, with all his crimes, to the reactionaries who
defeated him.

2. *unambitious:* not ambitious for the best things. Napo-
leon was a slave to his own passions, an 'Anarch' (*Ode
to Liberty* 175).

5. *had stood:* would have been still standing.

7–10. Awkwardly expressed. Perhaps Shelley intends us
to understand both (1) I prayed that Massacre, etc.,

47 should stifle, and (2) Massacre, etc., would have stifled (i.e. Napoleon's tyranny would have produced an internal revolt if he had not first been defeated from the outside). Other signs of hasty and careless writing are the ungrammatical 'shouldst' (3) and the lack of concord between 'a . . . foe' (12) and what follows.

14. *Faith:* religious Faith, the Christianity of the day as Shelley understood it.

48 SUPERSTITION

Abstracted from *Queen Mab* (VI. 72–102). See head-note to *The Dæmon of the World*, p. 251.

1. *Thou.* In *Queen Mab*, the Fairy Queen, Shelley's mouthpiece, is addressing Religion, more or less synonymous for him with superstition.

16–17. *yet still . . . blood.* In contrast to the 'bloody Faith,' as Shelley saw it, of Christianity and other later religions. His prejudice is seen in his ignoring of human sacrifice in early religions.

31–2. These two lines are substituted for a single one in *Queen Mab*: 'Converging thou didst bend and call it God!' *Queen Mab* continues

> The self-sufficing, the omnipotent,
> The merciful, and the avenging God!
> Who, prototype of human misrule, sits
> High in Heaven's realm, upon a golden throne,
> Even like an earthly king . . . .

Cf. Jupiter in *Prometheus Unbound*.

49 SONNET

Shelley often dreamed and wrote of retiring from the world and sailing to found in some remote place a perfect community of two (*Epipsychidion* 407–587) or a few sympathetic spirits. So naturally this sonnet (Sonnet VI in *Canzoniere*: Temple Classics edition of *Vita Nuova* and *Canzoniere*, p. 162) would appeal to him. Guido Cavalcanti and Lapo Gianni were fellow-poets of Dante's in Florence, and Vanna and Lagia were presumably their ladies.

1. *Lapo:* incorrectly spelt 'Lappo' in the first edition.   **49**
5. *And:* 'So' in Mrs. Shelley's editions. This would be a more accurate translation.
7-8. Not a very good translation. The original means 'so that . . . living ever in one mind, our desire might increase to stay together.'
10. *Bice.* Shelley can hardly have forgotten that Bice (Beatrice) was Dante's own love; so perhaps 'my' is a misprint for 'thy.' The text used by Shelley means 'Lady Vanna, and then Lady Bice, with her on number thirty' (of Dante's list of the sixty most beautiful ladies in Florence). The now accepted text means 'Lady Vanna and Lady Lagia . . .,' which removes the difficulty. 'Bice' is of course a dissyllable in Italian.

TRANSLATED FROM THE GREEK OF MOSCHUS   **50**

Moschus was a Greek pastoral poet of the second century B.C. This is one of the three short extracts (or possibly complete poems) from his Bucolics that have been preserved. The Elegy on Bion, once supposed to have been written by Moschus, was one of the sources of *Adonais*.

   There is no exact equivalent in the original for Shelley's 'tranquil deep,' 'unquiet mind,' or 'calm spirit.' His translation moves the poem a little from a timid man's search for pleasure towards an unquiet man's search for inner calm.

τὰν . . . βάλλῃ: the beginning of Moschus' poem—'When the wind blows gently over a calm blue sea.' κ.τ.λ.: 'and the rest.'

THE DÆMON OF THE WORLD   **51**

Shelley wrote *Queen Mab*, a long philosophical poem with extensive notes, in 1812–3, and in 1813 had 250 copies printed for private distribution. During the next two years he extensively revised sections I, II, VIII, and IX, and made slight revisions in other sections. He published the revised sections I and II as *The Dæmon of the World*

51 in the *Alastor* volume. The revised sections VIII and IX
were first published in 1876, and will be found as *The
Dæmon of the World*, Pt. II in modern editions of his
poems.

His reason for not publishing *Queen Mab* regularly in
1813 was probably a quite justified fear of prosecution;
but by 1821, when the first of the pirated editions
appeared, he wanted to suppress it for other reasons.
He wrote to *The Examiner* (22 June 1821): 'A poem,
entitled *Queen Mab*, was written by me at the age of
eighteen [really twenty], I dare say in a sufficiently in-
temperate spirit—but even then was not intended for
publication, and a few copies only were struck off, to be
distributed among my personal friends. I have not seen
this production for several years; I doubt not but that
it is perfectly worthless in point of literary composition;
and that in all that concerns moral and political specula-
tion, as well as in the subtler discriminations of meta-
physical and religious doctrine, it is still more crude and
immature.' In spite of this and of the imprisonment of
one publisher, at least fourteen pirated editions appeared
during the next twenty years, and *Queen Mab* was during
this time and probably until late in the nineteenth
century much the most popular and influential of Shelley's
works.

The general plan of *Queen Mab*, similar to that of
Volney's *Les Ruines* (see note to *Alastor* 107–30), is that
the Fairy Queen descends in her magic car to the bedside
of the sleeping Ianthe, transports her soul to a vantage
point from which she can see and be instructed about the
whole history of mankind—past (section II), present
(sections III–VII, with special emphasis on the evils of
monarchy, tyranny, economic exploitation, and religion),
and future (sections VIII–IX)—and finally restores her
soul to earth so that she may help to bring into being the
perfect future she has been shown.

In his revision Shelley aimed to improve the quality of
the writing and to make the poem publishable by omitting
or toning down some of the most offensive passages. Some
improvements were made, but the fire was somewhat

damped down. To meet the young radical Shelley one **51** should go to the original *Queen Mab.*

'The didactic,' Shelley told Hogg in a letter (7 Feb. 1813), 'is in blank heroic verse, and the descriptive in blank lyrical measure. If authority is of any weight in support of this singularity, Milton's *Samson Agonistes,* the Greek Choruses, and (you will laugh) Southey's *Thalaba* may be adduced.' Of these *Queen Mab* most resembles *Thalaba.* In revising the descriptive parts Shelley moved towards more regular measures, even inserting some rhymed stanzas (78–107).

Title. Shelley may have felt that the associations surrounding Queen Mab were too light and fanciful for this to be an appropriate name for the supernatural being whom he was using as his mouthpiece. So the Fairy Queen becomes the Dæmon of the World. Glossing the statement 'There is no God' in *Queen Mab* VII. 13 he had written: 'This negation must be understood solely to affect a creative Deity. The hypothesis of a pervading Spirit coeternal with the universe remains unshaken.' We may think of the Dæmon as this pervading Spirit as it manifests itself in the world, as the Soul of the World. This is quite in accordance with the meaning of δαίμων in Greek. It was the early Christians' identification of the pagan gods with devils that impressed on the word *demon* the evil associations which it now usually bears. Platonic (see *Timaeus* 30b) and Neoplatonic ideas about a World Soul are combined rather uneasily in this poem with ideas derived from French materialist philosophers of the eighteenth century.

Epigraph. 'And she is not permitted to reveal as much as she is suffered to know. All time is gathered up together: all the centuries crowd her breast and torture it.' Lucan is describing the priestess Phemonoe, possessed by the god Apollo in the cave at Delphi.

31. *Ianthe.* It is probably vain to seek for any special **52** significance in this name, used also for Shelley's eldest daughter and found probably in Ovid (*Metamorphoses* IX. 715). Ianthe is not individualized, and in this sort of poem does not need to be. The characters are not im-

52 portant. The setting is a device for getting us to a position where the author may expound his views on life, giving them authority by putting them in the mouth of a supernatural instructress speaking to a virtuous human soul.

34. *Henry*. At the end, Ianthe's soul is re-united to her body, and she finds Henry kneeling by her bed, lovingly watching her sleep (*Queen Mab* IX. 232-8). Otherwise he takes no part in the action.

59. *Its shape*: the figure in the chariot, the Dæmon. The description which follows reminds us that this figure was originally the Fairy Queen.

53 62. *indue*: put on.

78-107. This lyric, spoken by the Dæmon, is new.

80. *Folds*: presumably 'conceals,' as in *P.U.* II. v. 62. Ianthe's sight is to be cleansed of the limitations of mortality so that she may see what even the wisest poets glimpse only dimly.

54 100. *snake*. A snake, especially when depicted lying in a circle with its tail in its mouth, is a common emblem of eternity. Cf. *P.U.* II. III. 97 and IV. 567.

102-7. Ianthe's soul is to leave her body and all the insubstantial things of earth, which merely mimic, are imperfect copies of, the eternal forms. Platonic ideas are being used here, which do not fit well with other parts of the poem, such as lines 175-88. Shelley was constantly shifting between a dualism of soul and body and a monism which abolishes the distinction between the two. The dualism is even more extreme in the corresponding passage in *Queen Mab* (I. 139-56). See note on *Adonais* 370.

55 150-3. To the corresponding passage in *Queen Mab* (I. 242-3) Shelley added a note: 'Beyond our atmosphere the sun would appear a rayless orb of fire in the midst of a black concave. The equal diffusion of its light on earth is owing to the refraction of the rays by the atmosphere, and their reflection from other bodies. Light consists either of vibrations propagated through a subtle medium, or of numerous minute particles repelled in all directions from the luminous body.' In lines 154-8 he uses the

second of these ideas of the nature of light. The wave- 55
particle duality in the nature of light has, in fact, long
been a fundamental dilemma for physicists.

189. *thy*. The poet is now addressing the reader. In 56
Queen Mab this was the beginning of section II.

254–84. In the corresponding and much longer passage in 58
Queen Mab (II. 97–250) the Fairy tells the Spirit of
Ianthe about various past civilizations, stressing exploita-
tion and superstition. Here Shelley tries to convey the
same view of the past in a more condensed way and by
description of what Ianthe sees rather than by explana-
tion. She sees emblems of exploitation and war (263–9)
and then, presumably, the Pope with his three-fold crown,
upholder of a religion which, allegedly, causes men to live
in hypocrisy and self-contempt. Cf. *P.U.* I. 5–8.

291. *Necessity's:* in *Queen Mab* (II. 257) 'Nature's.' To 59
Shelley at this time Necessity (the impersonal law which
governs the universe) and Nature or the Spirit of Nature
were more or less the same, and both were preferable to
the idea of a personal God as conceived, in his view, by
Christianity. Cf. *Queen Mab* VI. 197–200:

> Spirit of Nature! all-sufficing Power,
> Necessity! thou mother of the world!
> Unlike the God of human error, thou
> Requir'st no prayers nor praises . . . .

Shelley was somehow able to combine belief in Necessity
with denunciation of tyrants and praise of the virtuous.
In *Queen Mab*, and decreasingly in later works, Shelley
was influenced by William Godwin's *Enquiry Concerning
Political Justice* (1793), which he read with enthusiasm in
1810 and often re-read. Godwin believed that 'man is
perfectible'; not that he will ever attain to a static per-
fection, but that he has 'the faculty of being continually
made better' (*Political Justice*, I. 92). And he believed in
Necessity, in the operation of impersonal laws which
would bring about, in the long run, a gradual improve-
ment in the human condition, a movement towards a
state of equality and freedom. The idea of Necessity was,
of course, not new. Shelley—and Godwin—were familiar

59 with the Greek idea of Necessity or Fate, the impersonal power to which even the gods were subject. Shelley's criticism of existing institutions and his vision of Utopia in *Queen Mab* were both largely Godwinian, but the total effect is different. Godwin's faith was in reason and benevolence, Shelley's in imagination and love.

61   PROMETHEUS UNBOUND

Shelley was twenty-six and had reached maturity as a poet when in September 1818, at Este near Venice, he began *Prometheus Unbound*. He wrote quickly; for on October 8th he wrote to Peacock that the first act was finished. During the winter he travelled south to Naples and then back to Rome early in March, doing much sight-seeing. Probably not much of the *Prometheus* was written, but it continued to be in the centre of his thoughts, and he was absorbing imagery for it from the things which he saw. In beautiful spring weather in Rome he wrote quickly again, and on April 6th wrote to Peacock 'My *Prometheus Unbound* is finished ... It is a drama, with characters and mechanism of a kind yet unattempted; and I think the execution is better than any of my former attempts.' At that time he regarded the poem as finished in three acts. The fourth act and some other additions were written several months later, and were finished by the end of 1819.

Prometheus Unbound is a complex poem, and several levels of meaning can be found in it. The meanings must be felt as they are embodied in the words. Any summary would be an over-simplification; so none will be attempted. But it may be helpful as a preliminary to have a look at a few of the ingredients from Shelley's reading and experience which contributed to form the poem.

(1) The principal source is *Prometheus Bound*, the only surviving play of a trilogy written by Aeschylus (525–456 B.C.), probably late in his life. Every student of Shelley should read this so as to see for himself what Shelley took over, how he modified it, and what he

added. The story is briefly that by the help of Prometheus, **61**
Zeus (= Jupiter) has recently overthrown the older
gods (the Titans, of whom Prometheus himself was one),
and has wished to destroy the race of men, but has been
prevented by Prometheus, who stole fire from heaven for
men, taught them all arts, and gave them hope. By com-
mand of Zeus, Prometheus is chained to a rock by
Hephaestus (god of fire, especially of the smithy fire),
and is visited by the daughters of Oceanus, who remain
as a chorus; by Oceanus himself, who pities him but
says he is rash and proud in resisting Zeus; and by the
mortal maiden Io. She also has reason to complain of the
tyranny of Zeus, for his ruthless love of her and the
jealousy of Hera have caused her to flee through the world
in the form of a heifer pursued by a gadfly. Prometheus
foretells her sufferings and the descent from her of a
glorious archer, Herakles (= Hercules), who shall
deliver him from captivity. Last comes Hermes (= Mer-
cury), demanding that Prometheus tell the secret of the
fatal marriage which, unless prevented, is destined to
lead to the downfall of Zeus. This secret is that the off-
spring of Thetis, a sea-goddess whom Zeus will wish to
marry, shall be greater than his father. Prometheus refuses
to reveal it, and is cast into Tartarus, a region of Hell.
Zeus is shown as a tyrant, but it is emphasized that his
rule is new. Prometheus is a noble rebel, but is also rash
and proud. The confrontation is not between absolute
good and evil; the possibility is left open for a reconcilia-
tion, to be effected in *Prometheus Unbound*, of which only
fragments survive. (In a letter written on 8th October
1818 Shelley asked Peacock what there is in Cicero about
this play. Cicero in *Tusculan Disputations* II. x. 23–5
quotes thirty-five lines from it.)

Shelley ordered Aeschylus' plays from his bookseller
at the end of 1812, and in the next year mentioned Pro-
metheus in a note to his immature poem *Queen Mab*:
'The story of Prometheus is one likewise which, although
universally admitted to be allegorical, has never been
satisfactorily explained . . . . Prometheus (who represents
the human race) effected some great change in the condi-

61 tion of his nature, and applied fire to culinary purposes; thus inventing an expedient for screening from his disgust the horrors of the shambles. From this moment his vitals were devoured by the vulture of disease . . . . All vice rose from the ruin of healthful innocence.' At that time Shelley was a vegetarian, and he took this interpretation over from a book by J. F. Newton, *Return to Nature; or, A Defence of the Vegetable Regimen* (1811). This eccentric and second-hand interpretation is irrelevant to our present purpose except that it may be worth noting that Prometheus is said to represent the human race and to have been responsible for a fall from primitive innocence.

During the following years Shelley's letters and his wife's journal several times mention readings of Aeschylus, and by 1818 Shelley was a fluent reader of Greek. He was constantly preoccupied by the themes of liberty, of man's perverseness in bowing before tyrants to whom he had himself given power, and of man's capability to achieve a far nobler and happier state than his actual one. Several of his poems contain the figure of a noble rebel suffering and enduring in the hope of bringing this happier state into being. So Prometheus' services to men, his sufferings and endurance under tyranny, his confident hope of eventual release, and the fact that he had been largely responsible for putting his oppressor in power were features of the myth which would especially appeal to Shelley, and which he saw how he could use in his own way.

Shelley's use of Aeschylus led him into difficulties. The meanings he saw in the story were different from those which Aeschylus saw, and some of the elements he took over did not fit well into his scheme. At the same time it gave richness beyond what any story newly invented would have had. Myth is inexhaustible. We must not expect to be able to sum up the significance of the story or of the characters in any simple statement.

(2) Plato (428–347 B.C.) was one of Shelley's favourite authors. From 1817 on he was constantly reading him, and in the summer of 1818, not long before starting the *Prometheus*, he translated the *Symposium*. At this time he

was reading the original, independent of any translator or **61**
commentator. But earlier, at Oxford with his friend Hogg,
he had read Plato in translations, including those of 'the
learned and eccentric Platonist, Thomas Taylor' (Hogg,
Life, I. 121). During the three years before leaving
England he saw much of T. L. Peacock, a friend of
Taylor's, and he was much interested in Peacock's poem
Rhododaphne (finished 1817), which is full of Neoplaton-
ism derived from Taylor. The Neoplatonists were
philosophers who flourished in the third and second
centuries B.C., mainly in Alexandria, and whose specula-
tions blend Platonic ideas with oriental mysticism. Taylor,
in his voluminous and influential translations and com-
mentaries on Plato and the Neoplatonists, treats the latter
as the true interpreters of Plato, whereas most modern
scholars try to distinguish true original Platonism from
later 'contaminations.'

Some Shelley scholars say that the influence of Plato
and especially of the Neoplatonists on Shelley has been
exaggerated; and it is true that he cannot conclusively
be shown to have read many of the books which some
commentators have thought were his sources. So we must
tread carefully. But we can say with confidence that he
knew some dialogues of Plato well, and that he knew
something of Neoplatonism through Peacock and by
other indirect means. He also knew something of oriental
mysticism through the works of the scholar Sir William
Jones, through a novel *The Missionary* (1811) by Sydney
Owenson, and through Edward Moor's *Hindu Pantheon*
(1810). There is kinship between visionary writers of all
times and places; so likenesses may be due to similarity
of experience rather than to influence. But it is clear that
images and ideas derived from Plato and related writers
helped Shelley to express his own intuitions, his own
vision. When we read of 'shadows' or of 'things which
seem' contrasted, if only by implication, with the 'real'
world of 'forms' or 'ideas,' Plato is in the background.
The unbinding of Prometheus makes possible on one
level the achievement of a just society, conceived roughly
on Godwinian lines; on another the penetration behind

61 veils of illusion to, or at least towards, knowledge of the
real. See notes on *P.U.* II. III. 59–60, III. III. 49–53, and
on *Adonais* 460.

(3) Science. As a boy and as a young man Shelley
was much interested in science. He was fond of experi-
menting with electricity and chemicals, and he read
quite a number of scientific books. At school he heard
lectures from Adam Walker, whose *A System of Familiar
Philosophy* (1799) contains bold and imaginative specula-
tions about the relationship of electricity, light, and heat,
which he regarded as manifestations of a single active
principle. He read books by Sir Humphry Davy, the
great chemist, and by Erasmus Darwin (grandfather of
Charles Darwin), in whose poems a wide range of the
scientific knowledge of the day was brought together
with his own advanced speculations about evolution.
After 1813 there is little evidence of scientific reading by
Shelley, but his early knowledge remained with him and
fused with other elements of his experience. He delighted
in things which flow and pervade, like light and scent
clouds, water, and wind. He must have been glad, there·
fore, to find in the latest scientific books that matter was
being thought of, not as solid and inert, but as instinct
with energy in every particle. His knowledge helped his
imagination to convey a sense of the universe as a single
living whole, and to show how man, liberated from
tyranny, might use his power over nature beneficently.
(Shelley's sense of the vitality of material things may
sometimes be felt to be at odds with the Platonic picture
of their being mere 'shadows.' It goes better with the
Neoplatonic picture of all things emanating from a central
fire.)

(4) Politics. There are few detailed references to con-
temporary history in *Prometheus Unbound*; but one needs
to bear in mind the general situation in Europe at the
time when it was written. Though born into a wealthy,
landed family, Shelley from early youth had been a
radical, a questioner of the established order in morals,
politics, and religion. People of his type in the preceding
generation had been first inspired and then disillusioned

by the French Revolution. At first it seemed that old **61** tyrannies had been destroyed, and that a new era of liberty, equality, and fraternity was dawning. Then the revolutionaries themselves became tyrants, and were overthrown. In 1818 most of Europe was ruled by repressive, conservative governments, though new revolutions seemed liable to break out at any time. Many former liberals had retreated to Conservatism, or out of politics. Shelley had been born too late to share their hopes or their disillusionment. Recent events had shown him that if a really new order were to come into being, a more radical change was needed than the overthrow of a tyrannical ruler or group of rulers—a change in mental attitudes. In *The Revolt of Islam* (1817) he had shown an unsuccessful revolution; now he wanted, among other things, to show a successful one, to show what were the necessary prerequisites for achieving it and what a society in which man realized his full potentiality might be like. In doing so he was not being naively optimistic. He was showing a vision of the ultimate goal, not saying what he thought likely to happen in the immediate future. He thought that men needed to be inspired by a vision of an ideal and by faith that progress towards that ideal is possible, as well as to be guided by a programme of practicable reforms, such as he put forward in his pamphlet *A Philosophical View of Reform*, written soon after *Prometheus Unbound*. In that pamphlet he wrote: 'Our present business is with the difficult and unbending realities of actual life, and when we have drawn inspiration from the great object of our hopes it becomes us with patience and resolution to apply ourselves to accommodating our theories to immediate practice.'

(5) Scenery. After crossing the Alps on his way to Italy in March 1818 Shelley wrote: 'The scene is like that described in the Prometheus of Aeschylus: vast rifts and caverns in the granite precipices; wintry mountains, with ice and snow above; the loud sounds of unseen waters within the caverns; and walls of toppling rocks, only to be scaled, as he describes, by the winged chariot of the Ocean Nymphs.' In the valley below, the subjects

61 of the tyrannous King of Sardinia, lived 'in a state of the most frightful poverty and disease. At the foot of this ascent were cut into the rocks at several places stories of the misery of the inhabitants, to move the compassion of the traveller. One old man, lame and blind, crawled out of a hole in the rock, wet with the perpetual melting of the snow above, and dripping like a shower bath.' (Mary Shelley's *Journal*, 26 Mar. 1818; this entry was written by Shelley.) Mrs Shelley says that this scenery gave him the idea of his Prometheus. He certainly used his memories of it in Act I. In Italy also he found splendid scenery and buildings, and among them much human misery and oppression—for instance gangs of chained prisoners working in the streets of Pisa. He was much impressed by the scenery round Naples, at once beautiful and awesome. He went up Mount Vesuvius, seeing rivers of lava gush from its sides and black bituminous vapour hurled up into the sky; he went to Lake Avernus, and through the cavern of the Sybil, and to the ruins of Pompeii. These and other scenes, as well as the things he was seeing around him in Rome while writing Acts II and III, have left their traces in the poem. Also Shelley was influenced by the many works of art which he saw during his travels.

Aeschylus gave him the story. His own experience (as a rebel against his father and against society), the contemporary political situation, and the influence of Godwin (whose perfectibilism and necessitarianism and conception of a just society he still, with modifications, believed in) and of Plato contributed to the significance he saw in it. His scientific knowledge and memories of particular places helped to give a solid base to his imaginings.

NOTES ON THE TITLE PAGE

A Lyrical Drama. In drama we expect to find action, movement, the development and clash of characters; in lyric, song-quality and the expression of emotion. A lyric may properly be more static than a drama. If it deals with an action it will probably celebrate (or depre- **61** cate) it, or unfold the meaning of it rather than try to enact it. So the sub-title warns us that we are not to expect the continuous dramatic tension we would look for in a play designed for the stage. We are to expect a dramatic structure and some dramatic scenes, but we shall not be surprised if we find passages whose object is rather to celebrate, to convey emotion, to show significance than to advance action. The dramatic poem not intended for the stage was a form characteristic of the Romantic period, used by Byron (*Manfred*, *Cain*), Goethe, and many lesser writers.

Audisne haec . . . 'Do you hear this, Amphiaraus, hidden under the earth?' A line from the lost Aeschylean drama *Epigoni*, quoted by Cicero (*Tusculan Disputations*, II. xxv. 61) in an anecdote about Dionysius of Heraklea. Dionysius when subjected to pain became a renegade from the Stoic creed, to the disgust of a fellow-Stoic Cleanthes, who used the quotation to call upon their dead master Zeno to witness the betrayal. Amphiaraus was a seer, who was saved by Zeus from pursuers by being miraculously swallowed by the earth, after which he became an oracular god. As his note-book shows, Shelley is addressing the line to Aeschylus, calling upon him to hear a new treatment of the Prometheus legend. Aeschylus is being invoked as the dead master and seer (like Zeno and Amphiaraus); and, if the Ciceronian context is relevant, he is perhaps also being challenged, albeit humorously, by the suggestion that he made his Prometheus a renegade (like Dionysius) from the true doctrine about suffering.

PREFACE   **63**

The first four paragraphs were written probably soon after the completion of the first three acts; the last five were added in answer to a review of *The Revolt of Islam* in the April 1819 number of the *Quarterly Review*, which Shelley received in October. (This review is reproduced in *Contemporary Reviews of Romantic Poetry*, ed. John Wain (1953).)

63 12-13. *The 'Prometheus Unbound' of Aeschylus:* lost, except for fragments. Shelley almost certainly misjudged his predecessor, who probably showed Prometheus driving a successful bargain with a Zeus who had learned to rule more justly. But what Aeschylus may be conjectured to have done is irrelevant here. Shelley was entitled to adapt the myth in his own way.

64 27-30. *The imagery . . . expressed.* Passages in the poem which may exemplify this include I. 10–23, 195–202, 465–72, 483–94, 657–61; II. v. 72–110; III. I. 3–17.

65 4. *One word . . .* In his answer to the *Quarterly* reviewer Shelley gives most attention to the charge—given no great prominence in the review—that he was an unsparing imitator, especially of Wordsworth, 'to whose religious mind it must be matter, we think, of perpetual sorrow to see the philosophy, which comes pure and holy from his pen, degraded and perverted . . . .'

14. *extraordinary intellects.* A MS draft in the Huntington Library shows that he had in mind especially Byron, Coleridge, and Wordsworth.

66 15. *poetry is a mimetic art.* Compare passages such as I. 743–9 and III. III. 49–53, where greater stress is laid on the creative power of the artist.

67 16. *Let this opportunity be conceded . . .* In his last two paragraphs Shelley briefly answers the main argument of the *Quarterly* reviewer, who attacked him as a dangerous subverter of the established order in morals, politics, and religion.

17. *a Scotch philosopher:* Robert Forsyth in his *The Principles of Moral Science* (1805).

22. *Paley and Malthus:* clergymen and supporters of the established order. About William Paley (1743–1805), an influential, rather complacent theologian, Shelley exclaimed disgustedly in an early letter: 'Paley's Moral Philosophy begins—"Why am I obliged to keep my word? Because I desire Heaven and hate Hell." '

W. R. Malthus (1766–1834) in his *An Essay on the Principle of Population* (1798) maintained that population always tends to increase faster than food supplies, and was disliked by liberals because of his allegedly too

easy acceptance of the need for wars and disease as **67**
means of carrying off the resultant surplus. Malthus
was for Shelley 'the apostle of the rich' because his
population theory was thought to show that no radical
improvement of the condition of the poor would ever
be possible. Even liberals were thrown into despondency
about the possibility of reform by his very influential
book. See note on III. 1. 19. Malthus's *Essay* was in
part an answer to perfectibilitarian speculations in
Godwin's *Political Justice*. Godwin later wrote *Of
Population: An Answer to Mr Malthus's Essay* (1820).
26. *Didactic poetry . . . happiness.* Compare *A Defence of
Poetry*: 'The great instrument of moral good is the
imagination; and poetry administers to the effect by
acting upon the cause . . . Poetry strengthens the faculty
which is the organ of the moral nature of man, in the
same manner as exercise strengthens a limb. A poet
therefore would do ill to embody his own conceptions of
right and wrong, which are usually those of his place and
time, in his poetical creations, which participate in
neither' (*Works*, VII. 118). In eschewing didacticism
Shelley is not denying a moral function to poetry, but
only saying that it must act in the way proper to it.
1-6. *Should I live . . . model. A Philosophical View of* **68**
Reform, written by May 1820 though not published
until 1920, was a partial fulfilment of this ambition.
8. *candid:* as elsewhere in Shelley carries the older
meaning, 'impartial, well-disposed' rather than the
modern 'frank, outspoken.'

ACT I   **69**

Stage Direction. Shelley alters the locale from the
Caucasus mountains near the Caspian Sea, as in
Aeschylus, to the Indian Caucasus, the Hindu Kush
mountains which run west from the Himalayas through
North India and Afghanistan. That area was thought by
some to have been the original homeland of the human
race, and was associated with the golden age; so it was
appropriate that a second golden age should be inaugu-
rated there.

NOTES

69 *Prometheus.* The name in Greek means 'forethought' or
'forethinker.' He was one of the Titans, the pre-Olym-
pian gods, children of Ouranos (heaven) and Gaia
(earth). Mrs Shelley, in her note on the poem, says that
he is 'the emblem of the human race'; and most com-
mentators have followed her in interpreting him as repre-
sentative of humanity, or of what is best in humanity, of
what man potentially is. In some passages, however, he
is clearly differentiated from men; and Wasserman
(*Shelley's P.U.*, pp. 31–4) interprets him as the One
Mind, in relation to which individual human minds are,
in Shelley's thought, ultimately illusory. (See III. III.
23–5 and note.) It is best to start without preconcep-
tions, and feel our way as we go along. He is not an
allegorical abstraction, whose meaning can be neatly
defined, but a character in a myth.

1. *Monarch.* Jupiter (= Zeus). In mythology he is the
son of Kronos, whom he overthrew, becoming the chief
of the gods, though still subject to Fate. In *Prometheus
Unbound* he remains a character in the drama, a tyrant
not just a symbol of tyranny. We need to keep this
obvious fact in mind, while recognizing that there is
also truth in saying that he is the embodiment of the
evil which seems dominant in the world, of tyranny in
the moral, political, and religious spheres.

One thing he stands for (4–9) is men's false idea of
God. God, as conceived of by, for instance, in Shelley's
view, orthodox Christianity, becomes a tyrant, filling his
followers with fear, self-contempt, and barren hope (of
heaven after death, attained by submission— a hope
which prevents them from improving their state now).
Cf. Blake's Nobodaddy and Urizen.

Dæmons. Not necessarily evil. Since Plato, usually
beings intermediate between gods and men.

2. *One:* Prometheus.

9. *eyeless in hate:* blind with hatred. Goes with 'thou'
in line 10.

10–23. There is a characteristically Shelleyan mixture
here of what we would normally regard as abstract and
concrete. The scene is suggestive of a mental state, and

mental events are treated as substantial entities. This **69**
is consonant with his philosophy, as expounded in his
essay *On Life*. 'The view of life presented by the most
refined deductions of the intellectual philosophy, is
that of unity. Nothing exists but as it is perceived. The
difference is merely nominal between those two classes of
thought, which are vulgarly distinguished by the names
of ideas and of external objects' (*Works*, VI. 196).

24. *no hope.* Prometheus does not strictly have no hope, **70**
since he knows (47–50) that each day brings nearer the
hour of Jupiter's downfall. But he does not know when
this deliverance is to come. He is in the position of the
idealist who has faith in human perfectibility, but sees
no immediate cause for hope in the situation in which
he finds himself.

31–43. One of the best descriptive passages in the
poem. Characteristically Shelley stresses cold—not
mentioned by Aeschylus. Later the nature of the new
state of being inaugurated by Prometheus the fire-
bringer is to be expressed through images of heat, light,
and electricity. It is also characteristic of Shelley to
make perceptible, in the phrase 'crawling glaciers,' some-
thing which is known, but which is not normally appre-
hended by the senses.

34. Cf. *Prometheus Bound*, 1016–23. 'The winged hound
of Zeus, the ravening eagle' is to come each day to devour
Prometheus' liver which will grow again each night.

48. *Their.* Locock prints this MS reading in preference **71**
to the 1820 edition's 'The.' 'Each day and night brings
its own train of "wingless, crawling Hours".'

53–9. The first great turning-point in the poem. Through
years of suffering Prometheus has learned compassion,
and he hates no more. This change, though he does not
know it, is the necessary precondition of his release. The
transition from lines 50–2 is perhaps too abrupt to be
convincing.

59. *recall:* remember, call to mind. It has been disputed
whether the word means also 'revoke.' Prometheus'
change of heart would lead one to suppose that he
wishes to have the words repeated in order that he may

71 revoke them. But it is immaterial whether the word does have this meaning here; for it is in any case clear that Prometheus does revoke the curse in so far as it was an expression of hatred and desire for revenge. It is significant that he no longer remembers the words, whereas Earth and others preserve them and meditate on them in secret joy (184–5). At the same time lines 69–73 show that he still wishes his words to have power, still wishes for the downfall of Jupiter, though no longer in a vengeful spirit.

65. *without beams.* See *The Dæmon of the World* 150–3 and note, p. 254, and lines 82–3 below.

74–106. Voices from the elements say that never had they heard anything so awful as Prometheus' curse. They sympathize with him, but their words imply that the results of the curse have been evil.

74. Orthodox opinion in Shelley's day, calculating from the Bible, still placed the creation of the earth in about 4000 B.C.; but scientists knew it was far older. Shelley's guess is as accurate as could be expected at that time.

78. *parched:* dried up, evaporated.

72 82–3. Whereas in the upper, tenuous air the sun is 'without beams' (lines 64–5 above), near the earth the atmosphere refracts, bends the light, and so contributes to the production of colour, which is really a property of the light rather than of the objects on which it falls. See Grabo, *Newton among Poets*, pp. 90–1, 153.

99–102. The combination of wound, blood, rending, darkness over the day, a loud cry stirs memories of Gospel accounts of the Crucifixion. See *Luke* 23: 45–6.

73 107–90. The progress of the action is perhaps unduly held up by discussion of the difficulty of getting the curse repeated. But a sense of suspense is created, and a sense of the horror that has followed from Jupiter's enthronement, and from the curse itself.

107. *The Earth.* In Act I Earth is similar to the Greek goddess Gaia, mother of the Titans and of all things that spring from the earth. Without undue confusion different parts of the physical earth may be treated as parts

of her body (I. 152–6) or as her sons (at I. 113 'thy sons'   **73**
are the mountains, winds, etc., rather than the Titans).
114–7. 'But of wretched mortals he [Zeus] took no heed,
but desired to bring the whole race to nothingness and
to create another, a new one, in its stead. Against this
purpose none dared make stand but I myself' (*Prometheus
Bound* 232–6). Shelley goes further in making the con-
tinued existence of the earth itself dependent upon
Prometheus. It is possible to read into this the philo-
sophical idealism of the young Shelley who in his essay
On Life expressed agreement with 'those philosophers
who assert that nothing exists but as it is perceived'
(*Works*, VI. 194). But probably we should be content
with the simple statement that Prometheus has pro-
tected earth and men from destruction.
121. *frore:* very cold.
123. *Asia:* daughter of Oceanus and bride of Prometheus,
from whom she is now separated. See note to II. I. 1.
130. *Brethren!* Prometheus and the lawns and streams
(or at any rate the spirit that animates them) are sons
of Earth. Such traditional mythological conceptions
accorded with Shelley's feeling of a living universe and
with scientific theories which stressed the continuity of
all life and of animate and inanimate nature.
137. *And love:* could mean (1) And lovest, (2) And Love   **74**
also is moving near, (3) And I love. (1) seems most likely.
137–8. Earth has two voices—of the living and of the
dead, or more accurately (149–51) of the immortal and
the mortal. The gods cannot hear the latter, which is
referred to also as earth's 'inorganic voice' (135). Earth
hopes that Prometheus, being more than god, may be
able to; but he cannot. The significance of all this is
obscure, though Wasserman has tried to explain it in
Shelley's P.U., pp. 51–3.
141. *wheel of pain.* This, like many other passages,
mingles mythology (Ixion's wheel) with science (the
obliquity of the earth's axis). See note on II. IV. 52.
151–2. Are we to infer from this question that Prome-   **75**
theus has not yet recognized the presence of his mother
Earth, that at 113 he called upon her without realizing

75   that it was her voice which had already spoken? Or is it just that he has now become confused by her speaking in her inorganic voice?

157–62. This must refer not to the birth of Prometheus, but to his first appearance as a rebel against Jupiter, whom he had previously helped.

177–8. Cf. Adam Walker, *A System of Familiar Philosophy* (1799), p. 203. 'The atmosphere is a thin fluid . . . principally made up of heterogeneous matter exhaled from the earth.' Earth's breath is poisoned by her hatred —another illustration of the fact that the ill effects of tyranny are produced not only by the tyrant, but by the victims also if they return evil for evil. Indeed Earth does not say that the evils she has suffered have been caused by Jupiter at all.

There are several references in the poem to exhalations, of both good and evil kinds, bursting from the earth and from the characters and then forming the atmosphere around them (e.g. I. 829–32; II. i. 73–8, II. v. 26–7, 54–9, 61–3; IV. 323–4, 557–61). Though in II. iv. 100–1 evil is a plague rained down, more characteristically both evil and good emanate from a centre within. For the symbolic meaning of this imagery see Wasserman, *Shelley's P.U.*, chap. v; for its physical basis G. M. Matthews, 'A Volcano's Voice in Shelley' (*Shelley: A Collection of Critical Essays*, ed. G. Ridenour (1953), pp. 111–32).

76   192–217. *Zoroaster:* Persian religious leader, about the eighth century B.C.; taught that the universe is ruled by two powers, but that the eventual victory of the Good Spirit (Ahura Mazda or Ormuzd) over the Evil (Ahriman) is assured. The source of this story about him is not known, but stories of such 'doubles' are quite common in the literature of the Romantic period, when men became more interested in exploring inwards into the depths of their own minds. Shelley himself had strange visions—perhaps projections of his own thoughts or emotions; and towards the end of his life saw an image of himself. The appearance of one's double was sometimes taken as a sign of approaching death.

Shelley's world underneath the grave presumably **76** owes something to the classical Hades and to traditional ideas about the soul, astral bodies, etc. What is distinctive about it is that it is inhabited not only by phantasmal persons, but also by mental experiences which have a life of their own. Following Jung we might call it the collective unconscious.

207. *Demogorgon.* See note to II. III. 2. Presumably this is only the Phantasm of Demogorgon. This world underneath the grave is different from the realm of Demogorgon we are to visit in II. III–IV.

222–39. Ione and Panthea are daughters of Oceanus **77** and younger sisters of Asia. Ione is sensitive, sympathetic, usually the first to sense what is coming; Panthea is more intelligent and ready to explain, and she acts as an intermediary between Asia and Prometheus. They serve usefully as a chorus, describing and commenting on the events. In so far as they are symbolic they may be thought of as lesser aspects of that which is represented by Asia (see note on II. I. I). While Prometheus harboured hatred in himself he was necessarily separated from love in its fullness, but lesser degrees of love remained with him. Her name ('deity in all') connects Panthea with Asia in the latter's capacity as goddess of nature. Attempts to define these figures more closely (e.g. Ione as Hope, Panthea as Faith or Memory) have not been convincing.

235–7. The Phantom holds a sceptre to steady his proud steps, as he approaches over the cloud. This seems preferable to taking 'stay' to mean 'stop' (any one from approaching him proudly).

258–60. It has been suggested that there is a likeness **78** between Prometheus' description here of the Phantasm and his own earlier description of himself in the curse (262), and that in cursing and hating Prometheus became like Jupiter. In that case, there is an appropriateness, not intended by Prometheus, in the Phantasm of Jupiter repeating the words—words which are proper to Jupiter rather than to the now changed Prometheus. The situation—almost a self-cursing—is appropriate in another

78   way; for the evil man does curse and punish himself by the very fact of being evil (cf. I. 403–5).

79   273–4. Cf. I. 381–2, II. IV. 43–6. Prometheus' helping Jupiter to power is taken over from the original myth. The significance in Shelley has usually been understood to be that man (Prometheus, here at any rate, being assumed to represent the mind of man) enslaves himself to tyrannies of his own creation—repressive moralities, unjust rulers, a God of wrath. These tyrants only seem to be omnipotent, only seem to be externally imposed. A possibly more adequate way of putting it is to say that, in so far as the poem is allegorical, different aspects or states of the human mind are embodied in Prometheus, Asia, and even in Jupiter.

277. *Its* MS; *In* 1820.

80   294–5. 'Both good and evil being infinite as the universe is, and as thou art, and as thy solitude is' (Forman).

302–5. Prometheus is so changed that he does not recognize his own former words. But his withdrawal of any desire for vengeance implies no weakening. Ironically the revocation of the curse, a desire for vengeance, is the precondition of it, as desire for Jupiter's downfall, becoming effective. Earth, speaking (306–11) for ordinary, earth-bound common sense, cannot understand this. Nor does Ione (314). Both in the curse and in its partial withdrawal Prometheus is regarding Jupiter as a person, a sentient being who can suffer and be spared suffering. Line 305 is, perhaps deliberately, rather vague. It is open to us to say that Jupiter is not really a 'living thing,' but a negation which will disappear in the Promethean day. But that is not the way Prometheus is thinking at this stage. He is renouncing his wish that the enemy who has tortured him unjustly for thousands of years should suffer in return.

81   325. *Mercury* (= Hermes). Son of Maia and Zeus, messenger of the gods. Unlike Aeschylus' Hermes, he is an *unwilling* servant of tyranny, one who recognizes good (356–60), but serves evil because it appears to be stronger. After Earth has thought Prometheus' change

a surrender it is appropriate to show what a real sur- **81**
render to evil is.

326. The Furies. The Greek Erinyes were avenging
spirits, perhaps originally personifications of curses,
which were thought to have a magical effect. It is appro-
priate that Jupiter should be shown pursuing vengeance
immediately after Prometheus has renounced it.

The Erinyes often acted upon the mind; so it is only
an extension of the Greek conception that Shelley
should make his Furies personifications of torturing
thoughts. They take their form 'from our victim's
destined agony' (470); except as mental experiences of
the victims they have no real existence. They come
'from the all-miscreative brain of Jove,' but he was
given power by Prometheus: so, in common experience
evil thoughts may seem to come from outside, but are
creations, even if involuntary, of the mind itself.

344–9. Mercury threatens to drive the Furies back to **82**
Hades, where flow the rivers Phlegethon and Cocytus
('streams of fire and wail'; 'wail' is a noun), and to raise
instead various mythical monsters. The Sphinx's
appearance at Thebes led to Oedipus' unwitting marriage
to his mother ('unnatural love') and to his cursing his
sons to make them kill one another ('more unnatural
hate').

349. *love*. Locock notes: 'In the MS. "love" is changed
to "hate," and then back to "love," with the following
remark: "The contrast would have been completer if
the sentiment had been transposed: but wherefore
sacrifice the philosophical truth, that love, however
monstrous in its expression, is still less worthy of horror
than hatred . . ." "Still," of course, is "nevertheless." '

353. *unwilling*: goes with 'thee.'

371–4. The fatal secret—that Thetis' offspring shall be **83**
greater than his father, so that if Jupiter unites with her
he will be overthrown, like his predecessor, by his son—
is important in Aeschylus, but does not fit well into
Shelley's scheme. In the new conditions produced by
Prometheus' change in Act I and by what happens in
Act II, Jupiter's fall is inevitable; it is not due to any-

83 thing Jupiter does, and it could not be prevented by him. Shelley tries to give the secret some meaning in III. I.; but at this stage we must just accept that Prometheus is being tempted to compromise with evil because of its apparent power, and so to perpetuate its rule. We should bear in mind that, for all he knows, he may by holding out be condemning himself to innumerable more years of pain (424).

Wasserman (*Shelley's P.U.*, pp. 85–8) points out that we are not told in *Prometheus Unbound* what the secret was, and thinks that we should not carry over our knowledge from the source here.

387. *thought-executing*. Cf. Shakespeare, *King Lear* III. II. 4, where it is usually glossed 'doing execution with the rapidity of thought.' Here it could mean 'thought-destroying' or, more likely, 'executing the thought' (of Jupiter).

84 398. *the Sicilian's ... sword.* Damocles, a flattering courtier, was forced by Dionysius I, ruler of Syracuse, to dine under a naked sword suspended by a single horse-hair so that he might realise the insecurity of a king's happiness. Here mankind is being compared to Damocles, and the possibility that Prometheus will yield to Jupiter, thus making mankind's enslavement eternal, is the suspended sword.

403–5. Triumphant Justice will meet crimes against herself with pity rather than punishment, evil-doers having already punished themselves too much by the misery of being evil.

86 437–8. Leaving Prometheus to the Furies, Mercury departs—suggestive of those who live in comfort, not bearing to confront themselves with the sufferings caused by the Governments and the policies they support. If his mission to extort the secret were being taken seriously his departure would be strange; one would expect him to try again after Prometheus had been weakened by torture. Shelley seems not really interested in the secret, but only in Prometheus' mental experiences. In comparison with Aeschylus (the Furies do not appear in *Prometheus Bound*) he places far more emphasis on

mental, as opposed to physical, suffering. In the rest of **86**
this Act he is little indebted to Aeschylus.

479. *lidless:* unclosed, wakeful. **88**

483–91. Evil thoughts and desires are as intimately
present to Prometheus as the animal life which sustains
his body. Shelley did not think that the conquest of
evil was easy, even for the best. Yet, the Fury goes on—
rather undramatically, expressing Shelley's view rather
than what she might be expected to say herself—evil
cannot touch the essential inner self, the 'soul within
our soul,' which is what man should, and can, be.

522. The second group of Furies which arrive now are **89**
to show Prometheus visions of external evils, whereas
the first have been concerned with internal.

530. *Kingly conclaves.* This is sometimes taken to refer to **90**
the Congress of Vienna (1814–15), which, from Shelley's
point of view, imposed reactionary regimes on Europe.
But strictly a conclave is a *secret* meeting. Shelley is
referring to the small, behind-the-scenes meetings at
which, whether at the Congress of Vienna or at most
other times, the real decisions are taken.

535. *might break.* To speak might weaken the force of
that which is to be shown rather than merely described.

539. *Tear the veil!* The MS has a stage-direction here:
'The Furies having mingled in a strange dance divide,
and in the background is seen a plain covered with
burning cities.' Prometheus is not merely to be told
about various dire events, he is to see them. The veil
cannot be, as has been suggested, that which separates
present from future. The imagined time in which
Prometheus Unbound is set is not the classical era, but
some undetermined time in the future; the events
Prometheus is shown are in the past. He experiences the
Crucifixion, the French Revolution, and their conse-
quences as equally present. If the veil is more than a
piece of stage furniture one might say that it separates
the individual consciousness from the collective con-
sciousness of the race.

546–52. *One:* Christ. *sanguine:* blood-stained. The cities **91**
are burning in religious wars.

91   561. *thee:* Prometheus, not Christ; but the images in
562–5, usually associated with Christ and now applied to
Prometheus, bring the two together. Prometheus
experiences a kind of crucifixion in seeing the ill-effects
that have flowed from attempts to benefit the human
race.

567. *disenchanted nation:* France, released from an evil
spell by the Revolution.

572. *'Tis another's.* The legioned band are now no
longer children of Love, but of Hatred; unity is lost in
internal struggles, and France again falls under tyranny.

93   606. *like to thee.* Cf. Shelley's note on *Hellas* 1090–1:
'The sublime human character of Jesus Christ was de-
formed by an imputed identification with a Power,
who tempted, betrayed, and punished the innocent
beings who were called into existence by His sole will;
and for the period of a thousand years, the spirit of this
most just, wise, and benevolent of men has been pro-
pitiated with myriads of hecatombs of those who ap-
proached the nearest to His innocence and wisdom....'

609. *hooded ounces:* hunting leopards, hooded until
released at their prey.

618–31. This is the climax of the temptation. The
Fury is all the more impressive for speaking in a level,
apparently reasonable tone, and because most of what
she says is true. The temptation is to despair, in view of
the apparent impossibility of improving things to
acquiesce in things as they are. Prometheus' answer
silences the Fury because it shows that he is willing to
accept any amount of suffering as being better than
acquiescence. It is those for whom the miseries of the
world are *not* misery who are to be pitied.

618–9. 'Superstitious fear lingers in every man's mind
after he has stopped believing in the cause of it'
(Matthews).

95   658–61. The Spirits live both in 'the dim caves of
human thought' (in individual human minds) and in its
(human thought's) 'world-surrounding æther' (? in the
one, universal mind, of which individual minds are
perhaps part. Or perhaps the idea is simply that human

thought creates the atmosphere in which men live). **95**
The Furies have shown the power of evil; the Spirits
show the persistence of good even in the face of the
worst, a persistence which gives hope of good's final
triumph. The first four Spirits tell of hopes for the
future from man's steadfastness in opposing tyranny,
from his capacity for self-sacrifice, from the sage's,
especially the political philosopher's, learning and vision,
and from the poet's imaginings. The Spirits perform
the work of angels, but Shelley rejects the idea of angels
who descend from heaven as emissaries of a ruling,
personal deity. The Spirits 'ascend' from within rather
than come down from on high.

662. *as in a glass:* as in a fortune-teller's crystal ball or
other magic means of foretelling the future. Cf. IV.
213.

717. Spread beneath the wrecked fleets was a hell of **97**
death.

743–8. A characteristic Shelley passage. The poet is **98**
concerned not just to observe and describe the surface
of things, but to penetrate by imagination to the reality
to which earthly beauty points. Some modern critics
would prefer him just 'concretely' to describe the bees.

760. *skiey grain.* 'Grain' is used to mean a purple dye,
but also other colours of dye. The wings are of the
colours of the sky, orange and azure, etc.

765. *planet-crested.* The planet is presumably Venus. **99**
The idea of a star as a crest is found again in III. ii.
27–8.

766–7. This is not merely fanciful, but is related to
contemporary scientific speculation. In Shelley's day
light, heat, and electricity were regarded as very subtle
fluids made up of minute particles capable of permeating
and passing through grosser matter. It was the special
theory of Adam Walker that these three are all one,
different manifestations of a single energy which is the
cause of all motion and so of all life. He thought that
this energy is radiated from the sun as electricity and con-
verted into light and heat in the atmosphere and on
earth. He thought that all suns give out this energy,

99 and that all bodies attract to themselves any of it that comes within the field of their gravitational pull. 'By this giving and taking the whole universe is filled with light and motion' (*Philosophy*, p. 3). For Shelley Love is the animating principle in the spiritual world, as for Walker light - heat - electricity is in the material. Furthermore, for Shelley, the distinction between material and immaterial is, in the last analysis, unmeaning. So he does not just say love is *like* a certain material force. Love scatters the liquid joy of life; the force which gives life to the Moon *is* Love (IV. 369); the earth gathers Love as it rolls through the skies (IV. 520–1). In the material realm Love manifests itself in this animating, fertilizing force.

770. Locock follows the MS in omitting the full stop after 'night' found in 1820 and many later editions.

772. Cf. Plato's *Symposium* 195, as translated by Shelley: 'Homer says that the goddess Calamity is delicate, and her feet are tender. "Her feet are soft," he says, "for she treads not upon the ground, but makes her path upon the heads of men" ... The same evidence is sufficient to make manifest the tenderness of Love. For Love walks not upon the earth, nor over the heads of men, which are not indeed very soft; but he dwells within, and treads on the softest of existing things, having established his habitation within the souls and inmost nature of Gods and men; not indeed in all souls—for wherever he chances to find a hard and rugged disposition, there he will not inhabit, but only where it is most soft and tender.'

Desolation is felt most keenly by the most tender-hearted. Love is shadowed by pain, for it raises hopes that are not fulfilled. The thought may seem inappropriately expressed by one of the Spirits called to cheer Prometheus. Is Shelley self-indulgently slipping into a favourite mood? Or was it necessary to stress again the present shadowing of Love by Pain in order to add force to the prophecy of the Promethean age? Perhaps the point is that the very fact that the tender-hearted find the present conditions painful is a sign of the possi-

bility of another order of things coming into existence. **99**
789. The at-oneness of Prometheus and the chorus is **100**
stressed by this line being metrically part of the stanza
(789–800).

831. *æther*. A medium more subtle than air, filling the **101**
interstices in interplanetary space and within matter;
thought in the 19th century to be the medium through
which gravity, heat, light, etc. are transmitted. Cf.
Boswell, *Life of Johnson*, 1 July 1763: 'My mind was
strongly impregnated with the Johnsonian æther.' Asia
is being thought of here in her capacity as Venus
Genetrix.

832. *would fade*. (1) Underlines the love between Pro-
metheus and Asia. (2) ? Suggests that the flourishing,
indeed the continued existence, of the material world is
dependent upon mind (Prometheus) operating on and
through the forces of generation (Asia).

ACT II. SCENE I   **102**

Asia. Daughter of Oceanus and bride of Prometheus.
Whatever symbolic meanings may be attributed to her,
she, like Prometheus, is not merely an allegorical
abstraction. She is a character in the drama, with an
important part to play in the action. She has suffered
during her separation from Prometheus, and she loves
him. In relation to him she is the antitype of the soul
within his soul (see *Alastor* 151–82 and notes). While
hatred existed within him, he was necessarily separated
from her; but now their union is possible.

At first she seems a person, with human character-
istics, limitations, yearnings. Later she is invested with
the characteristics of the ocean-born Aphrodite (Venus),
goddess of love and of the generative spirit in nature. She
is the 'shadow of beauty unbeheld' (III. III. 7), a mani-
festation of eternal Beauty and Love; in Platonic terms
a dæmon, one of that class of beings who are inter-
preters and mediators between gods and men. Writers
in the Platonic tradition often associate water with the
material world of generation, light with the eternal

102 world; so Asia is appropriately both a daughter of
Ocean (in that she dwells in the world of time and
change) and a 'child of light' (in that through her the
eternal Love flows into that world, in her it is revealed).
There is no incompatibility between these different ways
of looking at her. Compare the treatment of Emilia in
Epipsychidion and of Beatrice in Dante. See F. A.
Pottle, 'The Role of Asia in the Dramatic Action of
Shelley's *Prometheus Unbound*' (*Shelley: A Collection of
Critical Essays*, ed. G. Ridenour (Prentice-Hall 1965),
pp. 133–43).

Shelley preferred to call Prometheus' wife Asia, as
in Herodotus, rather than Hesione, as in Aeschylus,
perhaps because of the associations of the word. Hunger-
ford (*Shores of Darkness*, p. 131; see also p. 23) says:
'It was commonly believed that the continent Asia
was the cradle of civilization. Asia in the play could thus
represent the pristine culture, associated with Pro-
metheus, which had prevailed before that culture had
been contaminated with evil. She would be the state of
love and nature in which civilization could flourish.'
Furthermore, by calling his Venus-figure Asia Shelley
perhaps intended to bring together eastern and European
mythologies and to point to likenesses between them. In
books on Indian mythology he had read of Lakshmi,
described by Edward Moor (*Hindu Pantheon*, p. 32) as
'the daughter of Ocean' and 'the sea-born goddess of
beauty.'

17–25. One cannot be sure that this is more than merely
descriptive. But after the description of the coming of
spring and of dawn, suggestive of regeneration, the
emphasis on the fact that the dawn is not only putting to
flight the darkness but also blotting out the star, a thing
of beauty, is rather unexpected, and may be significant.
The suggestion could be that what has been aspired to
as a distant ideal is now to be brought close, made actual
in the light of day. Later, in *The Triumph of Life* 412–31,
the fading of the morning star in the light of the sun is
used to suggest the loss of vision of the ideal in the
light of common day. But at the time of writing *Pro-*

metheus Unbound Shelley was more optimistic than he 102
later became about the possibility of bringing together
the ideal and the actual.

26. *Aeolian.* Aeolus was god of winds. The wind pro-
ducing music from something it blows upon is a common
image in Shelley.

31. *shadow.* Cf. II. i. 70. For Prometheus, Panthea is 103
the shadow of Asia; for Asia she wears the shadow of
Prometheus.

32. *spherèd:* the sun has risen so that its whole sphere is
visible.

43. *Erewhile:* before the fall of Prometheus. The follow-
ing lines suggest a state of primitive at-oneness with
nature. Cf. Asia's description of the Saturnian age
(II. iv. 34–8).

52–5. This seems to refer to a longer period than that
since her dream of the night before. Panthea has in some
way been the intermediary between Asia and Pro-
metheus throughout the period of her vigil with him. It
seems there are three stages—'erewhile,' a primitive
Eden of innocence; a state of experience, full of care,
but in which contact with love is not wholly lost; 'now,'
when the possibility of full reunion with love has been
opened.

56–108. We have seen Panthea leaving Prometheus at
dawn immediately after witnessing his ordeal and
actively sympathizing with him in it. Now we are to
hear of her night of sleep and dreams—apparently the
same night—immediately before her departure to Asia.
We need not trouble about the inconsistency. Panthea's
first dream is another way of describing the same event
which has been presented in different terms in Act I.
In casting out hatred and successfully going through his
ordeal Prometheus has thrown off that which had ob-
scured his true self, 'that form which lives unchanged
within,' seen by Panthea in all its glory in her dream.

101–5. Ione has been through a similar experience in 105
relation to Panthea, as Panthea has in relation to Pro-
metheus—a dissolution of the sense of individual,
separate identity.

105 114–61. In Panthea's eyes Asia is able to see, and to interpret (as her sister has not been) the first dream, and then to see the second, which Panthea is then able to recall. Asia then remembers a similar dream of her own. The strange mingling of consciousnesses and the wordless communication between Prometheus, Panthea, and Asia are characteristic of Shelley, and consonant with his view that 'the existence of distinct individual minds ... is ... a delusion' (essay *On Life*; *Works*, VI. 196).

The first dream is merely prophetic; the second demands action.

106 134–9. The almond tree blossoms very early, anticipating the spring. Asia and Panthea are not to be discouraged by the fall of the early blossoms, but to follow where the spirit voices lead. So, it is implied, men should not be discouraged by the failure of abortive attempts to transform society, such as the French Revolution.

140. *Hyacinth:* a youth loved by Apollo. A flower (variously identified; not that now called by the name) with petals marked Ai (woe) sprang from his blood.

107 162. *Echo*. At first merely repeats what Asia has said; but soon the spirit voices go beyond that. The spiritual powers which have spoken through dreams and through nature now speak directly, though, since they are still called Echoes, one should perhaps think that they correspond in some way to thoughts in Asia's mind. Shelley slides from past to present, inner to outer in such a way as to suggest that there are really no hard and fast lines of division.

109 189/90, 195/6: *Echoes* 1820; *Echo* MS.

190–3. We have heard (I. 707) of a prophecy which begins and ends in Prometheus. Now we hear of some as yet unrealized potentiality which can be made actual only by Asia, whose part in the action is therefore as necessary as his. Not just undaunted resistance, not just renunciation of hatred, but something more positive is needed to bring the new order into existence. Critics who have complained that the essential action of the play is over in Act I have underrated Asia's part. The

109 beginning and the ending are not the whole. See F. A.
Pottle, 'The Role of Asia in the Dramatic Action of
Shelley's *Prometheus Unbound*.'

ACT II. SCENE II 110

Literally Asia and Panthea pass through lush, wooded
scenery to a volcanic mountain; symbolically they go
through the sensuous world to that power which lies
behind it. Compare the journey of the poet in *Alastor*
(420–68) through a dense forest to a well, the mysterious
source of life.

Stage Direction. Fauns: minor Roman pastoral deities,
depicted as men with the ears, horns, tail, and usually the
feet of goats.

4. *curtained:* a variation of the veil image, so common in
Shelley. The forest, emblematic of earthly life, is shut in
from eternity, but fertilizing influences and glimpses of
that which lies beyond enter it.

7–23. As in some others of Shelley's long sentences, the
syntax is irregular, but the meaning is plain. Nothing
pierces the interwoven bowers of the forest except when
a cloud of dew hangs a pearl ... or when a star, having
found a cleft, scatters drops of light before being borne
on its way.

10. Hangs a pearl in each pale flower.

24–40. In the singing of the nightingales, associated
with love and with poetry, joy is shadowed by pain;
both the sensuous richness of the temporal world and
its incompleteness, its pointing beyond itself, are sug-
gested.

34. *stream.* In the MS 'strain,' printed in 1820 and many 111
editions, is altered to 'stream.'

38. *lake-surrounded* (MS): preferable to 'lake-surround-
ing' (1820). The flutes are imagined as being played in
a boat or on an island in the middle of a lake.

44. *deep* MS; *sweet* 1820.

46. *boats.* Boats are often in Shelley emblematic of the
soul's earthly vehicle; souls are fated to enter the realm
of matter, to descend the separate streams of individual

111 lives (cf. *Alastor* 494–514) back to the Ocean (of universal being).

50. *destined.* The MS has a dash after 'destined' (noun, those who are destined) and no stop at the end of the line; 1820 has no stop after 'destined' (adjective) and a comma at the end of the line.

51–63. Shelley is using his experience of supposedly healing exhalations from the earth (at Bath and in southern Italy) and of volcanic mountains. We see steam rising from the earth, sweeping along and driving 'all souls'—now, in particular Asia and Panthea—along the path they are fated to follow. Characteristically this 'plume-uplifting wind' is also a 'stream of sound,' the sound being given motive power. The souls are awakened from slumber (in the world of generation) by sound— in II. I Asia and Panthea were impelled to start their journey by Echoes from the spirit world—and are driven towards the mountain of Demogorgon and the re-entry into eternity.

60–1. The MS has a dash after 'hurrying' and no other punctuation. 1820 has no stop after 'hurrying' and a comma after 'behind.'

112 64–97. Written as an afterthought, perhaps at the same time as Act IV, in which Shelley was concerned to associate the whole material world with the regeneration wrought by Prometheus. The Fauns add to the cycles already mentioned, of souls and of water, those of electricity and of chemical elements from the earth to the atmosphere and back (70–82). Their talk suggests that the Spirits are personifications of the elements of matter. Silenus (wood-god, with the gift of prophecy, tutor of Dionysus) and the Fauns (half-man, half-goat) and nightingales and spirits represent different levels of being, all longing for the deliverance of Prometheus.

70–82. Cf. Walker, *Philosophy*, pp. 231–2. He notes that much 'inflammable air' (hydrogen) is released from plants in ponds in hot weather. When the bubbles which the sun sucks from the plants come out of the water they burst and the hydrogen which they contain, being very light, ascends to the upper air, which is

heavily charged with electricity, and there ignites and 112
appears as meteors or falling stars. Lines 81–2 describe
the return of atmospheric electricity to the earth.
90. *thwart:* testy, cross-grained.

2. *Demogorgon.* Mrs Shelley says that he is 'the Primal
Power of the world.' The name is probably a corruption
of the Greek word δημιουργός. In Plato (*Timaeus,*
28–40) the Demiourgos is the beneficent fashioner of
the world after the pattern existing in the divine idea.
Later, the Demiourgos degenerated into a mysterious
and terrible power dwelling in the depths. Lucan refers
to 'Him, at the sound of whose name the earth ever
quakes and trembles. He looks on the Gorgon's head
unveiled .... He dwells in a Tartarus beneath your view'
(*Pharsalia* VI. 744–8). At the beginning of his *De
Genealogia Deorum* Boccaccio writes of Demogorgon
as the father and the chief of all the gentile gods. He im-
agines himself descending through a narrow passage in
Mount Taenarus or Aetna to Demogorgon's dark
dwelling-place in the bowels of the earth. He says that
belief in him arose, not among the learned, but among
Arcadian rustics who, seeing the vital forces of nature,
imagined an animating principle and named it Demogor-
gon. Shelley's friend T. L. Peacock in a note to his poem
Rhododaphne (1818) quotes Boccaccio as his authority on
Demogorgon, who 'was the genius of the Earth, and the
Sovereign Power of the terrestrial Daemons.' Demogor-
gon is mentioned by Spenser (*Faerie Queen* I. I. 37; I.
V. 22; IV. II. 47) and Milton (*Paradise Lost* II. 964–5).
  The name was suitable for Shelley as being mysterious
and impressive in itself and as conjuring up the idea of
a being with great but not clearly-defined powers. The
vagueness made it easier to mould him to his own
purposes. With reservations we may say that he repre-
sents the impersonal laws which govern the universe.
He acts only after Prometheus and Asia have acted. In

113 his final appearance in Act IV he does not say that he is going to do anything, only that in certain circumstances certain actions will lead to certain consequences. Compare Shelley's earlier conception of Necessity (*The Dæmon of the World* 291 and note, p. 255).

3–10. Boccaccio placed Demogorgon's dwelling in Etna (volcano) or Taenarus (seat of an oracle). Shelley combines the two, and makes the gaseous exhalation of the volcano oracular—i.e. productive of a state of inspired frenzy in which the inhaler might become the mouthpiece of a god. He had not long before been to Mount Vesuvius and had written to Peacock (21 Dec. 1818): 'The mountain is at present in a slight state of eruption; and a thick heavy white smoke is perpetually rolled out, interrupted by enormous columns of an impenetrable black bituminous vapour, which is hurled up fold after fold, into the sky; and fiery stones are rained down from its darkness.' Vesuvius was 'after the glaciers, the most impressive exhibition of the energies of nature I ever saw. It has not the immeasurable greatness, the overpowering magnificence, nor above all, the radiant beauty of the glaciers; but it has all their character of tremendous and irresistible strength.'

3. *meteor-breathing*. Meteors were thought to be exhalations from the earth rather than to come from outside the atmosphere. See *The Sensitive Plant* II. 10 and note.

9. *Mænads*. Women inspired to ecstatic frenzy by Dionysus, to whom they cried 'Evoe! Evoe!' Dionysian worship was associated with release from the conventions of daily life, the liberation of the instincts, the sense of at-oneness with nature and with the god. Dionysus' Roman name was Bacchus. It is probable that Shelley read about this time Euripides' *Bacchæ*, which tells of the terrible incursion of the divine power of Dionysus/ Bacchus and of the vain efforts of Pentheus to resist it. Cf. *P.U.* III. III.154, IV. 473–5; *Ode to the West Wind* 21; *Ode to Liberty* 92.

10. *contagion:* either (1) to the world, to the conventional, the voice of youthful enthusiasm seems pestilential; (2) as in *The Revolt of Islam* IX. IV. 8, the word does

not carry its usual association with disease—enthusiasm **113**
is, in a good sense, contagious.

12–16. Shelley preferred the notion of a God of limited
power to that of a God who is omnipotent and permits
evil. But he did not claim to know the answers to the
ultimate questions; the sentence is in the conditional
mood. Here, and throughout this and the following
scene, we should think of Asia as a loving person more
than as a goddess or as a representative of Love or of any
other quality. Possessed by wonder she could fall down
and worship the earth; she is perplexed, indignant,
brave; her understanding is limited.

24. *midway, around.* The line was at first left incom- **114**
plete, and later these rather weak words were added to
fill it up. Here, and in other passages, we see signs of the
speed with which Shelley wrote, achieving magical
effects but not the consistent excellence of some more
careful writers.

47–50. Locock follows the punctuation of the MS,
Shelley's dashes being appropriate to express Asia's
confusion.

59–60. Cf. 12–16. The phenomenal world is only a **115**
shadow; but now Asia and Panthea are passing through
the veil which divides things which only seem from the
reality. Behind all the 'shadow' imagery lies, of course,
the famous myth of the cave in *Plato's Republic*, VII.
514–7. Plato imagines men as being chained in an under-
ground cave, seeing only the shadows of things thrown
on to a wall by the light of a fire behind them, and
imagining that these shadows are the reality. But
Shelley's characters are descending into a cave in order
to confront 'things that ... are,' whereas in Plato's
myth it would be the ascent from the cave into the light
of the sun which would represent the attainment of
knowledge of the intellectual world. So we must be
careful to understand the images as they occur in their
contexts in Shelley without bringing in more from
Plato than is relevant.

66. *lightning:* cf. *The Cloud* 18 and note, p. 330.

70. *stone:* i.e. lodestone.

115 74. *prism.* Down here there is no light for the air to refract into colours. The splitting of the light is a common image in Shelley, suggestive of our normal inability to see the white radiance of eternity. Cf. *Adonais* 463.

116 90–8. Asia and Panthea have been bound, and are being guided by the spirits. Asia's submission is essential in order that the Eternal (Demogorgon) may release into life the destined downfall of Jupiter. 'Resist not ...' implies the possibility of resistance. Asia is to co-operate by submission.

No single interpretation of this descent will be adequate. Among other things it is a descent into the depths of the mind itself.

ACT II. SCENE IV

117 12–18. This sentence is syntactically irregular, either 'which' or 'when' (12) having no verb attached to it. Locock conjectured that since 'fills' will do in either clause Shelley inadvertently made it do for both.

Cf. Shelley's essay *On Love*: 'There is eloquence in the tongueless wind, and a melody in the flowing brooks and the rustling of the reeds beside them, which by their inconceivable relation to something within the soul awaken the spirits to a dance of breathless rapture, and bring tears of mysterious tenderness to the eyes, like the enthusiasm of patriotic success, or the voice of one beloved singing to you alone. ... So soon as this want or power is dead, man becomes the living sepulchre of himself, and what yet survives is the mere husk of what once he was' (*Works*, VI. 202).

118 19–28. This sentence also is oddly constructed. Shelley had been shocked by the sight of convicts chained together walking through the streets of Italian cities; so mention of 'the great chain of things' (the chain of necessity, of cause and effect) would conjure up for him a picture of the actual chains on the prisoners. The idea of one evil by necessity leading to another passes into the picture of each man reeling towards death loaded by

the chain of his own criminal or remorseful thoughts. **118**
28. *He reigns*. No explanation is given as to how the
world created by an Almighty and merciful God came
under the rule of evil. In a note to *Hellas* Shelley wrote:
'That there is a true solution of the riddle [of the origin
of evil], and that in our present state that solution is
unattainable by us, are propositions which may be
regarded as equally certain.' One should not assume too
hastily that he who reigns is Jupiter: Asia wants to get
behind Jupiter to the ultimate evil power whom he
serves (100-9). Nor should 'Almighty God' be identified
with Demogorgon. The ultimate powers are unknow-
able. Shelley may have been influenced by various cos-
mological theories—for instance the Zoroastrian, of
which he learnt in Peacock's fragmentary poem
Ahrimanes (written probably 1813-15; Peacock en-
visaged a primal power who delegates authority in turn
to good and evil gods, Oromazes and Ahrimanes). But
primarily he is dramatising his own direct experience—
the feeling on the one hand that the world and humanity
are of divine origin, the recognition on the other of the
present dominance of evil power. In his essay *On the
Devil and Devils* he wrote: 'the Manichean philosophy
respecting the origin and government of the world, if
not true, is at least an hypothesis conformable to the
experience of actual facts. To suppose that the world
was created and is superintended by two spirits of a
balanced power and opposite dispositions, is simply a
personification of the struggle which we experience
within ourselves, and which we perceive in the opera-
tions of external things as they affect us, between good
and evil. The supposition that the good spirit is, or
hereafter will be, superior, is a personification of the
principle of hope, and that thirst for improvement
without which present evil would be intolerable'
(*Works*, VII. 87).
32-100. This follows, though with important differences,
Prometheus' account of his dealings with Jupiter and
his gifts to mankind in *Prometheus Bound*, 196-254
and 442-506. Compare also the account of the reigns of

118 Oromazes and Ahrimanes in Peacock's *Ahrimanes*, I. XVIII–XXVII. (Peacock, *Works* (Halliford edition), VII. 272–5).

32. *Heaven and Earth:* Ouranos and Gaia, parents of Kronos (Time) or Saturn and of the other Titans.

33. *Love.* Cf. Plato's *Symposium*, 178, as translated by Shelley: 'Hesiod says, that first "Chaos was produced; then the broad-bosomed Earth, to be the secure foundation of all things, then love." '

33. *Saturn* (= Kronos =, in some interpretations, time). The origin of evil—or at least of imperfection—is placed at the very beginning of the temporal order; for the Saturnian age, though to some extent a golden one, is shown as very limited. The envy belongs properly to Saturn.

119 39. *birthrights* MS; *birthright* 1820.

43–4. Jupiter has been interpreted as representing the specific evils which men have themselves created, and from which they could, in theory, release themselves. As soon as man becomes self-conscious, begins to gain control over his environment, and to join together in societies, there comes the possibility of the new powers being abused. The development of the new powers and the abuse of them go together; Prometheus gives power to Jupiter.

Mrs Shelley in her note on *Prometheus Unbound* wrote: 'The prominent feature of Shelley's theory of the destiny of the human species was, that evil is not inherent in the system of creation, but an accident that might be expelled. ... Shelley believed that mankind had only to will that there should be no evil, and there would be none.' But his view was not quite so simple as this. See III. IV. 198–204 and note, p. 304.

52. *unseasonable seasons.* It was a common idea that in the golden age there was perpetual spring. Later (in Christian writings, after the Fall) the earth began to librate on its axis, producing the succession of the seasons. Cf. Ovid, *Metamorphoses* I. 113–24; Milton, *Paradise Lost* X. 668–70; Notes to *Queen Mab* VI. 45–6.

61. *Nepenthe:* a care-dispelling drug. *Moly:* drug given

by Hermes to Odysseus to counteract the potion of **119**
Circe. *Amaranth:* unfading flower.

66. *chase* MS; *prey* 1820.

75–84. In Aeschylus, Prometheus' emphasis is on the **120**
practical rather than, as here, the fine arts.

80. *mimicked:* imitated. *mocked:* created forms *more*
beautiful than the merely natural. The artist does not
just imitate nature, but through the imagination has some
apprehension of the ideal world of pure forms. Cf. I.
747–8.

83–4. 'Women with child gazing on statues . . . bring
forth children like them—children whose features
reflect the passion of the gaze and the perfection of the
sculptured beauty; men, seeing, are consumed with
love' (Swinburne, 'Notes on the Text of Shelley,' *Complete Works* (Bonchurch edition), XV.361). Cf. IV.
412–14.

88. *wide-wandering stars:* planets, or possibly comets.

89. *lair:* position in the Zodiac.

112–3. Demogorgon's statement may seem contra- **121**
dictory to what has gone before. But it is dramatically
appropriate that his utterances should be cryptic.
Perhaps what he implies is: 'If you [Asia regarded here
in her human rather than her divine aspect] think, as
men do, in terms of a personal ruler, then you must conclude that the world, as things are, is governed by
Jupiter. But you should not think in these terms. The
world is governed by impersonal principles—Fate,
Time, Occasion, Chance, and Change—to which all
things are subject except Love.'

126–8. The destined hour arrives immediately after
Asia has been led to the insights expressed in 119–23.
Once she has come to the full realization of the power of
love (latent in herself and in everybody) then the hour
must come.

155. *night.* At II. III. 30 it was dawn, and again at the **123**
beginning of II. v it is dawn. It is night here only in the
sense that it seems to be so from the deep inhabited by
Demogorgon.

157. *An ivory shell.* Associates Asia with Venus, and

123 looks forward to II. v. 20–30. Asia is now to be revealed in her divine aspect, as Venus, as eternal love (there is here no distinction, as elsewhere in Shelley, between the lower Venus Pandemos and the higher Venus Urania).

124   ACT II. SCENE V

3. *warning.* ? That Jupiter is soon to be overthrown. The positive side of the coming revolution must coincide with the negative.

11–14. The light is emanating from Asia, just as in his transfiguration light emanated from Prometheus (II. i. 63–5). It is a release of light from within, a revelation of what they essentially are, rather than a flowing down upon them of light from above. See note on I. 177–8.

125 20–6. The sea-born Aphrodite, the Greek goddess of love and fertility, whose attributes were taken over by the Roman Venus, came to land on the island of Cythera floating on a shell.

21. *hyaline:* glassy sea.

26–7. See note on I. 766–7, p. 277.

32–7. Venus was the goddess not only of human love, but also of the generative principle active in nature.

126 48–71. It is clear from Asia's next lyric and from a passage in the MS, here omitted, that the voice in the air is that of Prometheus.

The lyric takes the progressive revelation of Asia to a point where words fail. The presence of that 'beauty unbeheld' of which the visible Asia is the 'shadow' is felt, but necessarily it can neither be seen nor expressed. Though the imagery of light is still used it is seen to be inadequate. The atmosphere is 'divinest,' yet it shrouds; others, who can be seen, are fair, but they are less than she whom none beholds; she can communicate something of her nature, for her voice is low and tender, and yet the liquid splendour of light folds her from sight.

The many l's in this lyric contribute to the effect in a characteristically Shelleyan way.

72–110. Asia's answer to Prometheus was added as an afterthought. It expresses their spiritual reunion. We

are not to see Prometheus' release until III. III. In a **126**
drama events must be shown successively. But we
should regard Asia's transfiguration, Jupiter's downfall,
Prometheus' release and reunion with Asia as aspects
of a single spiritual happening.

Reversing the direction taken by the child in Words-
worth's *Ode, Intimations of Immortality*, who daily
farther from the east must travel, they pass backwards
through time out of time into 'a diviner day,' the eternal
world.

108–10. These lines are awkward syntactically, but **127**
something would be lost—the sense of progressive
revelation—if the phrases were rearranged into a
normally-constructed sentence. The inhabitants of the
diviner day are shapes too bright to see—for those first
entering this realm; but Asia and Prometheus come to
rest there; now they can see; Asia sees that Prometheus
himself is a being of the same kind as these shapes; they
belong there among the divine beings who walk upon
the sea and chant.

ACT III. SCENE I   **128**

11. *pendulous:* hanging suspended over; cf. Shakespeare,
King Lear, III. IV. 69–70:
> 'Now all the plagues that in the pendulous air
> Hang fated o'er men's faults light on thy daughters!'

19. *fatal child.* See note on I. 371–4. By this time we
have been led to believe Jupiter's fall to be inevitable,
as a result of what has been done by Prometheus and
Asia, and we are unwilling to accept that it is due to
anything he himself does. Nevertheless he can be made
to co-operate in his own fall; and dramatic irony can
be produced by making him expect the opposite from
what happens.

It is not clear why he hopes that his union with
Thetis will produce a son who, clothed in the might of
Demogorgon, will subdue man. If he knows (42–4) that
the fruit of their union will be mightier than either of
them, why does he expect to be able to control this

128 mightier one ? And if he knows this why did he need to try to wrest the secret from Prometheus ? Dramatically it is enough that he displays proud over-confidence at the very moment of his downfall. By union with the 'bright image of eternity' (36) he hopes to be able to extend his tyranny eternally. It is the nature of the proud to overreach themselves, and so to contribute to their own downfall.

Mr C. E. Pulos (*PMLA*, LXVII (March 1952), 113–24) conjectured that the fatal child 'may . . . be a symbol of Malthusianism,' quoting in support Shelley's reference in the Preface to *The Revolt of Islam* to 'sophisms like those of Mr. Malthus, calculated to lull the oppressors of mankind into a security of everlasting triumph.' On this theory Jupiter represents here the ruling classes. He has found in Malthusianism a new reason for thinking that necessity, the might of Demogorgon, is on his side. One cannot be sure that Shelley had any such precise reference in mind; but doubtless he would agree that the ruling classes' confidence, confirmed by their understanding of Malthus, that their rule was in the nature of things was an example of the state of mind dramatized here in Jupiter. (See note on Preface, p. 264.)

25. *Idæan Ganymede:* a beautiful youth, from Mount Ida near Troy where his father Tros was king. He was caught up to Olympus by an eagle from Zeus, and became cup-bearer to the gods.

26. *dædal:* well-wrought, richly adorned. Dædalus was a legendary artist, craftsman, and inventor.

129 36. *Thetis:* daughter of Nereus, a sea-god. In the original story she became the wife of Peleus and mother of Achilles. The union is described in characteristically Shelleyan terms. Cf. *Epipsychidion* 115, where Emilia is 'an image of some bright eternity'; and *P.U.* II. I. 75–82 and 101–6, where Panthea and Ione experience a sense of dissolution, of loss of individual identity. The difference here is that Jupiter wishes to control, to possess, and so Thetis feels the dissolution as poisonous.

39–41. Cf. Lucan, *Pharsalia* IX. 762–88, where the body of the soldier Sabellus was dissolved, through the

bite of a serpent; and Ovid, *Metamorphoses* II. 308–9, **129**
where Semele, having begged Jupiter to appear in his full
splendour, was consumed by the flames. *seps:* a very
poisonous snake.

48. *Griding:* combines suggestions of 'piercing' (the
original sense) with 'making a grating sound' (a meaning
arising probably from the sound of the word).

52. *direr name.* This has been interpreted as 'Necessity.'
But perhaps no more is intended than the name Demo-
gorgon itself. In Boccaccio, Demogorgon is said to be so
fearsome that no-one dared pronounce his name.

54. It is difficult to see how Demogorgon, who calls
himself 'Eternity,' can really be the child of Jupiter. We
may understand either (1) 'I am to you in the same
relation as you were to your father Saturn, whom you
overthrew.' Or (2) This particular manifestation of
Demogorgon, of Necessity, of the law of cause and
effect, is the child of Jupiter in the sense that he has
acted in such a way as necessarily to bring about his own
downfall.

55–8. Demogorgon is not going to take the place of
Jupiter. The Promethean age is to be one of freedom
and love, and Love has been shown to be the one thing
not subject to Fate (II. IV. 119–20).

63. The struggle which must be imagined here could **130**
not be presented dramatically. It is described at the
beginning of the next scene.

72–4. The image of a snake in combat in the air with a
vulture or eagle appears elsewhere in Shelley, most
prominently in *The Revolt of Islam* I. XXVII–XXVIII, where
it is the snake which represents the Good. Here the image
is hardly appropriate to the scale of the conflict.

76. *whelm:* throw violently.

ACT III. SCENE II   **131**

Stage Direction. Atlantis. Legendary island west of the
straits of Gibraltar, supposed by Plato in *Critias* to be
the seat of an ideal commonwealth. *Ocean.* Oceanus was
originally god of the great river which was thought to

131 encircle the (flat) earth, and to be, through subterranean channels, the source of all rivers. Here Ocean is god of the sea, but retains traces of the river-god. He reclines by a great river, and his task is to replenish the sea, as rivers do (lines 40–2). River-gods were often represented in art with amphorae or other such vessels for pouring (here the 'urns' of line 42). *Apollo.* Greek god of the sun, of medicine, and of poetry.

11–17. The verb from line 10 has to be carried forward. 'Yes; he sank like an eagle, caught . . .' It is ironical that the eagle, traditionally the minister of Jupiter and here standing for him, is blinded by the lightning, the weapon of Jupiter.

18. *heaven-reflecting sea.* The dialogue between the sun-god and the ocean-god suggests the at-oneness between heaven and earth resulting from the downfall of Jupiter. Parallels between sea and earth (20–1), sea and sky (24–8), and images of reflection (18, 32) and music (33–4) give a sense of a universe which is harmonious and alive in all its parts.

132 27–8. A star above the tip of a new ('light-laden' may mean lightly-laden as well as laden with light) moon suggests a boat guided by an invisible ('sightless') pilot with a star as his crest.

37–9. It is now time for the sun to rise. All the events so far have taken place during a single dawn. They have all been aspects of a single happening.

49. *unpastured:* unfed, as in *Adonais* 238.

133   ACT III. SCENE III

1–6. Shelley follows tradition in making Hercules release Prometheus, but he gives little prominence to the incident, the interest for him being in the internal drama. We should imagine Hercules leaving at line 6.

23–5. Prometheus and his companions are here clearly differentiated from men. In his suffering and in his regeneration he has been to some extent, in Mrs Shelley's words, 'the emblem of the human race'; but in his essential nature he is a god. Wasserman's contention

(*Shelley's P.U.*, pp. 31–4) that Prometheus is the One **133**
Mind should be considered, but is not entirely convinc-
ing. It seems to derive not so much from what is said
and done in the poem as from outside sources, especially
Shelley's essay *On Life*: 'The existence of distinct in-
dividual minds . . . is . . . found to be a delusion. The
words, *I, you, they,* are not signs of any actual difference
subsisting between the assemblage of thoughts thus
indicated, but are merely marks employed to denote the
different modifications of the one mind. . . . I am but a
portion of it' (*Works*, VI. 196).

42–3. The mountain Enna and the river Himera are in **134**
Sicily, associated with the pastoral poets and with
Persephone.

49–53. Cf. Plato, *Symposium*, 209–12, Socrates' account
of Diotima's discourse on Love. The mind can rise
from the love of particular beautiful objects, which are
'phantoms,' shadows of the ideal 'forms' in the real
world, to contemplation of Beauty itself; so enlightened
it casts the light from that real world upon its own
productions, which then are themselves 'immortal.'
'What must be the life of him who dwells with and
gazes on that which it becomes us all to seek? Think you
not that to him alone is accorded the prerogative of
bringing forth, not images and shadows of virtue, for he
is in contact not with a shadow but with reality . . .'
(*Symposium*, 212, as translated by Shelley). Cf. *P.U.*
I. 747–9. Shelley takes ideas and images from Plato, but
makes his own synthesis and gives a different emphasis
—on art rather than on moral virtue, though for him art
was an instrument of moral good.

58–60. Man's artistic productions are the mediators of
love between him and Prometheus. Prometheus and his
companions are to live in a cave on earth (not, as II. v.
98–110 might have suggested, in an eternal life wholly
separated from the world of time), and they are to be
able to exchange love with men. By their nature they
belong to the eternal world, yet they are still to be in
contact with the temporal.

65–7. Proteus was a sea-god and a prophet, with the **135**

135 capacity to take on any number of different shapes. Because of this last characteristic he has been held to be emblematic of the primal matter, or in general of nature. (In *The Triumph of Life* 271, Shelley wrote of 'the Proteus shape of Nature.') So perhaps the gift, and the voice hidden in the shell, may suggest the potentialities which are latent in the material world and which can be made actual by love. The shell is appropriately associated with Asia in her capacity as the sea-born Venus. See Wasserman, *Shelley's P.U.*, pp. 179–80.

136 111. Repetition of I. 150. Shelley was always unwilling to commit himself to dogmatic statements about life after death. Earthly life is a veil which will be lifted at death to reveal reality. Whether the individual mind will then exist as a separate entity he did not claim to know. 115. *seasons mild*. Cf. I. 141–2, II. IV. 52–3 and Note to *Queen Mab* VI. 45–6. 'The north polar star to which the axis of the earth in its present state of obliquity points. It is exceedingly probable from many considerations that this obliquity will gradually diminish until the equator coincides with the ecliptic; the nights and days will then become equal on the earth throughout the year, and probably the seasons also. There is no great extravagance in presuming that the progress of the perpendicularity of the poles may be as rapid as the progress of intellect; or that there should be a perfect identity between the moral and physical improvement of the human species.' He gives reasons for supposing that within recorded time 'the obliquity of the earth's position has been considerably diminished.'

137 124. *And Thou!* The Earth here turns from Asia to Prometheus. *cavern*. It is difficult to decide whether this cave is the same as that described earlier in the scene by Prometheus. Mainly concerned with mental states, Shelley was perhaps insufficiently interested in making the surface meaning clear and consistent. Whether we envisage one or two caves does not much matter; in either case different things are being suggested about the new life inaugurated by Prometheus' release. In the first passage the emphasis was on art; in the second it is on the release from false religious ideas and on the **137** physical consequences.

127. *temple*. Shelley may have had in mind the temple at Delphi, where oracles were uttered by the priestess in a state of trance induced, it was thought in his day, by vapours rising from a fissure in the earth, over which her tripos was placed. In some accounts the original oracular deity at Delphi was Gaia. Grabo (*Newton among Poets*, pp. 189–90) has identified 'crimson air' (133) as nitrous gas, much written about by scientists of Shelley's time, who did many experiments to show the effects of different gases in stimulating plant growth. However that may be, the main meanings are clear: the earth's exhalations are now not poisonous, but growth-inducing, and the cave of the mind is possessed not by religious superstitions, which produce strife and madness, but by calm and happy thoughts.

148. *Spirit*. It is natural to suppose, in spite of the disagreement of some commentators, that this is the same as the Spirit of the Earth which appears in the next scene. Contradictions can be resolved by supposing the Spirit capable of appearing in different forms.

152–3. They are to be guided from the Indian Caucasus **138** to Greece, passing Nysa, legendary scene of the nurture of Bacchus (Dionysus).

165. *Praxitelean*. Praxiteles was a Greek sculptor, who lived in the fourth century B.C. Of two statues in Rome attributed to him, Shelley wrote: 'These figures combine the irresistible energy with the sublime and perfect loveliness supposed to have belonged to the divine nature' (letter to Peacock, 23 March 1819).

168–70. In the Athenian festival in honour of the fire-gods youths raced from the altar of Prometheus in the Academy to the city, carrying lighted torches, the object being to arrive first without letting the torch out. Shelley's contemporary Thomas Taylor commented: 'This custom . . . was intended to signify that he is the true conqueror in the race of life, whose rational part is not extinguished . . .' (Pausanias, *The Description of Greece*, trans. Taylor (1794), III. 252).

138 170–2. A reminder of the present condition of humanity, in which anyone who hopes for a better future may have to bear the torch of hope to the grave in apparent defeat, not being able to transmit it to anyone. We must now envisage the race as a relay-race.

174. *far goal of time*. This could be taken to mean that Prometheus has carried the torch through the night of time to a goal at the end of time, the entrance to eternity. But it could mean simply that he has carried it through a long period of time. See note to IV. 14.

175. Now that Prometheus' temple has been located in the Academy (168–70) it is plausible to say that this line means that his cave must be in the nearby sacred grove of Colonus, and to bring in a whole train of associations with the two places. See Hungerford, *Shores of Darkness*, pp. 197–204. The Academy was a park and gymnasium, where Socrates and Plato taught and where the latter founded his famous school. The grove at Colonus was sacred to the Eumenides or Furies, but Sophocles (*Oedipus at Colonus* 39–40, 52–5) says that Prometheus also dwelt there; Oedipus came there to achieve his final purgation and entry into a higher life. Now the Furies, connected with guilt and vengeance, have been banished, and Prometheus will possess the place wholly. His gifts to men will be put to the best use, in the harmonious development of all their faculties, as was the aim of Greek education. Men, released from the sense of guilt, will, like Oedipus, find peace. Those for whom classical references are meaningful may find the scene enriched by letting such associations flow in; but they are not essential to the understanding of it. If Shelley had wanted to stress a particular location he would surely have indicated it earlier in the scene and more clearly. By his words he creates his own temple and cave, and gives them meaning; by leaving the location rather uncertain he allows himself to gather in associations from Delphi as well as from the Academy and Colonus and perhaps elsewhere.

Spirit of the Earth. Grabo (*Newton among Poets*, pp. 118–31) interprets the Spirit as atmospheric electricity. With due caution one may conjecture that the green star (3) may have been suggested by the green starlike light given out by the Leyden jar, an early kind of battery; that the Spirit's guiding of the earth through heaven (5–6) may derive both from the intelligences which in medieval and Renaissance literature are said to animate the spheres and also from Adam Walker's speculations about the effect of the sun's energy (manifested as electricity - light - heat) in causing the earth's motions; and that some of the imagery in lines 10–15 may derive from contemporary accounts of the electrical properties of phosphorescence, fog, the *ignis fatuus*, shooting stars, and meteors. With even more caution one may acknowledge the possibility that lines 16–19 and 24–9 may owe something to speculations about atmospheric electricity, drawn from the earth in water vapour and returning to it in dew and being quiescent at noon on calm days (28–9).

Perhaps more helpful is Wasserman's contention (*Shelley's P.U.*, pp. 72–6) that the Spirit 'performs . . . the role of Eros, or Cupid, son of Venus.' Cupid was sometimes represented as a 'wanton,' 'wayward' winged child; his ancestry was uncertain (23), though he was often said to be the child of Venus (24–5); he carried a torch kindled by love to guide lovers to their meeting (III. III. 148–53). Also he was at times written of as a great cosmic principle, the most powerful of all gods, bringing harmony out of chaos by uniting the elements. This combination may help to explain the combination of playfulness with the suggestion of great powers in the treatment of the Spirit.

Probably Shelley used his knowledge both of contemporary scientific speculation and of mythology in creating the Spirit, but he did so in his own way. The Spirit is a new creation.

19. *dipsas:* a snake whose bite was supposed to cause a **139** raging thirst.

139 29. *work is none*. Grabo's explanation of this has been
mentioned in the preceding note; but it may be simpler
to follow Locock and say that at noon 'the Earth can see
its way through space without guidance,' and so the
Spirit can have a siesta.

141 79–83. The nightshade has ceased to be poisonous, and
the kingfishers have become vegetarians instead of
eating fish.

86–96. These lines are written in pencil in the MS, and
were perhaps inserted when Shelley thought of adding
Act IV, to which they look forward.

142 106–8. The MS has no punctuation at the ends of these
lines. Zillman puts a colon at the end of line 105 and a full
stop after *down*, so removing the uncertainty as to how to
take line 107. I follow 1820, leaving the reader to decide
how to construe the sentence. I would construe: 'As,
dizzy with delight, I floated down, my coursers, winnow-
ing the ... air with ... plumes, sought their birth-
place ....'

111–24. The state of the MS indicates that these lines
were probably an afterthought—as lines 121–3 acknow-
ledge, a doubtfully justifiable one. Probably Shelley
wanted to work in a description of things he had seen in
Rome. In the Vatican Museum, in a domed room
specially made for it, there is—and was in 1819—a lively
sculpture of a *biga*, a two-horse chariot drawn by horses
linked together by a serpent with a head at each end
(an 'amphisbænic snake'). Around it are sculptures of
gods and other figures. Shelley probably had in mind
this room and also the Pantheon, which, unlike the
Sala della Biga, is a Temple and open to the sky. See
D. Reiman, 'Roman Scenes in *Prometheus Unbound*,
III. IV,' *Philological Quarterly*, XLV (Jan. 1967),
69–78.

143 130–204. Any representation of an ideal state is bound
to seem unrealistic and too easily attained. Shelley is
showing a vision of an ideal, not prophesying what he
thought likely to happen in the foreseeable future. Not
long afterwards he wrote *A Philosophical View of Reform*,
in which he advocated certain practical reforms, many of

which have been put into practice—reforms which were **143**
intended to improve, but not to abolish, the system of
government. He knew well enough that external
authority could not be abolished until man became 'king
over himself.' So in the first part of this passage (130–
63) he emphasizes the inner change within men and
women, and only then (164–96) the dismantling of
institutions.

136. Dante, *Inferno* III. 9.

147. A vampire is the spirit of a dead man which
comes from the grave, sometimes in the form of an
animal, and sucks the blood of sleepers so that they die,
and perhaps in their turn become vampires. According
to peasant superstition suicides were especially prone
to return from the grave as vampires; so the comparison
is particularly appropriate for 'a soul self-consumed.'

163. *nepenthe:* see II. IV. 61, and note.   **144**

170. *obelisks.* In Rome there were many Egyptian
obelisks among the palaces and tombs of the Roman
conquerors of Egypt. Reiman, in the article cited above,
maintains that Shelley was thinking of the hieroglyphics
on these obelisks, which were not in his day understood
and which would therefore form a good image for a
once-powerful faith now incomprehensible and dis-
regarded. He is surely right in thinking that Shelley
was using his experience of Rome, where so many
relics of past faiths are gathered, but it is not clear that
hieroglyphics could properly be described as 'monstrous
and barbaric shapes' (168). This phrase would more
naturally apply to carvings of gods and goddesses in
various preternatural forms.

172. Locock follows the MS in putting a comma after
'conquerors' (there is a colon in 1820) and inserts a
full-stop at the end of the line, where Shelley frequently
omitted punctuation. It is the Roman palaces and tombs
which are mouldering, while the older obelisks are
unworn. 'These' in the next line refers back to the
'shapes' (168).

180. *shapes.* The reference is more general than in line
168. These shapes are the emblems of all the tyrannies

144 and false religions associated with the reign of Jupiter and now overthrown. Shelley proliferates subordinate clauses in this passage (and elsewhere), perhaps unduly separating 'shapes' from the verb ('frown', line 189) of which it is the subject.

190. *veil*. Cf. III. III. 113 where life itself is a veil which is to be lifted at death to enable men to see the real world. Here, however, the veil is torn aside not by death, but during earthly life. What men in their state of delusion call life is not reality, but a painted veil projected from their own minds. The veil here represents the barriers which men create between themselves and the truth and which they could remove. More usually it represents the barriers which in life necessarily exist between men and the knowledge of ultimate reality. Shelley was both a reformer, wishing to guide men towards an ideal society on earth, and a visionary, yearning for a state of union and freedom beyond anything which could be attainable in any earthly society. The two sometimes get in each other's way. In the lines which follow we find the visionary beating against the bars of the paradise that the reformer has imagined.

145 193–8. I follow, in the main, the punctuation of the MS, that of 1820 being much lighter with no stops at the ends of lines 194 and 197. The MS punctuation gives great emphasis to the repeated 'but man.' Man is still man; he has not passed into any other condition; his true nature has been revealed.

198–204. If man is not exempt from chance and death and mutability it is difficult to see that he rules them like slaves and is free from pain. If not passionless he would surely, for instance, feel pain over the death of a loved one. Shelley the visionary knew that even after man had freed himself from all the evils he could free himself from he would remain subject to irksome limitations, his highest aspirations unfulfilled; but Shelley the reformer, the main writer of this scene, was unwilling to acknowledge this.

It was curious, though characteristic, to end the scene, originally the whole poem, in the conditional mood.

204. Under this line in the MS is written PROMETHEUS, **145**
which led one commentator to wonder whether Shelley
may have intended at one time to give his hero the
closing speech.

ACT IV

Some critics have thought this Act an excrescence, but
C. S. Lewis wrote: 'It does not add to, and therefore
corrupt, a completed structure; it gives structure to that
which, without it, would be imperfect' ('Shelley, Dryden
and Mr Eliot'; see Critical Extracts, pp. 355-6). Perhaps
Lewis was right in saying that Shelley's error was not in
adding the fourth Act but in not seeing that, having
done so, he could have shortened the third. The fourth
Act is the most purely Shelleyan part of the drama. In the
first Act the influence of Aeschylus is felt, and in all the
first three that of Milton (for instance, in Jupiter's
speech at the beginning of III. 1) and of Shakespeare.
Unseen Spirits: spirits of Air and of Earth (57).

14. This appears to mean that Time itself is at an end, **146**
and that the state we are to hear celebrated in this act
is a timeless eternity. But this is contradicted by what
follows. New hours come in; spirits say that their
singing 'shall build' (153); moon and earth still circle
the sun; at the end the possibility of the return of evil
is envisaged; time still seems to exist in the Promethean
day. Shelley may not always have drawn a clear line
between the millennium, an ideal earthly existence, and
the apocalypse, the final conquest of death and of time;
but on the whole we must take this Act as a celebration
of the former of these. So in the context we must under-
stand this first lyric as an elegy only over the past hours.
What we are to see is a state in which time is appre-
hended in a new way (see note to 105-10 below), not
one in which there is no time at all. See Milton Wilson,
Shelley's Later Poetry, Chap. VIII, and Wasserman,
Shelley's P.U., Chap. v.

34. *One:* Prometheus. Grabo (*Interpretation,* pp. 126–7)

146 would have us think also of the One, in the neo-Platonic system the ineffable, ultimate power. It is only in so far as they are emanations of the One that lesser beings have power over time.

147 47. *ye:* the new Hours.

57–80. The new Hours come in after the old have gone, and must, one would think, represent successive moments of time; yet they have existed already 'below the deep,' they appear all together, and they weave a mystic dance. Perhaps two conceptions of time are suggested—as successive moments, and as a whole existing within a timeless eternity. But one cannot be sure that Shelley intended anything of this kind. He was using a common motif from mythology. The Horae or Hours, often representing the seasons, were constantly depicted as joining in a dance, sometimes with the Graces. Both Horae and Graces were often shown as attendants on Venus.

148 61. *An hundred ages:* ? = generations = 3000 years, the time of Prometheus' bondage.

149 81. *Spirits:* presumably the same as the Spirits who consoled Prometheus in Act I.

82. *Wrapped . . . veils.* A characteristically Shelleyan mixture of sense impressions.

93–104. The stress is on unity—on the mind (not minds) of humankind, which is an ocean, a single whole. Shelley shows a vision rather than preaches a doctrine; but the bent of his mind was towards a Neoplatonic rather than a Christian heaven.

150 105–10. The passage of the Hours is delayed by Love and by Wisdom. In moments of love and in contemplation of wisdom men are so absorbed as to be heedless of time.

Cf. Note to *Queen Mab* VIII 203–7: 'Time is our consciousness of the succession of ideas in our mind. Vivid sensation, of either pain or pleasure, makes the time seem long, as the common phrase is, because it renders us more acutely conscious of our ideas. If a mind be conscious of an hundred ideas during one minute, by the clock, and of two hundred during another, the latter of these spaces would actually occupy so much greater **150** extent in the mind as two exceed one in quantity. If, therefore, the human mind, by any future improvement of its sensibility, should become conscious of an infinite number of ideas in a minute, that minute would be eternity. I do not hence infer that the actual space between the birth and death of a man will ever be prolonged; but that his sensibility is perfectible, and that the number of ideas which his mind is capable of receiving is indefinite.'

107. *loose*. Locock has 'sliding.' 'Sliding' is written above 'loose' in the MS, and 'loose' is underlined. Shelley sometimes used underlining for *stet*, and 'loose' is metrically better.

111–16. The outward-looking and the inner powers of the mind work in harmony. Eye and ear look out from temples high and what they report is converted within into sculpture and poetry; conversely the springs of inspiration within the mind are necessary for the upward flight of science.

116. *dædal*. See note on III. 1. 26, p. 294.

126. *beyond our eyes:* beyond the range of our vision.

139. *the bound:* of the earth's shadow, the 'pyramid of **151** night' (444).

140. *clips:* embraces.

206–8. The new moon sets with the sun. This leads on **154** to the picture of the new moon on sunset clouds in 214–17.

213. *Regard like:* look like, a rare intransitive use.

219–30. This is mainly visual, giving an impression of the moonlight—suggestive perhaps of sterility, of a frozen world, but at the same time strangely beautiful— in contrast to the varying colours of earth. But it probably owes something to scientific speculation as well as to observation. The whiteness is due to the absence of an atmosphere to refract light (cf. I. 82–3). Lines 225–30 probably refer to 'dark rays' discovered by the astronomer Herschel and described by Davy, whom Shelley read. These are the rays below red in the spectrum, which convey heat but are invisible, produce 'fire' but no

154 'brightness.' Davy speculated about the possible emanation of such rays from the moon.

The thinness of the new moon and the emphasis on whiteness may suggest potentiality. Life and colour are to be added as a result of union with the Earth. The potential is to become actual. See D. J. Hughes, 'Potentiality in *Prometheus Unbound,*' *Studies in Romanticism,* XI (1963), 107–26; reprinted in *Shelley: Modern Judgements,* ed. R. B. Woodings (1968).

155 236–61. Shelley wrote in *A Refutation of Deism*: 'Matter ... is not inert. It is infinitely active and subtle' (*Works,* VI. 50). He knew of the speculations of Dalton, Davy, and others about the structure of matter. A piece of matter was already coming to be thought of not as a solid and inert lump, but as composed of particles in constant motion round their own axes and round each other or both, and with spaces between them. So here the orb, which symbolizes the properties of the earth, is at once one seemingly solid sphere moving with solemn slowness and also it is seen to be made up of many particles whirling with unimaginable speed round each other and their own axes. Though in parts fanciful the description conveys a sense of the enormous energy in matter more than a merely scientific account would do.

246: *inter-transpicuous:* transparent.

256–61. A characteristic mingling of different senses moving towards an experience beyond the sensuous. Again not without a scientific basis. Walker wrote of the correspondence, which had been pointed out by Newton, between the width of spectrum occupied by the seven colours and the frequency-differences between musical notes.

156 269. *mocking:* echoing, imitating; as in *Alastor* 425.

270–87. Grabo (*Newton among Poets,* pp. 144–8) equated the 'azure fire' with blue electric flame and interpreted the whole passage as dealing with the Aurora Borealis and electricity in general. But primarily the piercing light coming from the Spirit's forehead suggests how mind guided by love (as we have seen, the Spirit has some of the attributes of Eros/Cupid) and released from the restraints of tyranny is going to lay bare the **156** secrets of the earth and use them for beneficent purposes. See lines 418–24 and note.

272. *tyrant-quelling myrtle.* Myrtle was used by the Greeks to crown victorious warriors. There is probably a reference to Harmodius and Aristogeiton, whose exploit in striking down the tyrant Hipparchus was celebrated in a song with the refrain 'I'll wreathe the sword in myrtle bough.' Here the light of the mind is the weapon which will end tyranny and ignorance.

273. *Embleming . . . now:* goes with 'beams' in the next line.

281. *Valueless:* not able to be valued. Shelley uses other such words in a similar way—e.g. sightless, viewless.

284–7. The sea is fed from springs within the earth, and the snow is produced from water vapour sucked up from the sea by the sun.

287–318. In the Promethean age mind will uncover not only the secrets of the earth's physical structure but also of human history and of prehistory. Shelley is looking backwards in time and ever deeper down into the earth. 'Over' in lines 302 and 308 is presumably being used in a sense for which we would normally say 'under.' The emphasis on weapons and on emblems of a hierarchical society among the relics of the human past (287–93) is no doubt intended to imply what is to be the different character of the new age. The next lines (296–302) probably derive from recent speculations about evolution, such as Shelley read in the works of Erasmus Darwin, and imply the possible continuity of human and pre-human life. In lines 302–14 Shelley is using recent geological discoveries, such as are contained in James Parkinson's *Organic Remains* (1804–11). See H. W. Piper, *The Active Universe* (1962), pp. 188–9 for further demonstration that this passage derives from scientific discovery and speculation, not from mere fancy.

The whole passage may be compared with Keats's *Endymion* III. 119–41, which Shelley read about the time he was writing this Act.

157 319. *The Earth*. Is this the same as the Earth in Act I
and in III. IV? Clearly not; that was a Hellenic goddess,
the Earth-mother; whereas here Earth is brother and
lover to the Moon. Is it then the Spirit of the Earth
of the early parts of this scene and of III. IV? More
nearly so; for the prophecy in III. IV. 86–90 is now
realized. But this Earth does not speak like the 'wanton'
child of the earlier scenes. We could answer that the
Spirit has grown to maturity through the experience of
love. But probably we are looking for a kind of con-
sistency we should not expect to find. Earth can meaning-
fully be treated as mother in relation to the creatures she
nourishes, as child in relation to Asia, where Asia repre-
sents the divine power of generation, as feminine in
relation to the sun and as masculine in relation to the
moon. Rossetti sums up: 'Earth and Moon, in their
large general character as members of the solar system,
are the essential speakers; but represented on the spot,
visibly and emotionally, by the Spirit of the Earth, a
boy, and the Spirit of the Moon, an infant girl, who are
touched into a kind of choral consonance with those
more potent entities.'

The earth's giving life to the moon is a myth devised
to symbolize and exemplify the new harmony in the
universe in the Promethean day, and is probably not
intended to be taken too seriously as a practical possi-
bility; but the substratum of scientific fact used in the
working out of the myth gives it a little extra solidity.
The moon is cold and lifeless because it has no, or little,
atmosphere and cannot therefore retain its heat. If, as
Erasmus Darwin (*Botanic Garden* II. 82, note) thought
might happen, an atmosphere could be generated there,
the heat radiated to it by sun and earth could be re-
tained, clouds would be formed and life might become
possible (356–69). The idea that such an atmosphere
might be produced by an increase in heat coming from
the earth is in accordance with Walker's theories as to
how the earth's own atmosphere was obtained—the
materials for it being drawn from the earth by the sun's
heat (*Philosophy*, pp. 225–39). Here, as in other passages,

a characteristically Shelleyan synthesis is produced by a **157**
mixture of new scientific speculation with ancient myth.
For treatments of the Golden Age, of the deterioration
of the earth as a result of the Fall or some other catas-
trophe, of the possible renovation of the earth through
the coming of the Messiah or some other Saviour, see
Virgil's Fourth Eclogue, *Genesis* 3: 17–19, *Isaiah* 11:
1–9 and 65: 17–25, *Romans* 7, Milton, *Paradise Lost* x.
668–78, *Queen Mab* VI. 39–46 and note; VIII. 58–68.

The different metrical forms are appropriate to
express 'the deep music of the rolling earth' and the
clear 'under-notes' of the moon.

369. Cf. I. 766–7 and note, p. 277. **159**

377. *has arisen.* The subject is still 'it' (Love).

379–80. Thought becomes creative only when impelled
by Love. 'Unremoved forever' presumably means
hitherto never removed.

385. 'Which' refers to Love, 'his' to man. **160**

388–93. The syntax is irregular. 'Hate, etc. leave man,
just as his sickness leaves a leprous child, who follows
a beast to healing springs and then, when it goes home
and its mother fears . . . .' One expects a concluding
verb of which the child should be the subject, but the
author has transferred his interest to the mother. One
might argue that the broken syntax appropriately
reflects the mother's agitation.

Shelley is using the story of King Bladud, the legend-
ary founder of Bath.

394–9. Men will control the elements as the sun by his
gravitational pull prevents the planets from flying into
space because of centrifugal force. Here again Shelley
conveys a more vivid sense of tremendous forces held
in balance than a merely factual description would do.

408. *A spirit.* In apposition to 'his will.' Man's will is
bad when it guides, when man is self-willed, but is
mighty when it acts in obedience to love, in accordance
with man's own true nature (cf. line 401). Shelley is not
preaching an easy anarchism. Freedom is attained only
by the obedience of the lower to the higher.

414. Cf. II. IV. 83–4. Looking on beautiful works of **161**

161 art mothers will form beautiful bodies to clothe the souls of their children.

415–17. Cf. II. iv. 72–3.

418–23. Not mere fantasy, but a prophecy of scientific advances that have happened. *lightning*. The energy which is manifested in lightning was already coming under man's control in his use of electricity. *the abyss:* the depths of the sea, or of the earth, or both?

See Hogg, *Life*, I. 59–63 for Shelley's early speculations about what man might be able to do by his increasing control over nature—e.g. greatly to increase the fertility of the soil by chemicals, to devise new means of heating houses, to make much greater use of electricity, to master the art of navigating the air. Hogg treats Shelley with amused irony, but time has turned the irony against Hogg.

436. Locock follows the MS in printing a dash (rather than a full-stop, as in 1820 and most editions) at the end of this line. Earth's sentence is unfinished, and we cannot be sure how he would have applied the simile— perhaps to the Moon (as the warmth of the sun has dissolved the cold dewdrop to vapour so the new warmth on the moon has dissolved its snow into fertilizing clouds). But the Moon interrupts and applies it to the Earth (as the cloud of vapour is derived from the earth and is lighted gloriously by the sun, so the light which enfolds the earth comes from his own joy and heaven's smile).

162 444. *pyramid of night:* the shadow of the earth cast by the sun, a cone of darkness surrounded by light (449). Cf. Pliny, *Natural History*, II. 7 'The figure of this shade is like that of a pyramid or an inverted top; and the moon enters it only near its point, and it does not exceed the height of the moon, for there is no other star which is obscured in like manner.'

447. *As*. For grammar, but not for sound, 'like' would be better.

163 470–2. Primarily conveys the emotional tone, but also has a basis in fact. The moon's orbit is irregular and its axis librates ('maniac-like'); it always turns the same face to the earth ('insatiate bride'). *maniac-*

like: in a state of rapture, completely possessed by love. **163**

474. *Agave:* daughter of Cadmus, and a priestess of Bacchus.

485–94. These lines are not in the MS, and are probably a late addition.

493–502. The at-oneness of Earth and Moon is expressed by the Earth completing the quatrain begun by the Moon, and then, for the first time, addressing her directly. Up to now the Earth has seemed absorbed in his own joy, and has paid little apparent attention to the Moon's speeches. (Rossetti thought that lines 493–4 belong to the Moon. Even if he is right—his arguments are not convincing—the main point is still valid.)

499–502. The colloquy of Earth and Moon ends with **164** these impressive, but strange and difficult, lines. 'Thy crystal accents' mingles sight and sound, giving a voice to the moonlight; 'pierce' adds the sense of touch. 'Caverns' suggests isolation. The Earth's love (man's love in general ?) has been shown so far as rather egotistical, self-absorbed—hence potentially self-destructive; whereas the Moon's has been more self-giving. Now their love is to be really mutual, a true mingling of male and female.

519–53. Demogorgon interpenetrates all nature. Each constituent of the universe answers him in a line which completes a stanza. Thus the metrical structure helps to convey a sense of the unity of all things when related to the power which animates them.

520–1. Cf. I. 766–7 and note, and IV. 369.

526. *birth:* race; a Graecism. **165**

534–8. Even the brightest beams of verse are inadequate to express the state of the happy dead. Perhaps they have become one with the universe; perhaps, like the mortal men they have left on earth, they still experience individual existence, subject to change.

539. *elemental Genii:* the elements, which are the constituents of all things, from the human brain to the lowest forms of existence, from the centre of the earth out to the farthest stars.

547. *feed:* substituted for 'throng' (printed in 1820) in **166**

313

166 the MS. More characteristic of Shelley and less common-place than 'throng.'

552. *dim night:* presumably the dim night of time *preceding* the immortal day of eternity.

555. *Earth-born's:* i.e. Prometheus'. *spell.* Since spell was used earlier (I. 61, 184) for Prometheus' curse, it has been alleged that this means that Prometheus did not really renounce his curse, which has in fact now been fulfilled. Perhaps 'spell' here should be connected with 'spells' in line 568 (charms, magically powerful instruments) and not with the curse at all. If a reference back to the curse is intended it must be to the endurance and hope expressed in it rather than to the hatred and desire for revenge which Prometheus did renounce.

167 565–8. During the reign of Jupiter a snake-like Doom lay coiled under the Eternal's throne (II. III. 96)—the potentiality of the downfall of Jupiter and the release of Prometheus. So now in the Promethean day the potentiality of the return of evil exists. The general meaning is clear, but it is difficult to see just how the image works. Up to 'should free/The serpent' we are led to envisage a serpent struggling to be free and in the end escaping from the 'infirm hand' of Eternity. The rest of line 567 makes us see a serpent trying to coil himself round Eternity. Perhaps one can say that the serpent by coiling himself round Eternity disarms her and so frees himself. Shelley was using the traditional image of 'the snake that girds eternity' (*The Revolt of Islam*, IV. IV)—that was indeed often an emblem of eternity itself (as in *The Dæmon of the World* 100)—and giving it a new meaning not easily imposed upon it. He was probably influenced by the first book of Boccaccio's *De Genealogia Deorum*, which he had already used for his portrayal of Demogorgon. After treating of Demogorgon Boccaccio goes on: 'Next of Eternity, whom the ancients supposed to be the companion of Demogorgon . . . . What Claudius Claudianus has written concerning her . . . may be quoted: "Far off, unknown, inconceivable by our minds, hardly to be approached by the gods themselves, is a cave of immense age, the hoary mother of the years, who gives forth the periods of time and recalls them into **167** her vast bosom. A serpent surrounds the cave, who consumes all things with quiet power; his scales perpetually grow afresh and, with his mouth turned back, he is devouring his own tail, thus in his course tracing his beginning." '

OTHER POEMS   **168**

These poems were written between the autumn of 1819 and the early summer of 1820. Some are slight occasional poems, some are among Shelley's finest works. All help to show his skill in handling a wide variety of different forms and metres.

Two of his main preoccupations at that time were:

(1) Politics. News, which reached him at the end of August, of the 'Peterloo Massacre' sharpened his already keen interest in the struggle between the conservative Governments which were dominant in most of Europe and the forces making for liberty. A peaceful demonstration of workers at Manchester was charged by mounted troops, six people being killed and many injured. He thought that the Government would try to establish 'a military and judicial despotism,' that the people were 'nearly in a state of insurrection,' and that civil war might be near (*Letters*, 3 Nov. 1819, 6 Nov. 1819). He wrote several poems, the most important of which is *The Mask of Anarchy*, in which he exhorted his countrymen to stand firm in the struggle, but to avoid violence. Soon afterwards he wrote his prose tract *A Philosophical View of Reform*. At the beginning of the following year the Spanish liberals rose against their reactionary king Ferdinand VII, and it seemed for a time that they would succeed in obtaining advances towards constitutional rule. Shelley's interest in these events is expressed directly in *An Ode* and *Ode to Liberty*, and underlies other poems, especially *Ode to the West Wind*.

(2) Poetry. The reading that autumn of an attack upon him in the *Quarterly Review* renewed his aware-

168 ness of his lack of outward success as a poet. His poems were being read by very few, appreciated by hardly any; and he was depressed about this not only because of a natural desire for appreciation, but also because he hoped to achieve practical effects through his poetry by acting on men's imaginations, to contribute in his own way to the struggle going on around him. He knew that in the last year he had written better poetry than ever before, but was it worth while if he was going to remain unread? See *An Exhortation, Ode to the West Wind* and *To a Skylark*.

A third, more private, facet of his life may have affected some of the poems, though it is not dealt with directly—his relationship with his wife. She had been greatly distressed by the deaths of their two children; and he felt at times that she had withdrawn from him into a remote melancholy. In November a son was born to them, and the situation probably improved; but there are indications that he still felt a coldness in her, an inability to give the full sympathy which he sought. Something of this may underlie, even if unconsciously, *The Sensitive Plant*; but the autobiographical element should not be overstressed.

In the best poems the personal and local elements are caught up in the larger themes, in the vision of a realm of 'love, and beauty, and delight' beyond this life of 'shadows.'

THE SENSITIVE PLANT

Written at Pisa early in 1820. Shelley may have been stimulated to write it in part by frequent visits at this time to the garden of his friends in Pisa, the Masons; and it is possible that the memory of a secluded garden which he and Hogg stumbled on during a walk near Oxford (Hogg, *Life*, I. 110–8) may have revived in him. On one level we can read the poem simply as a description of a beautiful garden, of the lady who tended it, of her death and its decay in winter. But it is not just

an ordinary garden. It is an 'undefilèd Paradise' (58) **168**
where flowers of 'every clime' grow 'in perfect prime'
(39–40). It has something in common with such paradisal
gardens as the Garden of Alcinous (Homer, *Odyssey*,
VII), Spenser's Garden of Adonis (*Faerie Queene*, III.
VI) and the garden in his *Muiopotmos*, and Milton's
Garden of Eden (*Paradise Lost*, IV); but, unlike them,
it is not abstracted from the normal world of change. It
images a certain psychological state, a fragile one, rather
like that suggested in Blake's *Songs of Innocence*.

The four-foot lines are made up, until the Conclusion,
of anapaests (xx/) and iambs (x/), usually two of each
to the line. Shelley seems to have been especially fond
at this time of using anapaests. See *A Vision of The Sea*,
The Cloud, *An Ode*.

See Wasserman, *The Subtler Language*, chap VII;
Bloom, *Shelley's Mythmaking*, chap. VI; Baker, *Shelley's
Major Poetry*, pp. 195–202.

PART I. 1. *Sensitive Plant*. A species of mimosa is called
by this name because its leaves curl away from the touch.
It has usually been taken to represent the specially
sensitive person with his aspirations towards an unattain-
able perfection. Wasserman, however, says that it is not
a special kind of man, but man. 'The Garden, exclusive
of the Sensitive Plant, is the total animate universe as it
is experienced by man, the Sensitive Plant' (*The Subtler
Language*, pp. 257–8). Perhaps one can say that it
images a state of being, shared to some extent by all
men, but more strongly experienced by some.

An autobiographical interpretation has been sug-
gested. Shelley himself is the Sensitive Plant, and he
finds his emotional life shrivelling as a result of the
withdrawal from him of his wife (death of the lady of
the garden) during the time of intense melancholy she
suffered after the deaths of their two children. This
interpretation is more convincing if put in more general
terms. The sensitive (or any) person flourishes and has
power of vision when living in an atmosphere of love,
but shrivels and sees things as hostile and ugly when
love is withdrawn.

168 16. *like the voice and the instrument.* The scent of the turf provides a background for the scents of the particular flowers as the musical instrument provides an accompaniment for the singer.

18–20. Narcissus pined away from love of his own reflection in water.

169 27–8. A characteristic mingling of different senses.

37. *tuberose; tube-rose* (1820). Probably pronounced as a disyllable by Shelley.

170 54. *fabulous asphodels:* the flowers which bloom eternally in the other world, in the Elysian fields.

72–3. In the MS there are only commas after 'all' and 'giver.' 'Wanted' could mean both 'was lacking in' and 'desired.' The Sensitive Plant was lacking in beauty which all the other plants had; for that very reason it desired it more, and so loved more than those plants who possessed and could give it could do.

72–8. These lines follow closely *Symposium* 200–1, in which Socrates persuades Agathon to agree that 'Love loves that which he wants but possesses not,' and that 'Love wants and does not possess beauty.'

172 PART II. 1. *a Power.* Shelley wrote to Leigh Hunt (19 June 1822): 'The Williams's are with us.—Williams one of the best fellows in the world, and Jane his wife a most delightful person—whom we all agree is the exact antitype of the lady I described in the Sensitive plant—though this must have been a *pure anticipated cognition* as it was written a year before I knew her.' On one level the lady is an idealized portrait of a woman, one who spreads about her an atmosphere of love and sympathy in which sensitive souls can flourish. She has also something in common with Milton's Eve, with Spenser's Venus in the garden of Adonis, and with Shelley's own Asia (*P.U.* I. 827–32). She is to the flowers as 'God is to the starry scheme.' For Shelley God was the animating spirit of the universe rather than the creator and father. On one level the lady may be thought of as a manifestation of that Spirit in its operations in the natural world.

5–8. Cf. Plato, *Republic* 403: (Socrates speaking) 'My own belief is, not that the good body by any bodily

excellence improves the soul, but, on the contrary, that **172**
the good soul, by her own excellence, improves the body
as far as this may be possible.'

10. *meteors.* Any phenomenon or appearance in the
atmosphere could be referred to as a 'meteor.' More
specifically the word was used for any luminous body
seen moving through the atmosphere. Many meteors
were thought to be exhaled from the earth rather than
to descend on it. Cf. *P.U.* II. ii. 79, II. iii. 3. Here the
bright flowers are 'meteors,' exhalations from the earth,
stars of this earthly Paradise. The association of flower
and star is common in Shelley. The flowers of earth
manifest in transient form the Spirit which is mani-
fested in more permanent form in the 'immortal' stars
(*Adonais* 256). It seems that the lady is visited 'while
the stars were awake' by a bright Spirit from Heaven;
during the day, while the veil of daylight conceals stars
and Spirit, the transient flowers bloom about her. Like
other such figures in Shelley she has relationships with
both worlds.

49. *ephemeris:* more commonly 'ephemerid'; the Mayfly, **174**
a slender, quick-moving insect, which lives in its winged
state for a very short time.

60. *she died!* Her death at the end of summer connects
her with the cycle of the seasons, but there is no indica-
tion that she is to revive in the next spring; so we cannot
think of her simply as a symbol of the spirit of animation
in nature. She is a particular woman, a particular mani-
festation of the spirit of animation.

A psychological change may be suggested—the passing
away of the poet's vision, or his power to see the world
'apparelled in celestial light'; or, more generally, the
necessary passage from Blake's state of Innocence to
Experience.

PART III. Depicts autumn and winter, decay and death.
Uglier and coarser things have greater power of survival
in these conditions. Suggests a state in which the vision
of Innocence has been lost, a state in which coarser
natures flourish more than the more sensitive.

1-4. The flowers lose their brightness, like stars

319

174 dimmed by moonlight or like waves at night before the rising of the moon.

176 66–9. Cancelled in the MS.

177 78. *unctuous*: ? causing an oily appearance. *meteors.* The word is being used in its widest possible sense, for any phenomenon in the atmosphere. See note on Part II. 10 above.

82. *forbid:* forbidden; perhaps used in the old sense 'laid under a curse, interdicted.' Cf. Shakespeare, *Macbeth* I. III. 21. 'Choppy finger' in line 91 also brings to mind this scene from *Macbeth*.

178 113. *griff:* claw.

Conclusion. The poet does not know whether the Sensitive Plant revives in the next spring. We are left with the feeling that it does not. In any case the consolation that is offered in face of mutability is not the cyclical return of spring. In the natural world mutability reigns. Beauty is transient; or rather man's limited power to apprehend it is so. But glimpses of love and beauty, even though they pass, are glimpses of permanent realities which cannot pass away. The theme was to be more fully and maturely embodied in *Adonais.*

180   A VISION OF THE SEA

Locock, considering this poem inferior to the others in the volume, maintained that Shelley's note 'Pisa Apr. 1820' in the Harvard MS notebook establishes only the date when it was written into the book, and that it may have been composed as early as 1816. But most commentators see no strong reason for supposing it to have been written long before the transcript. It can be linked with *The Sensitive Plant* in that in both two contrary visions are juxtaposed. The child, smiling and playing in the midst of the storm, delighted even with the tigers, is in a state of innocence (cf. *S.P.* I and II); the mother confronts the hostility and violence of nature, the terror of the world of experience, in more extreme forms than are shown in *S.P.* III. But one cannot say to what extent the poem was intended to be symbolic. It **180** reads rather as if it were the product of a nightmare.

The lines are made up normally of four anapaests, the first foot quite often and others occasionally being shortened to iambs.

5. *She*. The woman not mentioned again until line 66. We only gradually arrive at a clear picture of what is happening and of who is present. The rather confusing method of narration may be intended to convey the terror of the scene and the agitation of the speaker.

6. *ruining:* falling headlong (a Latinism). This MS reading is preferable to 1820's 'raining.' The waterspouts had seemed to be sustaining the heavens, but now they are bending and falling like the walls of a ruined building.

38–9. Presumably referring to the six members of the **181** crew who had been killed by lightning (61–3).

47. The sun is directly overhead at noon, as in *The Ancient Mariner*, lines 108–9. It is interesting, though not to its advantage, to compare this poem with Coleridge's, which Shelley had read; but one cannot say with confidence that he was influenced by it.

102–4. Locock puts a semi-colon after 'storm', and a **182** comma after 'waste'.

128–35. Cf. *P.U.* III. II. 18–34, where the picture of **183** the sea reflecting the calm of heaven follows an account of struggle, whereas here the struggle continues after the stilling of the sea.

139. *sunbows:* prisms, like small rainbows, formed by **184** sunlight on spray.

148. *centipede*. The very curious, surrealist image of sounds crawling over the ocean like centipedes perhaps supports the conjecture that this poem may be the product of a nightmare. If so it will be vain to seek in it for any consciously intended symbolism.

169. There is no evidence to show why Shelley left this poem unfinished. It may be that he was dissatisfied with it, as he well might be; but why then did he publish it? It may be that he could not bear to describe the probably disastrous dénouement. 'Here I was

184 obliged to leave off, overcome by thrilling horror,' he wrote at the end of his fragmentary essay on dreams (*Works*, VII. 67).

185   ODE TO HEAVEN

Dated 'Florence, December 1819' in the Harvard MS notebook. There is also a transcript in the Bodleian.

As usual in Shelley 'Heaven' is used in its literal meaning as the firmament, the whole expanse of space in which earth and the stars are set and which appears to us as a dome.

First Spirit. Celebrates the apparent eternity of Heaven, which continues to sustain the varying forms of life that come to being within it and pass away.

21. *that Power:* primarily the sun, with perhaps some suggestion of the being (God, the Good, the One as it is present in nature) which is manifested in it. Cf. Shelley's *Hymn of Apollo*.

> I am the eye with which the Universe
> Beholds itself and knows itself divine.

Cf. Plato, *Republic* VI. 508. The sun 'is that light which makes the eye to see perfectly and the visible to appear. ... The power which the eye possesses is a sort of effluence from the sun.' The sun 'is he whom I call the child of the good, whom the good begat in his own likeness, to be in the visible world, in relation to sight and the things of sight, what the good is in the intellectual world in relation to mind and the things of the mind.'

186 *Second Spirit*. 'A Remoter Voice' (Bodleian MS). It celebrates the powers of the mind, in relation to which the material universe is only a dimly-lighted cave (cf. *Republic*, VII. 514–7) from which it will be released at death into a state in which it will see the real world, not merely shadows.

Third Spirit. 'A louder and still remoter Voice '(Bodleian MS). It rebukes the presumption of the previous speakers. The material universe and the individual mind

are but fleeting manifestations of the One Spirit. Cf. **186**
Adonais 460–4.

Though the second and third speakers rebuke and
seem to contradict the ones before, the revelation is pro-
gressive and no speaker's insight is entirely invalidated
by what comes after. The Spirits form a Chorus.

38. *atom-born:* cf. Lucretius, *De Rerum Natura.* Follow-
ing Epicurus, Lucretius taught that man, the world,
and innumerable other worlds, formed from atoms, shall
pass away, the atoms alone remaining. Shelley may have
remembered Lucretius' ideas about atoms and the
formation and decay of many universes, but his emphasis
is quite different. For him it is the Spirit, of which indi-
vidual minds are a part, which shall persist.

48. *flower:* corresponds to the mind, celebrated by the
Second Spirit. The mind awakens to the realization of an
'unimagined world,' a reality greater than the material
universe which is only like a frail globe of dew. In spite
of his initial rebuke the implication of this Spirit's
final image is a vindication of the power of mind.

AN EXHORTATION 187

Mrs Shelley placed this among the poems of 1819, but
it is dated 'Pisa, April 1820' in Shelley's hand in the
Harvard notebook. It is probably the poem referred to
by Shelley in his letter to Mrs Gisborne on 8 May 1820:
'I send a little thing about poets, which is itself a kind of
excuse for Wordsworth.' Shelley was especially conscious
at this time of his own lack of fame, and perhaps also of
love. He recognizes the desire for these things as natural
in a poet, but the poem is more a vindication of the poet
who remains true to his principles than an excuse for
those who betray truth and liberty by reconciling them-
selves to the established order—as he thought Words-
worth had done (sonnet *To Wordsworth*). A person in
Shelley's position might well have written bitterly on
this subject, but this poem has a pleasant lightness and
urbanity, characteristic of him.

187 1. *Chameleons.* The myth that they live on air arose probably from their power of existing for long periods without food. Though knowledgeable about science Shelley was quite willing to use myth when it suited him. Chameleons change colour in response to changes of light (8–9), temperature, and their feelings.

10–15. Poets on earth are as distant from their natural habitat as chameleons (who live in hot climates, chiefly on trees) would be if they were hidden in a cave under the sea. Chameleons change in response to their proper environment, the light, whereas poets change only because they are deprived of their proper food, love.

188   ODE TO THE WEST WIND

Written October 1819 at Florence. Neville Rogers (*Shelley at Work*, chap. XII) gives an interesting account of how this poem was written. The first stage was the jotting down in a notebook of some fragments of verse describing things Shelley saw during a walk in the Cascine woods by the Arno. For instance:

> A lone wood walk, where meeting branches lean
> Even from the Earth, to mingle the delight
> That lives within the light

> Twas the 20th of October
> And the woods had all grown sober
> As a man does when his hair
> Looks as theirs did grey and spare

> When the dead leaves
> As to mock the stupid
> Like ghosts in

> The gentleness of rain was in the Wind
> But all the earth and all the leaves are dry

These are as yet mere fragments, without any theme to

bind them together. Next Shelley began a poem in **188**
terza rima which has a theme but no compelling image
to give it life. Depressed as he was at that time by his
lack of external success as a poet he imagined someone
rebuking him for presumption in claiming to be a poet
at all:

> And what art thou presumptuous who profanest
> > The wreath to mighty Poets only due
> Even whilst like a forgotten name thou wanest
> > Touch not those leaves which for the eternal few
> Who wander o'er the Paradise of fame
> > In sacred dedication ever grew—
> One of the crowd thou art,—without a name . . .

But the fragment ends with the hope that

> > > > if I fall
> I shall not creep out of the vital day
> > To common dust nor wear a common pall
> But as my hopes were fire, so my decay
> > Shall be as ashes covering them. Oh, Earth
> O friends, if when my   has ebbed away
> > One spark be unextinguished of that hearth
> Kindled in

At this point he must have thought—spark—unex-
tinguished—how is it to be kindled to flame?—by a
wind. He saw how he could use what he had observed
in his walk to give life to the thoughts about his own
poetry and the state of the world, which had been pre-
occupying him. Thought, feeling, and sensuous experi-
ence ran together in his mind.

On October 25th he wrote a draft of the first three
stanzas nearly in their final form. He invented a sonnet-
like stanza out of the terza rima, ending in a couplet
instead of a tercet. He recast the poem in the form of
a prayer to the wind, making it more concrete and less
merely personal. These sections deal with the operation
of the wind on the surface of the earth, in the sky, and

188 on the sea, the symbolical application being left implicit. Then in another notebook he worked out the last two sections, making the symbolism more explicit and ending with the unextinguished hearth, the focal point round which the different elements which went to form the poem had coalesced.

There is a good essay on this poem in Francis Berry's *Poet's Grammar* (1958), pp. 143–56. Berry shows, among other things, how closely the poem conforms to the almost invariable structure of a prayer—Invocation (repeated), Listing of the attributes of the Person or Power addressed, Confession by the suppliant of his inadequacy and failure unless he is divinely aided, Petition.

F. R. Leavis examined stanza II in detail, and found it an example of Shelley's 'weak grasp upon the actual' (see *Revaluation*, Penguin Books, 1964, pp. 171-2). His argument has been answered by, among others, Desmond King-Hele in *Shelley: His Thought and Work*, pp. 215-16 and John Holloway in his *Selected Poems of Percy Bysshe Shelley*, p. 139.

11. *buds like flocks*. The same process of renewal causes flowers to put forth buds and flocks of sheep to be driven up to their mountain summer pastures.

189 16. Clouds are operated on by the wind in the same way as the leaves are—or at any rate appear to be so. As leaves are blown away from the main mass of the tree, so wisps of cloud are blown along in front of the main mass of cloud, appear to be 'shed' from it. This is the point of the comparison, not any visual likeness, though there is some, between small ragged pieces of cloud and leaves.

17. *tangled boughs*. Heaven and ocean can be said to be tangled in the cloud in that clouds are formed from water vapour drawn up from the ocean (and the earth) by the sun and condensed in the sky. Cf. *The Cloud* 73–4. Clouds are the product of a similar organic process to that which forms trees. On this reading the image, like the last one, is not primarily visual. (For a contrary view see Holloway, p. 139.)

Some commentators think that Shelley is referring

to waterspouts such as he had seen that summer at **189**
Leghorn. 'The storms ... showed themselves most
picturesquely as they were driven across the ocean; some-
times the dark lurid clouds dipped towards the waves,
and became waterspouts that churned up the waters
beneath . . .' (Mrs Shelley's note on *The Cenci*). Cf. 'the
black trunks of the waterspouts' in *A Vision of the Sea* 5.
This reading gives a precise visual content to the image
but does not seem appropriate to the context.

18. *Angels:* messengers. The little 'loose' clouds give
warning of the rain and lightning which are to follow.

18–23. From the horizon, which is dim because of the
cloud which obscures it, to the zenith the sky is
covered high up with cirrus cloud. The word *cirrus*
means a lock of hair. So there is some appropriateness in
the imagery on the literal level. But the main point of
bringing in the Mænad was not so much to make the
scene more vivid before our eyes as to introduce the
desired emotional tone. In this section more than in the
first the fearfulness of the coming storm is being empha-
sized. The wind is felt here more as the destroyer of the
dying year than as a preserver. And yet, as the Maenad
in all her frenzy is possessed by the god, so the wind is
felt to be the fearful agent of a possibly divine power, of
necessary change.

Stanza III. The previous winter Shelley had visited the
Bay of Baiae, and seen 'the ruins of its antique grandeur
standing like rocks in the transparent sea under our
boat' (letter to Peacock, 17 Dec. 1818). In Roman times
some of the Emperors had villas at Baiae, and the place
had a reputation for luxury and immorality. Shelley
seems to go out of his way here to stress the calm of the
Mediterranean's summer dreams, the beauty of the
palaces which will be hidden by the coming storm. As
an aristocrat and lover of art he was sensitive to the
beauty of the old European civilization represented by
'palaces and towers,' even though as a revolutionary he
longed to see this civilization swept away or transformed.

Stanzas IV–V. In the first three sections the wind has
been seen in relation to the natural world, and by implica-

189 tion to human society, as the necessary, if fearful, agent of change, blowing away that which is corrupt and dead, preserving the life which is to come to birth in the new spring. Now it is seen in relation to the poet himself. Some critics have thought the last few lines of stanza IV a blemish, but their self-pity is contained in a context in which it is transcended. In the final section his own ageing and death are accepted (58). It is not his personal fate that matters, but the fate of his ideas. He hopes that his dead thoughts (his *Revolt of Islam*, he had just heard, had apparently fallen still-born from the press) might still help to quicken a new birth, that his words (he had just sent to England the first three acts of his 'prophetic' *Prometheus Unbound*) might be a true prophecy of the spring which would surely come, in society and in men's personal lives as well as in nature.

191   AN ODE

Inspired by the 'Peterloo Massacre.' See introductory note to *Other Poems* (p. 315).

The metre is based on the number of stresses rather than the number of syllables to the line. The poem seems to demand to be read rhetorically, with great stress and in a loud voice as at a public meeting. It does not ask for, nor deserve, close attention.

7. ? If the survivors remember and speak for them, they will not really be dead.

21. *But:* except.

192 28. They are to achieve a more glorious victory, not over others but over the bad passions in themselves—pride, desire for revenge and for power (as Prometheus did in *P.U.* I).

34. *pansy:* from French *pensée*, thought; hence used for memory. The injured are not to keep their injuries in mind.

In a MS in the Bodleian there is an extra stanza: **192**

VI

   Gather, oh gather,
Foeman and friend in love and peace!
   Waves sleep together
When the blasts that called them to battle cease.
For fangless Power, grown tame and mild,
Is at play with Freedom's fearless child,—
The dove and the serpent reconciled!

Without this additional stanza, envisaging a state in which past injuries are forgotten, lines 34–5 form rather an obscure and unsatisfactory conclusion.

THE CLOUD

Though Mrs Shelley placed this poem among those of 1820 her statement about Shelley 'marking the cloud as it sped across the heavens, while he floated in his boat on the Thames' has been taken to imply that it must have been written, or at least begun, in England. But the position of the draft in one of his Italian notebooks shows clearly that it belongs, at any rate in its present form, to the same period as the other poems published with *Prometheus Unbound*.

It treats not of one particular cloud, but of a variety of different types and conditions of cloud, forming, changing shape, dissolving and re-forming. It conveys in a typically Shelleyan way a sense at once of continuity and change, and combines contemporary scientific speculation with poetic fancy.

Probably Shelley intended no more than a poem about a cloud, but one feels that his fascination with the changes of the cloud is connected with his sense of the flowing, transitory but indestructible nature of life itself. G. Wilson Knight writes: ' "I change, but I cannot die" refers to both the cloud and the central "I am" in humanity. . . . The cloud's transmutations are

192 felt as symbolic of (i) birth and (ii) resurrection: to Shelley, as to St Paul, these mysteries involving each other. The doctrine beautifully renders pantheism and the inwardness of human experience identical.' (*The Starlit Dome* (1941), p. 199.)

The metre is appropriate to the subject, the insistent beat of the rhymes corresponding to the continuity of natural processes, the variations within the lines to the ever-changing nature of clouds. Four-stress lines alternate with three-stress ones (except that the first two short ones have only two stresses). Iambs (x /) and anapaests (x x /) are combined in many different ways, the short lines ranging from five to nine syllables, the long from eight to twelve.

See King-Hele: *Shelley: His Thought and Work*, pp. 219–27.

11. *it:* the hail.

193 17–30. The part which atmospheric electricity plays in the formation and movement of clouds was much exaggerated by some scientists in Shelley's day. Adam Walker says that 'water rises through the air, flying on the wings of electricity.' Having established 'the identity of lightning and electricity,' he says that, especially in summer, clouds become strongly charged with positive electricity, 'while the earth, comparatively, may be in a negative state; the consequence will be a violent effort to restore equality by a storm of thunder and lightning; and the air near the earth will be found positive and negative, by fits, while the storm lasts' (*Philosophy*, pp. 356–8). So here the pilot is electricity, which guides the cloud over sea and land, seeking to be united to the negative electricity below, between which and it there is a natural attraction analogous to love. The electricity in the cloud may be discharged either violently in a storm (19–20) or gently in rain (29–30).

49. 'We can almost hear the photons pattering down' (King-Hele).

194 58. *these:* the stars.

64. *torrent;* adjective, as in *P.U.* III. III. 156; a not very happy Latinism.

71. *sphere-fire:* the sun. *soft:* appropriate description of **194**
the colours of the rainbow, which melt into one another.
75. *pores.* Walker, *Philosophy*, p. 306. Rain 'sinks into
the chinks and pores of the ground ... For, dead and
inanimate as our mother earth appears, we find her thus
fraught with veins and arteries like the animal body.'
Here it is the sea which is seen as an animal body sweat-
ing as the sun sucks moisture from it, which rises and
condenses in the air into clouds. The pores of the shores
are the outlets of the rivers and streams into the sea.
79. *convex.* 'The earth's atmosphere bends a ray of
sunlight into a curve ... convex to an observer in a
cloud looking down' (King-Hele).
84. *unbuild.* The blue dome left when clouds have dis-
solved in rain is unbuilt by the re-formation of clouds.

TO A SKYLARK   195

Written early in the summer of 1820 while staying in
the Gisbornes' house at Leghorn. Mrs. Shelley wrote:
'It was on a beautiful summer evening, while wandering
among the lanes whose myrtle hedges were the bowers of
the fireflies, that we heard the carolling of the skylark
which inspired one of the most beautiful of his poems.'
Shelley was oppressed by many worries at that time, and
would respond with special poignancy to the joy of the
lark's song, to the skylark-poet whose song, unlike his
own, was gladly listened to.

Only a few weeks before, he had read in Plato's
Phaedrus Socrates' discourse on the soul. The soul
'when perfect and fully winged ... soars upwards, and
orders the whole world; whereas the imperfect soul,
losing her wings and drooping in her flight, at last settles
on the solid ground .... The wing is the corporeal
element which is most akin to the divine, and which by
nature tends to soar aloft and carry that which gravitates
downwards into the upper region which is the habitation
of the gods' (*Phaedrus* 246). The lark, 'scorner of the
ground,' in its upward flight into invisibility suggests
the aspiring, then the perfected soul; pouring down

195 'from Heaven, or near it' its song, it suggests the inspired poet who should be a channel through which grace flows into the world. (Cf. Blake's use of the lark in his *Milton*, plate 35, lines 54–67.)Yet it is not merely, or primarily, a symbol. Primarily the poem describes lark-song and its effect upon Shelley on a particular occasion.

'Any one who has listened attentively to the soaring lark will recognize in the delicate hesitant poise of each stanza upon its prolonged floating last line, the lark-song with its extended trill' (Kathleen Raine, *Defending Ancient Springs*, p. 147). The short lines are basically three-foot trochaic (/x), the long ones six-foot iambic (x/).

2. (1) The lark is so high as to be invisible; one can hardly believe that a mere bird is the source of the song. (2)? The ultimate source of the song is *not* the bird, who, like the poet, is only an instrument.

21–5. Venus as morning star ('The sphere whose light is melody to lovers', *The Triumph of Life* 479) is so bright that it can be seen for a time after sunrise; it appears to narrow as daylight strengthens, and then is no more seen, but its presence may be felt. (Cf. *The Triumph of Life* 413–20.) The association of song and light is common in Shelley. It is characteristic of him to compare something intangible, the song of the unseen lark, not to something more concrete, but to something even more tenuous, the light of an unseen star.

196 36–55. The point of these comparisons is in the action, the showering out from some unseen source, more than in the things themselves.

198 86. *look before and after*: cf. Shakespeare, *Hamlet* IV. IV. 37.

199 103. *madness*: inspiration, as in Plato's *Phaedrus* 245: 'The third kind is the madness of those who are possessed by the Muses; which taking hold of a delicate and virgin soul, and there inspiring frenzy, awakens lyrical and all other numbers. . . . He who, having no touch of the Muses' madness in his soul, comes to the door and thinks he will get into the temple by the help of art— he, I say, and his poetry are not admitted.'

Written early in 1820, inspired by the rising in Spain which began on January 1st. Not long before, in *A Philosophical View of Reform*, Shelley had prophesied that the tyrannous actions of Ferdinand VII of Spain, 'in the present condition of understanding and sentiment of mankind, are the rapidly passing shadows, which forerun successful insurrection.' He places the rising in the context of world history. The recurring struggle between liberty and despotism had, as he saw it, reached a particularly crucial stage. Everywhere men were becoming less willing to accept their institutions as given, more disposed to question whether they were producing the desired results. The American and French Revolutions had shown what might be done. In 1815 the lid had been put back on, but the forces of revolution were boiling under the surface. Shelley saw the Spanish rising as a possible sign of the coming of the spring looked for in *Ode to the West Wind*.

The Ode form treated in this elaborate way, with long complex stanzas, was suited to the large, impersonal theme. This is public poetry, to be judged in a different way from the more personal poems in the volume.

Motto. *Childe Harold* IV. xcviii. 'a' should be 'the.'

1. *vibrated:* 'brandished' (Ellis); 'reflected' (Locock). A possible other meaning is 'vibrated with.' The spirit of liberty is animating the people of Spain like an electric current.

7–9. 1820 has a semicolon after 'strong' and a comma after 'among.' Locock put dashes round line 8 so that 'hovering in verse' may be taken with 'soul' rather than 'eagle.' Rossetti kept the 1820 punctuation and amended 'in verse' to 'inverse,' which goes well with 'eagle.' In any case both the soul and the eagle are hovering, in their different ways, over their prey.

11–13. The whirlwind of the Spirit caught up my soul and bore it to a region beyond the remotest star.

16–45. Cf. *P.U.* II. iv. 32–58. But there is here no suggestion of a Golden Age and a Fall. History is going

200 to be seen as a progress, even though interrupted by periods of reaction. Though Shelley made use of the myth of a Golden Age, his real view of history was that taken here. See *Essay on Christianity* (*Works* VI. 250).

18. *dædal:* skilfully made, richly adorned. See note on *P.U.* III. I. 26, p.294.

201 41. *sister-pest:* religion.

43. *Anarchs:* tyrants, rulers who obey no law but their own desire.

45. *astonished:* in Shelley's day meant 'stunned,' 'bewildered,' not just 'very surprised.'

202 58. *Parian stone:* marble from Paros, an island in the Aegean, used by many of the ancient sculptors.

60. *lidless:* open, wakeful.

74. *that hill:* the Acropolis, on which is the Parthenon.

75. *latest oracle:* Liberty was again speaking from Athens, in the rising of the Greeks against their Turkish rulers, in Shelley's own day.

76–9. Almost repeated in *Evening: Ponte al Mare, Pisa.* Cf. Wordsworth, *Peele Castle* 3-8.

203 92. *Mænad.* Euripides, *Bacchæ* 700–1. The mænads, possessed by the spirit of Bacchus/Dionysus, went out from Thebes, where Cadmus was king, to worship the god in the hills and woods, some of them giving suck to fawns or wolf-cubs.

93. *thy dearest:* Greece.

97. *Camillus.* Marcus Furius Camillus, second founder of Rome after the invasion of the Gauls (387 B.C.); 'saintly' perhaps because of his going into voluntary exile after being accused of distributing spoils improperly, and then returning to save Rome.

Atilius. Marcus Atilius Regulus, commander of Roman armies against the Carthaginians in the 3rd century B.C. It was later believed in Rome that, having been captured by the Carthaginians and sent to Rome to arrange peace terms, he advised the Senate to reject the terms, and voluntarily returned to Carthage to die under torture.

100–5. First wealth corrupted the Republic; the rulers, the senators, became tyrants. Then the Republic was

334

replaced by the rule of a single tyrant, the Emperor. **203**
Liberty departed, delaying only to hear some echoes of
Greek poetry in the works of such poets as Virgil and
Horace who would recite their poems in the Emperor's
palace on the Palatine hill.

111. *Naiad:* water nymph. **204**

115–20. *Scald:* a Scandinavian bard. The spirit of
Liberty was not, according to Shelley, active in the
war-like Scandinavian civilization nor among the Druid-
dominated Celtic peoples. Things became worse still
when Christianity united the western world.

121–35. Examples to show that the revival of liberty
and of art and culture are associated. Alfred in the late
ninth century not only helped to unite England and to
defend her from the Danes but also promoted a revival
of literature. A revival of the arts took place in Italy from
the twelfth century onwards, especially in the cities
which achieved a measure of independence from the
surrounding dominions of Emperors and Popes.

129. *anarchy:* tyranny (cf. line 43).

142. *leaden lance.* Cf. *A Defence of Poetry*: 'Dante was **205**
the first religious reformer, and Luther surpassed him
rather in the rudeness and acrimony than in the boldness
of his censures of papal usurpation' (*Works*, VII. 130–1).

148–50. Milton, blind but 'spirit-sighted,' saw beyond
the 'night' of the Restoration, when the power of King
and Church were restored, to a new dawn of liberty, and
may have expressed this hope obliquely in *Samson
Agonistes*.

151–8. Refers to the time between the Restoration and
the end of the eighteenth century. Europe was ruled by
strong monarchical and aristocratic governments, but
the spirit of liberty was alive and a current of free thought
was moving. There were both hopes and fears. Dawn is
seen on the hills, but the sun does not rise until the
Revolution.

159–65. The American Revolution.

171–8. Refers to the war of the conservative powers **206**
against the French revolutionaries, and to the rise and
fall of Napoleon. Napoleon, when fighting against

206 reactionary regimes, to some extent stood for the forces of liberty, but himself became an 'Anarch,' a tyrant. So the situation became confused, not a simple confrontation of good and evil.

186. *Pithecusa:* the island of Ischia in the Bay of Naples. *Pelorus:* in Sicily.

189–91. England is ruled by a plutocracy, which could be overthrown fairly easily in comparison with the military despotism which the Spanish revolutionaries are destroying.

192–5. The new revolutionaries, in Spain and (he hopes) England, should appeal to those who have already carried out a successful revolution in America. 'May all you (the Americans) have thought and done, the memory of which cannot be obliterated by time, be impressed upon us (Spain and England), as with a seal.'

194. *impress, as* Forman; *impress us* 1820. Locock accepts Forman's conjectural emendation.

196. *Arminius:* led German tribes to victory over the Romans in A.D. 9. Shelley believed that the Germans would soon join in the struggle for liberty. Though still ruled by kings they were already mentally free (203).

207 199. *Thy:* Germany's. *his:* Arminius's.

204. *thou:* Italy, most of it at that time under the rule of Austria.

212. *King:* replaced by asterisks in the early editions for fear of prosecution.

218. *gordian word.* An oracle declared that he who should unravel the intricate knot tied by King Gordius of Phrygia would become master of Asia; but Alexander cut through it with his sword. The implication is that kingship should be promptly abolished rather than gradually reformed.

221. *The axes and the rods:* the *fasces*, a bundle of rods tied round an axe, carried before Roman magistrates as a symbol of authority.

225. *reluctant:* struggling.

208 241. *He.* It is not clear that Shelley had any one particular in mind. Whoever taught man to master his circumstances made him King of Life.

244–5. Cf. Prometheus giving power to Jupiter.   **208**
254–5. If wealth takes away from those who toil and groan the gifts given by liberty and nature.
258. *Eoan:* eastern.
Among Shelley's papers a cancelled passage for this ode was found, which Locock took to be a preliminary draft for stanza XVIII.

> Within a cavern of man's trackless spirit
>   Is throned an Image, so intensely fair
> That the adventurous thoughts that wander near it
> Worship, and as they kneel, tremble and wear
> The splendour of its presence, and the light
>   Penetrates their dreamlike frame
> Till they become charged with the strength of flame.

ADONAIS   **211**

Shelley met Keats occasionally in London between December 1816 and March 1818, and admired his work; but, according to Leigh Hunt, 'Keats did not take to Shelley as kindly as Shelley did to him' (*Autobiography*, ed. J. E. Morpurgo (1949) p. 273). In July 1820, hearing of Keats's illness, Shelley wrote to invite him to stay at Pisa; but when Keats came out to Italy that winter he went to Rome, where he died on 23rd February 1821. Shelley had heard of his death by 19th April, and on 5th June wrote to the Gisbornes: 'I have been engaged these last days in composing a poem on the death of Keats. . . . It is a highly wrought piece of art, and perhaps better, in point of composition, than anything I have written.' Three days later he wrote to his publisher, Charles Ollier, that the poem was finished, and that he would send it 'either printed at Pisa, or transcribed in such a manner as it shall be difficult for the reviser to leave such errors as *assist* the obscurity of the "Prometheus." ' It was printed at Pisa during the next month. Shelley continued to think well of it, writing to Horace Smith in September: 'I am glad you like "Adonais,"

211 and, particularly, that you do not think it metaphysical, which I was afraid it was'; and to his publisher in the same month: 'The "Adonais," in spite of its mysticism, is the least imperfect of my compositions.' Ollier did no more than distribute the copies received from Pisa. The next edition was published at Cambridge in 1829 on the initiative of Monckton Milnes and Arthur Hallam, then undergraduates there. Mrs Shelley introduced into her edition of 1839 the changes noted in lines 72, 143, and 252, presumably with Shelley's authority.

According to the gossip which Shelley and Byron were too ready to believe, Keats's death had been brought about largely by distress over an unfavourable criticism in the *Quarterly Review*. Shelley was more resentful than he liked to acknowledge against the *Quarterly* for a hostile review of his own work. He had recently, in March, written his *Defence of Poetry*. So circumstances made Keats's death a suitable focus round which to gather some of the thoughts about poetry he had just expressed in prose and his sense of the world's hostility to the poet. Fortunately, as he worked on the poem, his personal injuries were largely eliminated, or swallowed up in the larger themes. There is not much in the poem about Keats as an individual. Read as biography it gives a false impression of the man and of the circumstances of his death. But we should not read it as biography. Keats is transformed into a generalized figure of the poet who brings light into an uncomprehending world; and the reviewer's hostility becomes a symbol of the world's incomprehension, its resistance to the light.

As a help in transforming the particular into the universal it was appropriate for Shelley to use a traditional form, the pastoral elegy. He took ideas especially from two such elegies, an elegy on Adonis attributed to Bion, and an elegy on Bion attributed to Moschus. (Bion and Moschus were Greek Bucolic poets who lived in the second century B.C.) In the former the poet mourns for Adonis, slain by a boar, and calls upon Aphrodite to rise and lament. She roams distracted through the wood, bare-footed, and 'the brambles tear her as she

goes, and draw her sacred blood' (cf. *Adonais*, XXIV). **211**
She pleads: 'Stay, Adonis . . . . Kiss me so long as life is
in the kiss, until thy spirit has passed into my lips . . .
and I shall guard that kiss as though it were Adonis'
self, since thou, hapless one, art fleeing from me. Far
away thou fliest, Adonis, and comest to Acheron. . . .
But I, poor soul, live, and am a goddess and cannot
follow thee (XXV–XXVI). Take thou my husband, Per-
sephone [Queen of the Underworld], for thou art
mightier far than I, and all that is fair comes down to
thee . . . . Why, rash one, didst thou go hunting? Why,
being so fair, wast thou so mad as to pit thyself against
the beast?' (XXVII). Aphrodite's tears and Adonis' blood
are turned to flowers as they fall to the ground (XXIV).
His body is carried to Aphrodite's bed, 'and weeping
Loves make moan about him, their locks shorn for
Adonis. One casts on him his arrows, one his bow, one a
feather from his wing, one his quiver. Here one has
loosed Adonis' sandal; these bring water in a golden
ewer; another bathes his thighs; another from behind
fans Adonis with his wings' (X–XI). Finally the poet bids
Aphrodite 'cease thy laments today; stay thy dirges.
Again must thou lament, again must thou weep another
year' (*The Greek Bucolic Poets*, trans. A. S. F. Gow
(1953), pp. 144–6). He is to be mourned another year.
This may point to the significance usually attributed to
Adonis as a fertility god who dies and is resurrected
each year.

In the other lament the poet calls upon rivers, flowers,
nightingales, etc. to join with various mythological
characters and with places associated with Bion and
other poets in mourning for Bion. He addresses Meles,
the name of a river near Smyrna, Bion's birthplace, and
of its god, supposed by some the father of Homer: 'Here
is for thee, most musical of rivers, a second sorrow . . . .
Of old died Homer, that sweet mouthpiece of Calliope
[the muse of epic poetry] . . . . Now for another son
again thou weepest, and wastest with a new grief' (cf.
Adonais IV–VI). When plants wither they 'spring up
another year, but we men, we that are tall and strong,

211 we that are wise, when once we die, unhearing sleep in the hollow earth, a long sleep without end or wakening' (XVIII–XX). He tells how Bion died: 'Poison came to thy lips, Bion; poison didst thou eat. To such lips could it approach and not be sweetened? What human was so brutal as to mix the drug for thee, or give it at thy bidding? He escapes my song [or, according to another translator, 'shall be nameless in song']. Yet justice reaches all' (Epigraph to Preface: XXXVI–XXXVII). (*The Greek Bucolic Poets*, pp. 134–7.)

Shelley uses these elegies and the pastoral elegiac conventions in general, for his own purposes and in his own way, in the first thirty-seven stanzas of *Adonais*; but thereafter the pastoral mode is thrown aside, and the chief source is Platonic/Neoplatonic philosophy. One of the chief critical questions about the poem is whether the two sections cohere.

Shelley had already used the Spenserian stanza in *The Revolt of Islam*, 'enticed,' he wrote in the preface, 'by the brilliancy and magnificence of sound which a mind that has been nourished upon musical thoughts can produce by a just and harmonious arrangement of the pauses of this measure.' To see different ways of using this stanza compare *Adonais* with, for instance, Thomson's *Castle of Indolence*, Wordsworth's *Guilt and Sorrow*, Keats's *Eve of St. Agnes*, Byron's *Childe Harold*.

See Baker, *Shelley's Major Poetry*, chap. VI; Hungerford, *Shores of Darkness*, 216–34; Wasserman, *The Subtler Language*, chap. VIII.

Title Page. Shelley translated the lines attributed to Plato:

> Thou wert the morning star among the living,
>   Ere thy fair light had fled;—
> Now, having died thou art as Hesperus, giving
>   New splendour to the dead.

The planet Venus appears sometimes as the morning star (Lucifer, 'lightbearer'), sometimes as the evening star (Hesperus).

Epigraph. See A. S. F. Gow's translation, p. 340 above:
'Poison came to thy lips . . . escapes my song.'

1. *It is my intention* . . . Never fulfilled. In November
Shelley wrote to Joseph Severn: 'I have little hope . . .
that the poem . . . will excite any attention nor do I feel
assured that a critical notice of his writings would find
a single reader.'

11. *twenty-fourth year.* Keats was in his twenty-sixth
year when he died on the 23rd of February 1821.

24. *The savage criticism.* The *Quarterly* review of
Endymion appeared in September 1818, after which
Keats went on to write nearly all his greatest work.
Probably he caught tuberculosis when nursing his
brother Tom that winter, but it did not move into an
active stage until the following autumn, and his first
haemorrhage was in February 1820.

29. *acknowledgments, from more candid critics.* Shelley
probably had in mind mainly Jeffrey's favourable article
in the *Edinburgh Review* for August 1820.

10. *calumniator.* Presumably the reviewer of Shelley's 213
own *Revolt of Islam.* His correspondence with Southey,
earlier wrongly reported to him to have been the author,
shows his indignation over this review (*Letters,* ed.
Jones, III. 203–5, 230–2).

19-20. *What gnat . . . camels?* See Jesus' rebuke to the
Scribes and Pharisees in *Matthew* 23: 24. The next
sentence alludes to another rebuke against hypocrisy, in
John 8: 3–11.

30. *I am given to understand . . . his care.* This much
exaggerated statement is based on a letter to Mr Gisborne
from the Revd Robert, self-styled 'Colonel,' Finch, not
a reliable source. The words in inverted commas in the
next sentence are inaccurately quoted from this letter.

ADONAIS   214

1. *Adonais.* Wasserman (*The Subtler Language,* 311–2)
suggests that in telescoping Adonai (in the Old Testa-

214 ment one of the names of God) and Adonis Shelley was suggesting that his hero is more than the fertility god Adonis. But perhaps in choosing a name, which needed to be like but slightly different from Adonis, he was guided mainly by sound. The name should be pronounced with four syllables.

215 10. *mighty Mother.* Shelley substitutes Urania the mother for Aphrodite the lover in the Adonis myth. The name Urania was, first, one of two titles sometimes given to the goddess Aphrodite, the other being Pandemos. Sometimes, as in Plato, *Symposium*, 180, these titles were interpreted as distinguishing heavenly from merely physical love. Secondly, Urania was, in classical mythology, one of the nine Muses, the Muse of Astronomy. By a natural extension from the idea of the 'heavenly' bodies the name came to be used, in Renaissance times, for the Muse of 'heavenly' or spiritual, sometimes specifically Christian, poetry. In *Paradise Lost* VII. 1–40 Milton invokes by this name a being who, he says, is higher than any of the nine Muses.

The mythical story Shelley is using is about Aphrodite, but in character and function his Urania is primarily a Muse. He had recently been stirred by Peacock's 'Four Ages of Poetry' to vindicate 'the insulted Muses,' to break a lance with him 'in honour of my mistress Urania' (Letter to Peacock, 15 Feb. 1821). Probably he intended the name to combine suggestions of the higher kind of love and of the higher kind of poetry (closely connected, in his view). See lines 29 and 232–5 and notes.

Compare also the 'mother of this unfathomable world' in *Alastor* (18–23). What is new is that Urania is shown as loving the poets whom she inspires.

11-12. *shaft . . . darkness:* the anonymous attack in the *Quarterly*.

25-6. As fertility god Adonis returns to the upper air in summer, and during winter sleeps in the underworld with Persephone, who, falling in love with him, at first refused to let him go. But Adonais is not going to be revived.

29. *Lament anew, Urania !* 'Lament anew, great poetry'

in an early draft (in a MS notebook in the Bodleian). **215**
He: Milton, who died after the Restoration had brought
back the power of the King and the established Church.
'His country's pride' is the object of 'trampled and
mocked'—rather an awkward inversion.

36. *third*. 'Homer was the first and Dante the second
epic poet . . . . Milton was the third' (*Defence of Poetry*,
in *Works*, VII. 130).

39–41. Not all aspired to such high poetry as the epic. **216**
Happier were those minor writers who lived to see their
merits recognized [?], and whose works survive, whereas
some major ones have been lost.

47. *widowhood*. The Muse may be thought of as mistress
or mother. Urania has been bereaved by the deaths of
the great poets of the past, and the period since the
death of Milton has been without any supremely great
poet. Perhaps it would be oversubtle to suggest that
Adonais is appropriately the son in that his work derives
its inspiration from the dead poets as well as from the
Muse.

48–9. Probably refers to Keats's Isabella, who wept
over the head of her murdered lover, preserved in a pot
of basil.

55. *Capital:* Rome.

58. *among the eternal*. In this context probably means
no more than 'among the many famous people buried
there.' *Come away!* Addressed not to Urania, but to
those gathered round the body, not yet beginning to
corrupt, of Adonais. We turn, rather abruptly, from
Urania at the end of stanza VI, and do not return to her
until stanza XXII.

63. *liquid:* pure, serene (as sometimes in Latin).

68. *His extreme way*. The personified figure of Corrup- **217**
tion is waiting to follow him on his last journey to
the grave, where the process of decomposition will
set in.

72. Improved from the Pisa edition, which reads:

Of mortal change shall fill the grave which is her maw.

73. *Dreams*. As Bion's Aphrodite is changed to Urania,

343

217 so the mourners are changed from Loves (Cupids) to Dreams, poetic imaginings and other mental states. In this stanza Shelley uses motifs from pastoral poetry in interesting and new ways, but in stanza XI he follows the elegy for Adonis more closely, with less happy effect. Actions which were appropriate for the Cupids are less so for Shelley's 'Dreams.' In stanza IX, and again in stanza XII he is using imagery in his own characteristic way; stanza XI is in comparison derivative and precious.

88. *ruined Paradise:* the brain of Adonais, the origin of this 'Dream,' which now fades without trace like a cloud which has given up all its rain.

218 94. *anadem:* wreath for the head.

101–3. The mouth which could put the Dream, the poetic thought, into words, and give it power to pierce beneath the resistant rational faculty of a reader to his emotions.

107. *clips:* embraces, surrounds.

219 121. *unbound:* an adjective. The clouds make the morning dim instead of fertilizing the ground.

127. *Echo:* a nymph who loved Narcissus; he repulsed her, and she pined away. Now, having, it is supposed, loved Adonais even more than Narcissus, she will not repeat the sounds that come to her, but only murmurs the remembered words of Adonais.

140. *Hyacinth:* a youth loved by Phoebus (Apollo) and accidentally killed by him.

141. *Narcissus:* fell in love with his own reflection in water, some say as a punishment for scorning Echo. *both:* Hyacinth and Narcissus, now thought of as the flowers into which these youths were transformed.

143. *faint companions:* 'drooping comrades' (1821).

144. *ruth:* compassion.

220 145–51. The nightingale does not so musically mourn for her mate, nor does the eagle so passionately complain over her empty nest as England wails for the death of Adonais. Keats had written an ode to the nightingale, and had scaled heaven by writing of the sun-god Hyperion. *Albion:* a poetic name for England.

154. Shelley here moves from the idea of nature sym- **220** pathizing in the death of Adonais (appropriate enough if the dead youth is partly to be identified with the fertility god Adonis) to the contrast between the bursting forth of spring and his death. Adonais is now to be clearly distinguished from Adonis. The writing becomes stronger and more impassioned as Shelley approaches his central theme.

159. *brake:* bush.

160. *brere:* briar.

167. *steam* (1821); *stream* (1829 and Mrs Shelley). Steam would in fact effectively diffuse the light from the 'lamps of Heaven' as suggested in 168.

172–80. The magical transformation of Adonis' blood **221** into flowers (anemones; in Greek the name means daughters of the wind) is changed to a statement which is literally, not just mythically, true. The physical elements of the body dissolve, but continue to exist, fertilizing new life. The things which we know live on, but the mind which knows them apparently dies, the sword being consumed before the sheath. The star/light —flower/fragrance comparison is a favourite one in Shelley. Cf. *The Sensitive Plant* I. 35–6. Especially characteristic is the sense-mingling in 'splendour [light] is changed to fragrance.'

179. *sightless:* unseen.

195. *their sister:* the Echo who repeated Adonais' poems (128).

208–16. Again motifs from the elegy on Adonis (Aphro- **222** dite's body torn by brambles, her tears and Adonis' blood turned to flowers) are modified and given new meaning. Urania, standing here for poetry and poets, is wounded by men's cruelty and insensitivity, but their malice cannot repel her. Poetry persists and paradoxically flourishes even as the consequence of the poets' wounds. Cf. *Julian and Maddalo* 544–5:

> Most wretched men
> Are cradled into poetry by wrong.

226–34. This follows the elegy on Adonis quite closely; **223**

223 but the familiar idea of a goddess being unable to lay aside her immortality to follow a mortal who dies is given a new twist by Shelley. For it is, we shall later find, Adonais who through death has entered eternity, whereas Urania is chained to time. Urania must remain within the realm of time in order to continue to inspire poets, who while on earth must derive inspiration from *incarnate* beauty.

235–43. Keats had challenged established opinion (represented by the powerful Tory *Quarterly Review*) by associating himself with 'modern' writers as against the practitioners of 'correct' verse in the eighteenth-century manner, and by making no secret of his liberal opinions nor of his friendship with the radical Leigh Hunt. He had done so when very young and before his powers of expression had reached maturity.

240. *mirrored shield:* such as Perseus used against Medusa.

242. *crescent:* growing.

249–52. As Apollo killed the dragon Python (his earliest exploit), so Byron cowed the critics who attacked his first volume of verse with his satirical poem *English Bards and Scotch Reviewers* (1809).

252. *lying low* Mrs. Shelley; *as they go* 1821.

224 253–61. The sun represents the great poet during his lifetime; the reptiles those who are dependent on him, whether as critics who dim his light or as imitators who share it; the stars the poets who have achieved lasting fame, whose light was temporarily obscured by the splendour of the new poet, who after death will become one of them.

264. *Pilgrim of Eternity:* Byron, author of *Childe Harold's Pilgrimage* and destined to be eternally famous; perhaps also a pilgrim in quest of eternity.

268–70. Thomas Moore, writer of songs, who had attacked British policy towards Ireland. It does not matter that Byron's attitude to Keats was contemptuous and flippant (though he admired *Hyperion*), nor that Moore does not seem to have been concerned about him at all. True poets, especially those on the liberal

side, had cause to mourn the death of a comrade, even **224**
if they did not know it.

271. *frail Form:* Shelley himself.

276. *Actaeon:* was turned into a stag for seeing Artemis
(Diana) naked, and pursued to death by his own hounds.

280. *pardlike:* like a panther or leopard. The panther **225**
was sacred to Dionysus, and Shelley appears here as
one of that god's followers.

291–2. Dionysus and his followers carried a light
spear, the thyrsus, tipped with a pine cone (here the
cypress for mourning) and often garlanded with ivy—
an appropriate emblem for an inspired poet. Cf. Plato,
Ion 533–4, translated by Shelley at about this time:
'thus the composers of lyrical poetry create those
admired songs of theirs in a state of divine insanity . . . .
Like the Bacchantes, who, when possessed by the God
draw honey and milk from the rivers . . . .'

Many have thought that Shelley gives too much pro-
minence to himself here, and that he overplays the part
of the sensitive martyr. But the passage needs to be
read in its context. In this part of the poem the *apparent*
weakness of the poet and what he stands for is stressed;
later we are to see things in a different perspective.

298. *partial:* opposite of impartial; taking one side,
involved.

301. *the accents of an unknown land.* Shelley wrote in
his essay *On Love* (*Works*, VI. 201) that when he had
tried to unburden his inmost soul 'I have found my
language misunderstood, like one in a distant and savage
land.'

306. *Cain's or Christ's.* Shelley was rejected by his con-
temporaries for his opinions and actions, as Cain and
Christ had been. He is not necessarily implying that the
three are in other respects alike. The world rejects
equally the murderer and the innocent.

307. *softer voice:* Leigh Hunt's. Keats had been attacked **226**
partly because of his friendship with the radical Hunt.
Shelley had been highly praised as a poet by *Black-
wood's Magazine*, but condemned for the evil principles
he shared with Hunt. His inclusion of Hunt here there-

226 fore was an act of defiance, a restatement of his stand on the liberal side, as well as a tribute to one who was closer to Keats than the others mentioned.

316. *poison.* See lines from the elegy on Bion quoted at the beginning of the Preface. We need not trouble about inconsistencies produced by combining the two elegies, nor ask exactly how Adonais died—struck by a shaft (11), killed by a dragon (238) or poisoned. These are symbols of the reviewer's hostility to Keats, and in general of the world's hostility to the light-bringer.

319. *nameless:* anonymous (reviewer). The unsigned *Quarterly* article was probably written by John Wilson Croker.

321–3. Keats's prelude (*Endymion*) silenced the envy, etc., of all hearers except the reviewer. Shelley seems to have been unaware of the *Blackwood* review of Keats's early poems by John Gibson Lockhart, which was more contemptuous than that in the *Quarterly*. Most other contemporary reviews of *Endymion* were quite favourable.

325–33. Cf. Prometheus' curse (*P.U.* I. 292–301).

327. *noteless:* insignificant, unremembered.

227 334. This is the turning point of the poem, which has up to now been a pastoral elegy mourning the death of a poet, who from a this-worldly point of view seems forever gone. Now his death is seen in a different context. From the viewpoint of eternity earthly life is a kind of death in comparison with the full life of the soul released from the limitations of mortality. Cf. Plato, *Gorgias* 492–3 (Socrates speaking): 'I think that Euripides may have been right in saying,

"Who knows if life be not death and death life";

and that we are very likely dead; I have heard a philosopher say that at this moment we are actually dead, and that the body is our tomb . . . .'

Though Shelley was, on the whole if not uniformly, successful in adapting the conventions of pastoral poetry to his purposes, his greatest writing comes when he soars free of them.

228 370–8. In this and the following stanza Shelley's sense

of the vitality and beauty of nature lead him away from **228**
the dualism he seemed to be approaching in stanza
XXXIX. Matter is not merely a corpse to be escaped from.
The ultimate Power wields the world with *love*; the
one Spirit bursts in beauty from trees and beasts and
men. Cf. *The Dæmon of the World* 102–7 and note. The
same two conceptions are still present, but Shelley is
now more able to make us feel them as halves of a
paradox, rather than as stark opposites.

370. *one with Nature.* In a different sense than has been
envisaged before. It is not that the physical elements of
his body are still a part of nature (172–3), nor that he
returns, as fertility god, to the earth each spring. He is
now part of that which is the ultimate source of all life.

384–5. Cf. Shelley's essay *On the Devil and Devils*: 'But
the Greek philosophers abstained from introducing the
Devil. They accounted for evil by supposing that what
is called matter is eternal, and that God in making the
world, made not the best that he, or even inferior intelli-
gence could conceive; but that he moulded the reluctant
and stubborn materials ready to his hand, into the
nearest arrangement possible to the perfect archetype
existing in his contemplation' (*Works*, VII. 88–9).

394–5. When love (of higher things) and the ordinary **229**
cares of life contend in the heart of the aspiring youth
the creative minds of the dead are a living influence
upon him. 'Life' is being used in a similar sense to that
found in *The Triumph of Life*. For the contention of Love
and Life see also Shelley's fragmentary story in Italian
Una Favola (*Works*, VI. 279–82).

397–405. *inheritors:* poets like Keats who died before
maturity. *Chatterton:* poet of extraordinary precocity, to
whom Keats dedicated *Endymion*; committed suicide in
1770 at the age of seventeen. *Sidney:* poet, courtier,
soldier; died heroically in battle in 1586 at the age of
thirty-two. *Lucan:* Roman poet, conspired against Nero,
and died in A.D. 65 at the age of twenty-six; thought,
perhaps wrongly, to have betrayed his fellow-conspira-
tors, but redeemed himself by the manner of his death.

410–14. This passage has been held to imply the possi-

229 bility of personal immortality. Adonais is to occupy a particular star, and to contribute his own individual note to the music of the spheres, one which has not so far been heard. The Neoplatonic metaphor of a spark flowing back to the fountain of light from which it came (338–40) has suggested a different kind of immortality, a merging of the individual in the One. Probably Shelley meant to leave the different possibilities open. But perhaps there is no real contradiction; for it is in the 'firmament of time' (388) that the stars burn on. The poets' souls flow back to the fountain, but in time they through their works continue to have an individual influence. On the other hand in 494–5 Adonais' soul is a star (or 'like a star'), not in the firmament of time but in the 'abode where the eternal are.'

414. *Vesper:* Hesperus. See verse on the title page.

230 415–23. It is foolish ('fond') to mourn for Adonais. We should consider the vastness of the universe, which we can encompass with our 'spirit's light,' and the relative insignificance of our earthly life in time. Hope (? of immortality) may lure us to the brink (? of death) and then our hearts may sink (? with doubt, awe); so we should keep our hearts light. This last exhortation shows a quality not always allowed to Shelley, his urbanity, his capacity to take even his own most exalted speculations lightly. In this part of the poem he is using Neoplatonic notions, but he is not committing himself to them as to dogmas.

417. *pendulous:* hanging suspended.

428–32. Men like Keats do not derive glory from being buried among those who preyed upon the world; they add glory to the surroundings. Empires and religions pass away, but the influence of creative minds lives on.

439–47. 'The English burying-place is a green slope near the walls, under the pyramidal tomb of Cestius, and is, I think, the most beautiful and solemn cemetery I ever beheld' (Shelley to Peacock, 22 Dec. 1818). Shelley's own son William was buried there, and his grief for him is remembered in 440 and 453–5. Little is known of Caius Cestius except that he was a Tribune of the People

in Rome in the first century A.D.; so this is the one place **230**
where his memory has taken refuge (446).

460–4. A brilliant brief statement of Platonic/Neopla- **231**
tonic philosophy. As the sun always shines, but the
shadows which it casts are always changing and passing
away, so in relation to the one, unchanging, ultimate
reality, all earthly things are only shadows. On earth we
see the light split into many colours as the eternal unity
is broken into many individual persons and things.

The passage exemplifies the dilemma of which it
speaks. The poet, wishing to express the deep truth
which is imageless (*P.U.* II. iv. 116), must use imagery.
All the beauty, natural and artistic, which he sees
around him transfuses something of the eternal glory,
but imperfectly—as his own words as well as those of
other poets do.

485. *now beams on me.* In stanzas LI to LIII the poet **232**
desired death as a means of escape from the sorrows of
the world and from the limitations of worldly knowledge,
as a means of reunion with the One Spirit. But here the
reference is not primarily to death, but to something
that can happen, is happening to him, even in life. The
eternal Beauty, though eclipsed by entry into the tem-
poral world, is not quenched; the Light shines on all
earthly things, and each can in some degree reflect it
('are' in 484 is ungrammatical, but it does not matter).
So, inspired by Adonais, the poet finds himself be-
coming a more nearly perfect mirror of that Light. 'The
clouds of cold mortality'—attachment to worldly things,
base passions, anything which would prevent him from
reflecting the Light—are being consumed 'now,' in this
life.

488. *my spirit's bark is driven.* This should not be taken
as a prophecy of his own death in a boat a year later. It
is a spiritual experience, and is happening in the present.
Shelley is approaching the state of mystic union—a kind
of death, but not physical death, not an escape. The
escapism in stanzas LI–LIII passes into something more
mature and spiritually advanced in stanzas LIV–LV. Cf.
the end of *Epipsychidion*, written shortly before.

Critical Extracts

SHELLEY

I am formed, if for anything not in common with the herd of mankind, to apprehend minute and remote distinctions of feeling, whether relative to external nature or the living beings which surround us, and to communicate the conceptions which result from considering either the moral or the material universe as a whole.

From a letter to WILLIAM GODWIN, 11th December, 1817.

JOHN GIBSON LOCKHART

It would be highly absurd to deny, that this gentleman has manifested very extraordinary powers of language and imagination in his treatment of the allegory, however grossly and miserably he may have tried to pervert its purpose and meaning. ... With him, it is quite evident that the Jupiter whose downfall has been predicted by Prometheus, means nothing more than Religion in general, that is, every human system of religious belief; and that, with the fall of this, he considers it perfectly necessary (as indeed we also believe, though with far different feelings) that every system of human government also should give way and perish. The patience of the contemplative spirit in Prometheus is to be followed by the daring of the active Demogorgon, at whose touch all 'old thrones' are at once and for ever to be cast down into the dust. It appears too plainly, from the luscious pictures with which this play terminates, that Mr. Shelley looks forward to an unusual relaxation of all moral *rules*—or rather, indeed, to the extinction of all moral feelings, except that of a certain mysterious indefinable *kindliness*, as the natural and necessary result of the overthrow of all civil government and religious belief. It appears, still more wonderfully, that he contemplates this state of things as the ideal SUMMUM BONUM. In short it is quite impossible that there should exist a more pestiferous mixture of blasphemy, sedition, and sensuality than is visible in the whole structure and strain of this poem—which, nevertheless, and not withstanding all the detestation its principles excite, will be considered by all that read it attentively, as abounding in poetical beauties of the highest order—as presenting many specimens not easily to be surpassed, of the moral sublime of eloquence—as overflowing with pathos, and most magnificent in description. Where can be found a spectacle more worthy of sorrow than such a man performing and glorying in the performance of such things ?

From: Blackwood's Edinburgh Magazine VII (Sept. 1820).

MACAULAY

The strong imagination of Shelley made him an idolater in his own despite. Out of the most indefinite terms of a hard, cold, dark, metaphysical system, he made a gorgeous Pantheon, full of beautiful, majestic, and life-like forms. He turned atheism itself into a mythology, rich with visions as glorious as the gods that live in the marble of Phidias, or the virgin saints that smile on us from the canvas of Murillo. The Spirit of Beauty, the Principle of Good. the Principle of Evil, when he treated of them, ceased to be abstractions. They took shape and colour. They were no longer mere words; but 'intelligible forms'; 'fair humanities'; objects of love, of adoration, or of fear. As there can be no stronger sign of a mind destitute of the poetical faculty than that tendency which was so common among the writers of the French school to turn images into abstractions, Venus, for example, into Love, Minerva into Wisdom, Mars into War, and Bacchus into Festivity, so there can be no stronger sign of a mind truly poetical than a disposition to reverse this abstracting process, and to make individuals out of generalities. Some of the metaphysical and ethical theories of Shelley were certainly most absurd and pernicious. But we doubt whether any modern poet has possessed in an equal degree some of the highest qualities of the great ancient masters. The words bard and inspiration, which seem so cold and affected when applied to other modern writers, have a perfect propriety when applied to him. He was not an author, but a bard. His poetry seems not to have been an art, but an inspiration.

> *From:* A review of *The Pilgrim's Progress* in *The Edinburgh Review* (Dec. 1830), reprinted in *Literary Essays Contributed to the Edinburgh Review* (O.U.P. 1913), p. 196.

MATTHEW ARNOLD

Poetry interprets in two ways; it interprets by expressing with magical felicity the physiognomy and movement of the outward world, and it interprets by expressing, with inspired conviction, the ideas and laws of the inward world of man's moral and spiritual nature. In other words, poetry is interpretative both by having *natural magic* in it, and by having *moral profundity* .... In Shelley there is not a balance of the two gifts, nor even a co-existence of them, but there is a passionate straining after them both, and this is what makes Shelley, as a man, so interesting: I will not now inquire how much Shelley achieves as a poet, but whatever he achieves, he in general fails to achieve natural magic in his expression; in Mr Palgrave's charming *Treasury* may be seen a gallery of his failures.

Compare, for example, his 'Lines Written in the Euganean Hills' with Keats's 'Ode to Autumn.' The latter piece *renders* Nature; the former *tries* to *render* her. I will not deny, however, that Shelley has natural magic in his rhythm; what I deny is, that he has it in his language. It always seems to me that the right sphere for Shelley's genius was the sphere of music, not of poetry; the medium of sounds he can master; but to master the more difficult medium of words he has neither intellectual force enough nor sanity enough.

> *From:* 'Maurice de Guérin,' delivered as a lecture in 1862, printed in *Fraser's Magazine* (1863) and in *Essays in Criticism* (1865). The second paragraph was printed as a footnote.

SWINBURNE

The poem of Keats, Mr Arnold says, *'renders* nature'; the
poem of Shelley *'tries* to render her.' It is this that I deny.
What Shelley tries to do he does; and he does not try to do
the same thing as Keats .... Shelley never in his life wrote a
poem of that exquisite contraction and completeness, within
that round and perfect limit .... This poem of the Euganean
Hills ... is a rhapsody of thought and feeling coloured by
contact with nature, but not born of the contact; and such
as it is all Shelley's work is, even when most vague and vast in
its elemental scope of labour and of aim. A soul as great as
the world lays hold on the things of the world; on all life of
plants, and beasts, and men; on all likeness of time, and
death, and good things and evil. His aim is rather to render
the effect of a thing than a thing itself; the soul and spirit of
life rather than the living form, the growth rather than the
thing grown. ...

Of all forms or kinds of poetry the two highest are the
lyric and the dramatic, and ... as clearly as the first place in
the one rank is held among us by Shakespeare, the first place
in the other is held and will never be resigned by Shelley.

> *From:* 'Notes on the Text of Shelley' in *Fortnightly
> Review* (May 1869), reprinted in *Complete Works*
> (Bonchurch Edition), XV (1926), 380, 397.

C. S. LEWIS

I have now to show that Shelley, with all his faults of execu-
tion, is a poet who must rank higher than Dryden with any
critic who claims to be classical; that he is superior to Dryden
by the greatness of his subjects and his moral elevation
(which are merits by classical standards), and also by the
unity of his actions, his architectonic power, and his general
observance of *decorum* in the Renaissance sense of the word;
that is, his disciplined production not just of poetry but of
the poetry in each case proper to the theme and the species
of composition. ...

Shelley's poetry represents a variety of kinds, most of them traditional. ... In all these kinds Shelley produces works which, though not perfect, are in one way more satisfactory than any of Dryden's longer pieces: that is to say, they display a harmony between the poet's real and professed intention, they answer the demands of their forms, and they have unity of spirit. Shelley is at home in his best poems, his clothes, so to speak, fit him, as Dryden's do not. The faults are faults of execution, such as over-elaboration, occasional verbosity, and the like: mere stains on the surface. ...

* * * * *

... Dante is eminently the poet of beatitude. He has not only no rival, but none second to him. But if we were asked to name the poet who most nearly deserved this inaccessible *proxime accessit*, I should name Shelley. Indeed, my claim for Shelley might be represented by the proposition that Shelley and Milton are, each, the half of Dante. ...

* * * * *

The fourth act [of *Prometheus Unbound*] I shall not attempt to analyse. It is an intoxication, a riot, a complicated and uncontrollable splendour, long, and yet not too long, sustained on the note of ecstasy such as no other English poet, perhaps no other poet, has given us. It can be achieved by more than one artist in music: to do it in words has been, I think, beyond the reach of nearly all. It has not, and cannot have, the solemnity and overwhelming realism of the *Paradiso*, but it has all its fire and light. It has not the 'sober certainty of waking bliss' which makes Milton's paradise so inhabitable —but it sings from regions in our consciousness that Milton never entered.

From: 'Shelley, Dryden, and Mr. Eliot,' in
Rehabilitations and Other Essays (1939).

JOHN HOLLOWAY

Shelley, more perhaps than any other poet, possesses an imaginative insight into nature as a world of events and processes, especially those which occur through a great volume of space. His imagination comes to life before the movements of the sun and the planets as tangible realities, the transmission of light or sound through the air, the development of things as they grow, the great cycles of interaction between sea, land, and air which are determinants of climate. It is a gift such as might start with the insight of science, but it has become the insight of a poet or an artist. . . .

*   *   *   *   *

. . . these later poems may be recognized as not a repudiation, but an extension and perhaps even a deepening, of the reformist enthusiasm which dominates the earlier ones. Plato's idealism, as a philosophical doctrine, went not with unrealistic dreaming but with a sombre and unflinching awareness of the savage realities which are integral to (though not the whole of) the public world. . . . The transition which [Shelley] made from Godwin to Plato was quite logical and imaginatively coherent. Perhaps the sharpest change, indeed, was one that personal experience and the current state of Europe were both teaching Shelley, at the same time as Plato was suggesting it: that to bring about the millenium is an almost hopeless dream, and moreover that if the millenium were to be realized it would probably prove transient. To the Platonic philosophy, however, the world of the millenium is not something to be brought about in the real world. Rather, it is a permanently co-existing contrast to that world, or at least to all of it that is evil. And here, perhaps, one can see how misleading it is, to say that Shelley's last works are progressively less and less about the real world. What in essence they do, what everyone, Platonist or not, can accept them as doing, is to employ the ideas of Plato as sustained *metaphors*, through which to reveal, with decisive emphasis, the actualities and the potentialities of life, and the gulf between these. In *Adonais* the contrast is between a world in

357

which a writer like Keats is ignored or reviled, and one in which the whole creation, in all its beauty and dignity, would mourn for his death and would unite with what he stood for. . . .

Few single works of literature depict either the actualities or the potentialities of life in full. Those of Shelley certainly do not. It is along these lines, though, that one can most easily see their wide and real significance. Their import is by no means to be mere re-statements of the doctrines of Plato; it is to show, with compelling intensity, what men have made of life against what they might make of it.

> From: *Selected Poems of Percy Bysshe Shelley* (Heinemann 1960), pp. xxi-ii, xxvii-xxviii.

G. M. MATTHEWS

Shelley is distinctive in that although he imagined and desired 'Elysian, windless, fortunate abodes' of social and sexual equality, where Nature would be wholly under man's co-operative control—where, in Platonic metaphor, the Many would be identical with the One—he accepted imaginatively the processes of change that alone could lead towards such a goal. The goal itself he knew to be unattainable, because his very acceptance of change gave him also a quite exceptional awareness of man's situation in infinite time, of the limited and relative nature of every human society and attribute. All other poets reject change emotionally even when their reason acknowledges it to be inevitable. Shelley's uniqueness is that in some of his best poetry his whole poetic personality sides with change, with the shadow of the sunrise, with the uncontrollable Wind, with Time that has shattered Ozymandias, with Demogorgon who will overthrow Jupiter. 'And yet to me welcome is day and night,' Prometheus cries, embracing the suffering that temporal existence inflicts on him. In the Platonic metaphors he often uses, Shelley does not normally look forward to escaping from the flux of reality into some transcendental permanent world, but seeks unity with the Ideal in its incessant struggle to realize itself through the transient things of Nature and of human society,

> bursting in its beauty and its might
> From trees and beasts and men into the Heavens' light.

To the individual man, however, the pain of transience is not diminished by taking the side of change; instead the co-existence of the two feelings contributes to that peculiar poignancy that is characteristic of Shelley's utterance. In his best writing, personal suffering is felt as a qualifying force that accompanies, without counteracting, the main affirmative movement of the poem. 'What if my leaves are falling like its own?' Shelley is almost invariably strongest in poems where the social, the natural, and the personal worlds coincide, weakest when he is most purely personal.

> *From: Shelley: Selected Poems and Prose* (The Clarendon Press, Oxford, 1964), pp. 43-4.

KATHLEEN RAINE

Shelley is at the present time perhaps the least understood of the major English poets. Reasons for this are not far to seek: the positivist philosophers who have so strongly influenced the climate of modern critical opinion are fond of applying to all that cannot (following the scientific method) be perceived by the senses or subjected to quantitative measurement the term 'meaningless.' But in fact their philosophy precludes the notion of meaning by definition, since meaning can never be 'positive,' being precisely that in any word or image which communicates a mental, and therefore immeasurable, attribute. Shelley, most Platonic of poets, becomes, in such terms, the most open to the charge of being 'meaningless' precisely in so far as he is most rich in that quality. Emptied of meaning, poetic figures stand only for their physical terms; and Shelley's richly metaphorical poetry, read as merely descriptive, or 'imagist' verse, seems superficial precisely to those readers who have least understood it.

The beauty of metrical form and symbolic image speak immediately to the imagination, or not at all; to the discursive reason 'meaningless,' beauty is, to that higher faculty, meaning itself.

*   *   *   *   *

No stupider judgment was ever passed upon Shelley than by Arnold, who called him an 'ineffectual angel.' There spoke the school-inspector who believes that 'good' is something done by busy people. Giving men material goods and material aid cannot make them better, only better off; the effect of poetry is to change us permanently in our nature; a transmutation by no means ineffectual. It would be hard to name a poet whose political and social propaganda—to put it at its lowest—has more effectively changed public opinion and altered the course of history. More far-reaching is the transforming power of poetry itself. Only those lacking in all sensibility to a poetry which speaks to the soul in its own language and of its native place and state can read Shelley unchanged.

From: Defending Ancient Springs
(O.U.P. 1967), pp. 139, 155.

Bibliography

I. *Alastor, Prometheus Unbound, Adonais*

Alastor and Other Poems was published in 1816. A facsimile, edited by Bertram Dobell, was published by the Shelley Society in 1885 (2nd ed., with corrections, 1887).

Prometheus Unbound with Other Poems was published in 1820. A. M. D. Hughes's edition (O.U.P., 1910; 2nd ed., revised, 1957) has a good introduction and notes. L. J. Zillman's variorum edition of *Prometheus Unbound* (University of Washington Press, 1959) reprints the text and all important variations in later editions and in the MSS, and brings together copious extracts from and summaries of critical and interpretative comment. L. J. Zillman's edition, *Prometheus Unbound: The Text and the Drafts* (Yale U.P., 1968), provides full evidence of the growth of the poem as revealed in the extant MSS.

Adonais was printed at Pisa in 1821. Facsimiles were published by the Shelley Society in 1886 and as one of the Noel Douglas Replicas in 1927. A reprint with modernized spelling and punctuation was edited with introduction and notes by W. M. Rossetti (O.U.P., 1891; revised 1903).

II. *Collected editions, selections and other works by Shelley*

Complete Works, edited by R. Ingpen and W. E. Peck (the Julian edition, 1926–30) is the most nearly complete edition. Large selections of the poetry and prose are contained in editions by A. S. B. Glover (The Nonesuch Press, 1951) and K. N. Cameron (Holt, Rinehart and Winston, 1951), the latter with introduction and notes. Smaller collections include *Shelley: Poetry and Prose*, ed. A. M. D. Hughes (O.U.P., 1931; this has extracts from critics and biographers as well as the editor's introduction and notes) and *Shelley: Selected Poems and Prose*, ed. G. M. Matthews (O.U.P., 1964; this has a good introduction and notes).

For the ordinary reader the best edition of the *Complete Poetical Works* is probably still that of T. Hutchinson (O.U.P., 1904, 2nd ed., corrected by G. M. Matthews, 1970). There is a large selection with introduction and notes by Neville Rogers (Houghton Mifflin, 1968; O.U.P., 1969), and a smaller selection edited by John Holloway with an excellent introduction and some notes (Heinemann, 1960). Advanced students may wish to consult editions of the poems by Mary Shelley (*Posthumous Poems*, 1824; *Poetical Works* (with notes), 1839), W. M. Rossetti (1870), H. B. Forman (1878), G. E. Woodberry (1892), and C. D. Locock (1911); and *The Shelley Notebook in Harvard College Library*, ed. G. E. Woodberry (Harvard U.P., 1929).

The prose is most easily available in the Julian edition and in *Shelley's Prose*, ed. D. L. Clark (University of New Mexico Press, 1954), which contains all the prose except the novels, translations, and letters. *Shelley's Critical Prose* has been edited by B. R. McElderry (University of Nebraska Press, 1967). F. L. Jones's edition of Shelley's *Letters* (O.U.P., 1964) is excellent. F. L. Jones has edited also Mary Shelley's *Journal* (University of Oklahoma Press, 1947), which contains writing by Shelley and is a principal source for his life and reading, and her *Letters* (University of Oklahoma Press, 1944).

III. *Biography*

Most readers will find enough for their purposes in Edmund Blunden's *Shelley* (Collins, 1946; O.U.P., 1968). The standard life is Newman Ivey White's long *Shelley* (Knopf, 1940; Secker and Warburg, 1947), which, having an excellent index, is useful for reference even for those who do not want to read it through. K. N. Cameron's *The Young Shelley* (New York: Macmillan, London: Gollancz, 1950) is good on the life up to 1813, and A. M. D. Hughes's *The Nascent Mind of Shelley* (O.U.P., 1947) on his early reading and intellectual development.

Memories of Shelley by those who knew him can be found in biographies by Thomas Medwin (1847) and T. J. Hogg (1851); and in Leigh Hunt's *Autobiography* (1850; 2nd ed., revised, 1859; edited by J. E. Morpurgo in The Cresset Library, 1949), E. J. Trelawny's *Recollections of the Last Days of Shelley and Byron* (1858), T. L. Peacock's *Memoirs of Shelley* (in *Fraser's Magazine*, 1858–62; ed. Brett-Smith, 1909). and in Edward Williams's *Journal* (ed. Garnett, 1902).

IV. *Criticism, etc.*

(i) *Recommended for use in schools and universities*

M. H. Abrams (editor), *English Romantic Poets: Modern Essays in Criticism* (O.U.P., 1960). Contains four essays on Shelley: C. S. Lewis, 'Shelley, Dryden and Mr Eliot', from *Rehabilitations and Other Essays* (O.U.P., 1939); F. R. Leavis, 'Shelley', from *Revaluation* (Chatto, 1949); F. A. Pottle, 'The Case of Shelley', from *P.M.L.A.*, LXVII (1952); and Donald Davie, 'Shelley's Urbanity', from *Purity of Diction in English Verse*, (Chatto, 1953). These essays, and John Holloway's introduction to his selection, are especially recommended since they deal with Shelley as a poet and raise the relevant critical questions about him. A large proportion of the other writings mentioned are mainly interpretative rather than critical.

Carlos Baker, *Shelley's Major Poetry* (Princeton U.P. and O.U.P., 1948). Perhaps the best comprehensive interpretation of the major poems.

A. C. Bradley, 'Shelley's View of Poetry' in *Oxford Lectures on Poetry* (Macmillan, 1909).

A. C. Bradley, 'Shelley and Arnold's Critique' in *A Miscellany* (Macmillan, 1929), which contains also essays on 'Odours and Flowers in the Poetry of Shelley' and on 'Coleridge Echoes in Shelley's Poems.'

Francis Berry, 'Shelley and the Future Tense' in *Poets' Grammar* (Routledge and Kegan Paul, 1958). Mainly about *Ode to the West Wind*.

H. N. Brailsford, *Shelley, Godwin and Their Circle* (Home University Library, 1913; O.U.P., 1951). A readable introduction to the radical thought of the period.

T. S. Eliot, 'Shelley and Keats' in *The Use of Poetry and*

the Use of Criticism (Faber, 1933). Should be read because of the eminence and the influence of the writer, but it should be remembered that he later came to take a more favourable view of Shelley.

D. W. Harding, 'Shelley's Poetry' in *The Pelican Guide to English Literature*, Vol. 5 (1957).

D. G. James, *The Romantic Comedy* (O.U.P., 1948), Part II. On Keats and Shelley.

Desmond King-Hele, *Shelley: His Thought and Work* (Macmillan, 1960). A good general introduction by a professional scientist.

(ii) *Recommended more particularly for university students*

P. H. Butter, *Shelley's Idols of the Cave* (Edinburgh U.P., 1954). Considers Shelley's recurrent images.

R. H. Fogle, *The Imagery of Keats and Shelley* (University of N. Carolina Press, 1949). Good general survey of Shelley's imagery.

Evan K. Gibson, 'Alastor: A Reinterpretation,' *P.M.L.A.*, LXII (1947), 1022–46.

H. L. Hoffman, *An Odyssey of the Soul: Shelley's Alastor* (Columbia U.P., 1933).

E. B. Hungerford, *Shores of Darkness* (Columbia U.P., 1941). Considers the interpretations of myths current in Shelley's time, and the use made of myth by, among others, Shelley in *Prometheus Unbound* and in *Adonais*.

G. Wilson Knight, *The Starlit Dome* (O.U.P., 1941), chap. III.

G. M. Matthews, 'Shelley's Lyrics' in *The Morality of Art*, ed. D. W. Jefferson (Routledge, 1969). Does not deal directly with many of the poems in this book, but is an excellent essay, showing the dramatic element in Shelley's lyrics.

Kathleen Raine, 'A Defence of Shelley's Poetry' in *Defending Ancient Springs* (O.U.P., 1967). Shows a poet's understanding.

George Ridenour (editor), *Shelley: A Collection of Critical Essays* (Prentice-Hall, 1963). Especially notable are 'Shelley's

Theory of Evil' by M. H. Rader, 'A Volcano's Voice in Shelley' by G. M. Matthews, and 'The Role of Asia in the Dramatic Action of Shelley's *Prometheus Unbound*' by F. A. Pottle.

Neville Rogers, *Shelley at Work* (O.U.P., 1956, 2nd ed., revised, 1967). An examination of Shelley's notebooks, showing the stages of composition of some poems, and the use Shelley made of his reading.

John Wain (editor), *Contemporary Reviews of Romantic Poetry* (Harrap, 1953). A small selection of the most important early reviews.

Earl R. Wasserman, 'The Sensitive Plant' and 'Adonais' in *The Subtler Language* (Johns Hopkins Press, 1959). Perhaps over-subtle at times, but interesting and original.

Earl R. Wasserman, *Shelley's Prometheus Unbound* (Johns Hopkins Press, 1965). Good on Shelley's use of myth and on his treatment of time.

Milton Wilson, *Shelley's Later Poetry* (Columbia U.P., 1959). Centres on *Prometheus Unbound*.

R. B. Woodings (editor), *Shelley* (Macmillan, 1968). Contains essays already mentioned by Pottle ('The Case of Shelley') and Matthews; chapters from the books mentioned by Pulos, Rogers, Bloom, Wasserman (*Prometheus Unbound*), Baker, and Wilson; and, among other things, 'The Political Symbolism of *Prometheus Unbound*' by K. N. Cameron, from *P.M.L.A.*, LVIII (1943) and 'Potentiality in *Prometheus Unbound*' by D. J. Hughes, from *Studies in Romanticism*, XI (1963).

W. B. Yeats, 'The Philosophy of Shelley's Poetry' in *Ideas of Good and Evil* (1903), reprinted in *Essays and Introductions* (Macmillan, 1961). Mainly on Shelley's symbolic images.

(iii) *Of more specialized interest; recommended for advanced students*

Harold Bloom, *Shelley's Mythmaking* (Yale U.P., 1959). More difficult than it need be, but contains interesting discussion of Shelley as a maker of myths.

F. S. Ellis, *A Lexical Concordance to the Poetical Works of Percy Bysshe Shelley* (Quaritch, 1892).

C. Grabo, *A Newton among Poets* (University of N. Carolina Press, 1930). On Shelley's knowledge and use of science.

C. Grabo, *Prometheus Unbound: An Interpretation* (University of N. Carolina Press, 1933). Places much, perhaps too much, emphasis on Neoplatonism.

J. A. Notopoulos, *The Platonism of Shelley* (Duke U.P., 1949). Only specialists will want to read this large volume through, but others will find it useful for reference.

C. E. Pulos, *The Deep Truth* (University of Nebraska Press, 1962). Emphasizes Shelley's scepticism.

Newman Ivey White, *The Unextinguished Hearth* (Duke U.P., 1938). Brings together all contemporary reviews of Shelley.

Index of Titles

Adonais 214
Alastor, or The Spirit of Solitude 19

Cloud, The 192

Dæmon of the World, The 51

Exhortation, An 187

Mutability 43

Ode, An (written October 1819) 191
Ode to Heaven 185
Ode to Liberty 200
Ode to the West Wind 188
On the Fall of Bonaparte 47
'O! There are Spirits of the Air' 41

Prometheus Unbound 69

Sensitive Plant, The 168
Sonnet, from the Italian of Dante 49
Stanzas (April 1814) 42
Summer Evening Church-yard, A 46
Superstition 48

'The Pale, the Cold, and the Moony Smile' 44
To A Skylark 195
To Wordsworth 47
Translated from the Greek of Moschus 50

Vision of the Sea, A 180

Index of First Lines

A glorious people vibrated again 200
A Sensitive Plant in a garden grew 168
Arise, arise, arise! 191
Away! the moor is dark beneath the moon 42

Chameleons feed on light and air 187

Earth, ocean, air, belovèd brotherhood! 19

Guido, I would that Lapo, thou, and I 49

Hail to thee, blithe Spirit! 195
How wonderful is Death 51

I bring fresh showers for the thirsting flowers 192
I hated thee, fallen tyrant! I did groan 47
I weep for Adonais—he is dead! 214

Monarch of Gods and Dæmons, and all Spirits 69

O! there are spirits of the air 41
O Wild West Wind, thou breath of Autumn's being 188

Palace-roof of cloudless nights! 185
Poet of Nature, thou hast wept to know 47

The pale, the cold, and the moony smile 44
The wind has swept from the wide atmosphere 46
Thou taintest all thou look'st upon! The stars 48
'Tis the terror of tempest. The rags of the sail 180

We are as clouds that veil the midnight moon 43
When winds that move not its calm surface sweep 50